Strategic Environmental Assessment in Policy and Sector Reform

ENVIRONMENT AND DEVELOPMENT

A fundamental element of sustainable development is environmental sustain-ability. Hence, this series was created in 2007 to cover current and emerging issues in order to promote debate and broaden the understanding of environmental challenges as integral to achieving equitable and sustained economic growth. The series will draw on analysis and practical experience from across the World Bank and from client countries. The manuscripts chosen for publication will be central to the implementation of the World Bank's Environment Strategy, and relevant to the development community, policy makers, and academia. Topics addressed in this series will include environmental health, natural resources management, strategic environmental assessment, policy instruments, and environmental institutions, among others.

Titles in this series:

The Changing Wealth of Nations: Measuring Sustainable Development in the New Millennium

Convenient Solutions to an Inconvenient Truth: Ecosystem-Based Approaches to Climate Change

Environmental Flows in Water Resources Policies, Plans, and Projects: Findings and Recommendations

Environmental Health and Child Survival: Epidemiology, Economics, and Experiences

International Trade and Climate Change: Economic, Legal, and Institutional Perspectives

Poverty and the Environment: Understanding Linkages at the Household Level

Strategic Environmental Assessment for Policies: An Instrument for Good Governance

Strategic Environmental Assessment in Policy and Sector Reform: Conceptual Model and Operational Guidance

Strategic Environmental Assessment in Policy and Sector Reform

*Conceptual Model and
Operational Guidance*

World Bank
University of Gothenburg
Swedish University of Agricultural Sciences
Netherlands Commission for Environmental Assessment

THE WORLD BANK
Washington, DC

CONTENTS

Figures

Tables

Acknowledgments

Undertaken in the context of the Paris Declaration on Harmonization and Alignment, this study was a collaborative effort of the Environment Department of the World Bank, the Environmental Economics Unit at the Department of Economics of the University of Gothenburg (EEU), the Swedish EIA Centre at the Swedish University of Agricultural Sciences, and the Netherlands Commission for Environmental Assessment (NCEA). The team that produced this report regularly informed the strategic environmental assessment (SEA) Task Team of the Organisation for Economic Co-operation and Development (OECD) Development Assistance Committee (DAC) on the progress of the review and received valuable feedback during Task Team meetings and other jointly organized events. It is expected that this report will provide guidance for applying SEA in development cooperation that supports policy and sector reform.

The team that produced this report was made up of Fernando Loayza (task team leader, World Bank), David Annandale (consultant), Anna Axelsson and Matthew Cashmore (Swedish EIA Centre, University of Agricultural Sciences), Anders Ekbom and Daniel Slunge (EEU), Mans Nilsson (consultant), and Rob Verheem (NCEA). This report is based on the findings of the evaluation of pilots under the World Bank's SEA pilot program; the evaluations were undertaken by David Annandale, Anna Axelsson, Matthew Cashmore, Anders Ekbom, Daniel Slunge, and evaluators Juan Albarracin-Jordan, Jiri Dusik, Paul Guthiga, Yin Jian, Wilfred Nyangena, and Ulf Sandstrom. The contribution of Geske Dijkstra, Sibout Nooteboom, and Ineke Steinhauer to the framework for the evaluation of pilots is also acknowledged.

The team greatly benefited from the advice of Kulsum Ahmed (World Bank), Fred Carden (International Development Research Centre, Canada), and Maria Rosario Partidario (University of Lisbon, Portugal), who were members of the evaluation's advisory group. Detailed comments were also provided by peer reviewers Diji Chandrasekharan (World Bank), Peter Croal (Canadian International Development Agency and chair of the OECD DAC SEA Task Team), Richard Damania (World Bank), and Gary McMahon (World Bank). The team further acknowledges the feedback received from the participants in the meetings and workshops held in Gothenburg (2007 and 2008), Rotterdam (2008), Washington, D.C. (2009), Geneva (2010), and Utrecht (2010). James Cantrell, Patricia Katayama, Cindy Fisher, and Nora Ridolfi, all of the World Bank, assisted in the publication and dissemination of this book. Grace Aguilar, Juliette Guantai, and Setsuko Masaki, all of the World Bank, provided administrative support to the team. The work was carried out under the general direction of James Warren Evans, director, and Michele de Nevers, sector manager, of the World Bank Environment Department; and as part of the work program of the World Bank's Environmental Institutions and Governance Team, led by Kulsum Ahmed.

This report would not have been possible without the collaboration of the governments and the World Bank's country offices where the pilot SEAs were carried out. The task managers of the SEA pilots, all from the World Bank— Diji Chandrasekharan, Adriana Damianova, Fei Deng, Peter Kristensen, Bryan Land, and Muthukumara Mani—kindly facilitated data collection, suggested contacts, and participated in interviews during the evaluation. Stakeholders from government departments, communities, nongovernmental organizations, civil society organizations, and the private sector generously provided their time and knowledge both during the SEA pilots and during the evaluation. The partners in this evaluation are most grateful to all of the stakeholders for their spirited participation. This appreciation and gratitude is extended to the Swedish, Dutch, Norwegian, and Finnish governments for their support of this evaluation and the World Bank's SEA pilot program, through trust funds from the Swedish International Development Cooperation Agency, the Trust Fund for Environmentally and Socially Sustainable Development, and the Bank Netherlands Partnership Program.

Abbreviations

AMGP	Africa Mineral Governance Program
CBA	cost-benefit analysis
CBO	community-based organization
CEA	cost-effectiveness analysis
CIDA	Canadian International Development Agency
CSO	civil society organization
CUA	cost-utility analysis
DAC	Development Assistance Committee (OECD)
DAP	Detailed Area Plan
DIEWRMP	Dhaka Integrated Environment and Water Resources Management Program
DMDP	Dhaka Metropolitan Development Plan
ECOWAS	Economic Community of West African States
EIA	environmental impact assessment
EEU	Environmental Economics Unit, Department of Economics, University of Gothenburg
EITI	Extractive Industries Transparency Initiative
HPCD	Hubei Provincial Communication Department
HRNP	Hubei Road Network Plan
IAD	institutions and development framework
IDRC	International Development Research Centre
I-SEA	institution-centered strategic environmental assessment
J4P	Justice for the Poor
KFS	Kenya Forest Service
OECD	Organisation for Economic Co-operation and Development
MSR	mineral sector review
MTAP	Mining Technical Assistance Project
NACEF	National Commission for Environment and Forestry
NCEA	Netherlands Commission for Environmental Assessment
NGO	nongovernmental organization
PAM	policy action matrix
PEI	Poverty-Environment Initiative
PSIR	pressure-state-impact-response
RAC	Resource Assessment Commission (Australia)
RAJUK	Capital Development Authority (Dhaka)

SEA	strategic environmental assessment
SESA	strategic environmental and social assessment
UNDP	United Nations Development Programme
UNEP	United Nations Environment Programme
WAEMU	West African Economic and Monetary Union
WAMGP	West Africa Mineral Governance Program
WAMSSA	West Africa Minerals Sector Strategic Assessment

Overview

AROUND THE WORLD, it is increasingly being recognized that for sustainability goals to be reached, efforts need to go beyond complying with standards and mitigating adverse impacts, to identifying environmental sustainability as an objective of the development process. This approach requires the integration of environmental, sustainability, and climate change considerations into policy and sector reform.

Because sector reform brings about significant policy change involving adjustments in laws, policies, regulations, and institutions, it is a sensitive political process often driven by strong economic interests. Policy makers are subject to a number of political pressures that originate in vested interests. The weaker the institutional and governance framework in which sector reform is formulated and implemented, the greater the risk of regulatory capture. The recommendations of environmental assessment are often of little relevance unless there are constituencies that support them and have sufficient political power to make their voices heard in the policy process. While strong constituencies are important during the design of sector reform, they are even more important during implementation. It follows that effective environmental assessment in policy and sector reform requires strong constituencies backing up recommendations, a system to hold policy makers accountable for their decisions, and institutions that can balance competing and, sometimes, conflicting interests.

Acknowledging the intrinsically political nature of sector reform, and in response to a mandate for strengthening strategic environmental assessment (SEA)[1] in its activities,[2] in the mid-2000s the World Bank embarked on a testing program for applying SEA at the policy level. Building on experience accumulated in sector reform in middle-income countries, the World Bank proposed an approach known as *institution-centered SEA* for incorporating environmental considerations in policy formulation (World Bank 2005, 2008). This proposed approach coincided with the development of the Organisation for Economic Co-operation and Development (OECD) Development Assistance Committee SEA Task Team's *Applying Strategic Environmental Assessment: Good Practice Guidance for Development Co-operation* (OECD DAC 2006), which describes SEA as a family of approaches using a variety of tools, rather than a fixed, single, and prescriptive approach. It acknowledges that SEA applied at the policy level requires a particular focus on the political, institutional, and governance context underlying decision-making processes.

The World Bank SEA Pilot Program

The World Bank established a pilot program to test and promote SEA applying institution-centered SEA approaches in policy and sector reform beginning in 2005. The main objectives of the program have been to test and validate policy-based SEA in different sectors, countries, and regions; to draw lessons on the effectiveness of this approach; and to yield tools and operational guidance that could be useful in applying SEA in policy and sector reform.

There are two components to the pilot program. The first has provided grants and/or specialized assistance to support eight SEA pilots linked to World Bank activities. Six of these pilots were completed and evaluated:

- *Strategic Environmental Assessment of the Kenya Forests Act 2005*
- *Sierra Leone Mining Sector Reform Strategic Environmental and Social Assessment (SESA)*
- *Dhaka Metropolitan Development Plan Strategic Environmental Assessment*
- *Strategic Environmental Assessment for the Hubei Road Network Plan (2002–2020)*
- *West Africa Minerals Sector Strategic Assessment (WAMSSA)*
- *Rapid Integrated Strategic Environmental and Social Assessment (SESA) of Malawi Mineral Sector Reform*

The second component of the SEA pilot program consisted of an evaluation of the pilots, conducted in partnership with the Environmental Economics Unit at the University of Gothenburg, the Swedish EIA Centre at the Swedish University of Agricultural Sciences, and the Netherlands Commission for Environmental Assessment. This book summarizes the main findings and results of this evaluation.

Main Findings

The lessons drawn from the pilots suggest that *SEA can, under conducive conditions, contribute to improved formulation and implementation of sector reform.* Largely, this contribution stems from the ability of the pilots to call attention to priority environmental and social issues affecting stakeholders. The evaluation also confirmed the importance of strengthening constituencies, as the pilots opened up participation in sector-reform dialogues to previously sidelined or weakly organized stakeholders. For example, in one of the most promising SEA pilots—WAMSSA, which focused on mining reform in the Mano River Union countries—stakeholders prioritized lack of transparency and weak social accountability linked to mineral resources exploitation as the most critical issue affecting sustainable development in the mining sector. The WAMSSA policy dialogue involved 10 mining communities in three countries, civil society organizations (CSOs) and nongovernmental organizations (NGOs), private mining companies, and government mining sector authorities. This dialogue is expected to continue during mining sector reform through a multistakeholder framework, which was recommended by the stakeholders themselves and later adopted by the countries as the social accountability mechanism for the World Bank's major program in support of mining sector reform in the Mano River Union.

In addition, it was found that *ownership, capacity, and trust are necessary conditions for effective environmental mainstreaming at the policy level.* In particular, strong evidence was found that SEA has positive outcomes only if it promotes ownership of the policy SEA process by governments, CSOs, and local communities. The evaluation confirmed that country ownership has several dimensions. Because government ownership involves a mandate to control the reform and accountability for results, when national agencies are put in charge of designing policies, they are equipped to deliver much more powerful measures than those that the World Bank or other agencies would be able to induce. It is important to note, however, that when weak sector ministries take ownership of SEA, there is a risk of regulatory capture and associated rent seeking. The WAMSSA pilot showed that arrangements such as multistakeholder frameworks can guard against this eventuality. Another dimension of ownership is linked to civil society and to potentially affected stakeholders. With well-designed institutional support and multistakeholder frameworks for addressing policy and development decisions in sector reform, SEA can help to reconcile different interests and to address regulatory capture by enhancing transparency and social accountability.

Another important finding emanating from the evaluation is that *long-term constituency building is needed.* SEA is but a small and bounded intervention in the continuous process of policy making, and so positive outcomes from the pilots could be short-lived. To sustain outcomes over the longer term, it is necessary to build constituencies that can sustain policy influence and institutional changes, which takes a long time to realize. Constituencies that can demand accountability with regard to environmental and social priorities need to be strengthened. Achieving this goal requires trust building and a common perception of problems. Under the right conditions, as stakeholders start to deal with the complex problems and responses to sustainable development issues and to share policy dilemmas and trade-offs that emerge, a common perception of problems and trust in each others' intentions may surface. As a corollary, the evaluation showed that when constituency building was weak in the pilots, the take-up of SEA recommendations was limited.

A final finding is that *contextual factors are of overriding importance in determining whether the main benefits of policy SEA are attained.* In some cases, these factors may be aligned in such a way that pursuing policy SEA is not meaningful. This can happen when—as in the case of the Sierra Leone pilot—a newly elected government decides to slow down reform processes initiated by a previous administration. In all cases, however, preparation and planning must make sure to adapt and adjust the SEA process in view of these factors. In addition, windows of opportunity that close may open over time. In Sierra Leone, for example, interest in mining reform has renewed. SEA may at this point have an opportunity to influence sector reform as long as there are constituencies that can take up the now three-year-old recommendations.

A lesson related to the issues of ownership and constituency building is that *the potential benefits of policy SEA must be clearly articulated.* Developers of SEA must recognize that incumbent actors have certain interests when engaging in SEA activities. Their participation will occur when the benefits of engaging are greater than the risks and costs. Policy-based SEA must first and foremost be understood as a strategic decision support process that will enable governments to engage in better policy making, and not merely as an environmental safeguard. Speaking directly to the development priorities of the country, SEA at the policy level not only works toward improving policy making from an environmental mainstreaming perspective, but also supports better planning and policy making from an overarching development point of view. As sector review analyzes the potential economic and growth impact of sector reform, SEA could offer a complementary analysis that explores the economic and growth implications of environmental and social priorities. This perspective on SEA makes it much easier to establish country ownership.

Guidance for Applying SEA in Sector Reform

A major purpose of the pilot program and the evaluation was the development of operational guidance that policy makers, CSOs, NGOs, and SEA practitioners could use for applying SEA in policy and sector reform. Despite the fact that sector reform is complex and nonlinear, and that SEA is a time-bounded process, the evaluation suggests that effective SEA at the policy level could follow three stages, as follows:

1. *Preparatory work for policy SEA*. Before implementation of policy SEA can begin, there is a need to understand the context within which it will take place. Various questions need to be asked to ensure that the goals and intentions of the specific SEA process are understood by the major stakeholders. The most important questions relate to issues, initiatives, or questions to be addressed; the scale of the process; and the assessment of windows of opportunity. As clearly shown by the pilot SEA in Dhaka, a reluctant lead agency can set back the general development of the approach. As a general rule, sector agencies should lead policy SEA.

2. *Implementing policy SEA*. This stage involves the following steps:
   Situation analysis and priority setting. SEA at the policy level starts with a situation assessment that accounts for the main environmental and social issues prevailing in a region or associated with a sector; the goal is to inform deliberations on priorities by stakeholders. Stakeholders are invited to react to the situation analysis; raise specific and relevant environmental and social concerns; and choose the SEA priorities. The choosing of SEA priorities by stakeholders is critical because it opens up the policy process to their influence. On the one hand, SEA priorities reflect the concerns and preferences of stakeholders, who now have a strong incentive for constituency building or strengthening. On the other hand, SEA priorities are a demand from stakeholders to policy makers to give the reform a specific environmental and social direction and thus sow the seeds for social accountability. Accordingly, special care should be taken to ensure that the voices of the vulnerable and weak in society are effectively heard in priority setting.
   Institutional, capacity, and political economy assessment. The next stage in applying SEA in policy and sector reform is to assess the extent to which existing systems have been able to manage the chosen priorities. A first step is often a thorough review of the policy, institutional, legal, and regulatory frameworks, and of the existing capacities associated with the management of environmental and social priorities. This is followed by an assessment of the effectiveness of these frameworks and capacities for addressing the priorities, which facilitates the identification of institutional weaknesses and capacity gaps. This analysis is complemented by an assessment of the effect that sector reform may have on the identified weaknesses and gaps. The analysis requires considering the potential reactions of stakeholders and the potential conflicts that may adversely affect the reform. Finally, these assessments are validated by the stakeholders to expose them to the complexities of sector reform, and to call attention to the need for finding common ground in order to prevent or manage potential conflicts.

Recommendations. Finally, policy SEA should formulate specific policy, institutional, legal, regulatory, and capacity-building recommendations for overcoming the weaknesses and gaps, and for managing the political economy constraints, determined during the assessment. Validation of the recommendations by stakeholders further strengthens constituencies because it enhances ownership and encourages stakeholders' participation in follow-up and monitoring. Ultimately, this step promotes greater accountability on the part of policy makers.

3. *Environmental and social mainstreaming beyond policy SEA.* After completion of the policy SEA report, certain follow-on interventions should be established to ensure that the recommendations are implemented and that environmental and social mainstreaming becomes a continuous process. At a minimum, stakeholders should be informed about the results of the SEA through mechanisms appropriate for different audiences. To the extent possible, dissemination and discussion of the results by the media should also be promoted. Any monitoring and evaluation framework should be designed as a continuation of the multistakeholder dialogue established during the SEA. At this point, the dialogue should allow for reflection on what was or was not achieved by the SEA and the sector reform.

Ways Forward

SEA can be an effective approach for assisting with the implementation of policy and sector reforms that foster sustainable development. Therefore, *the main recommendation of this report is to move forward with further testing and a staged scaling up of SEA at the policy level.* It is suggested that scaling up be undertaken in three phases over approximately 10 years. The main expected outcome is this: better policy making and successful environmental and social mainstreaming in selected countries as a result of greater capacity for undertaking SEA in policy and sector reform; increase in trust among stakeholders; and strengthened country ownership. The expected development impacts would be contribution to sustainable economic growth, mitigation of and adaptation to climate change, and improvement in environmental and social management of key sectors in selected countries.

The proposed scaling up would focus on promoting the following:

- *Country ownership.* There is strong evidence from the evaluation of the pilots that unless country ownership is ensured, SEA of policy and sector reform is unlikely to be effective. Therefore, the proposed scaling up suggests that donors, the World Bank, and other multilateral institutions should encourage partner countries to undertake SEA for informing policy making. However, as has happened with environmental impact assessment, financial support to client countries would be required during the first stage of testing and experimentation, until SEA becomes ingrained in the regular process of sector planning and policy making. It is suggested that a policy SEA fund be established to provide low-income countries with grants, specialized advice, and technical assistance to facilitate their undertaking SEA of policy and sector reform.

- *Capacity building on policy SEA in sectors critical for economic growth and climate change.* The evaluation also provides ample evidence that SEA effectiveness is constrained by the punctuated, short-lived nature of sector-reform design when SEA typically takes place. In this new phase of piloting policy SEA, a more strategic approach is consequently suggested. Capacity building should focus on raising awareness of SEA as an approach for improving planning and policy making by supporting the accumulation of SEA skills in key sectors of the economy at the level of public agencies, consultants, and civil society. The idea is to set in motion a process that ensures that proposed institutional, legal, regulatory, capacity, and policy adjustments originating in individual SEAs reinforce each other, thereby creating a virtuous cycle of environmental, social, and climate change mainstreaming. Countries could participate in the proposed program on a self-selection basis provided that they are interested in applying SEA in sectors critical for economic growth and for mitigation of and adaptation to climate change.
- *A system of incentives that rewards successful reform and gradual environmental, social, and climate change mainstreaming.* The evaluation has also shown that unless there are incentives for sustaining the mainstreaming effort and strong constituencies that demand it, the process may be derailed or thwarted by vested interests.
- *An alliance of donors and partner countries for environmental, social, and climate change mainstreaming.* In the context of the Paris Declaration on Aid Effectiveness, the proposed program aims at seizing the window of opportunity that seems to be opening for fostering policy SEA with the development of the World Bank Group's New Environment Strategy, the scaling up of the Poverty-Environment Initiative (PEI) of the United Nations Development Programme and the United Nations Environment Programme, and environmental and climate change mainstreaming initiatives being undertaken by other multilateral and bilateral development agencies. It seems that the time is ripe for the establishment of a broad environmental mainstreaming alliance, which would clarify the roles and niches of the different interested parties. The World Bank could add its more specialized experience in sector reform to a potentially influential alliance. The alliance would help partner countries learn from one another's experiences in applying SEA in policy and sector reform

to address common and global challenges such as climate change. The result would be to render SEA implementation globally more efficient.

If this proposal for scaling up is not fully realized, SEA could still make an important contribution to enhancing sector reform. The evidence provided by this evaluation suggests that donors and partner countries should join efforts to foster SEA in policy and sector reform under the following conditions:

- Country ownership is ensured
- SEA is undertaken along with sector-reform design and not as an isolated exercise
- Follow-on activities recommended by the SEA can be supported during sector-reform implementation

Notes

1 SEA describes analytical and participatory approaches that aim to integrate environmental considerations into policies, plans, and programs and to evaluate the interlinkages with economic and social considerations (OECD DAC 2006, 30).

2 This mandate was provided by the Bank's Environment Strategy of 2001.

References

OECD DAC (Organisation for Economic Co-operation and Development, Development Assistance Committee). 2006. *Applying Strategic Environmental Assessment: Good Practice Guidance for Development Co-operation.* Paris: OECD Publishing.

World Bank. 2005. *Integrating Environmental Considerations in Policy Formulation: Lessons from Policy-Based SEA Experience.* Report 32783. Washington, DC: World Bank.

World Bank. 2008. *Environmental Sustainability: An Evaluation of World Bank Group Support.* Independent Evaluation Group. Washington, DC: World Bank.

CHAPTER 1

The World Bank's Pilot Program on SEA

ENVIRONMENTAL DEGRADATION CONTINUES to be a consistent concern around the world. In addition, converging challenges associated with surging food prices, global climate change, and species extinction have made it clear that current economic development trends are unsustainable.

The predominant approach to dealing with environmental and climate change problems has been to treat them as unwanted side effects of economic development. This approach has worked to some extent where it has been possible to effectively regulate commercial and domestic activities. However, in most developing countries, administrative infrastructure has not been able to keep pace with economic activity, and so ecosystems are suffering.

There is growing recognition that for sustainability goals to be reached, efforts need to go beyond complying with standards and mitigating adverse impacts, to gradually decoupling environmental degradation from economic growth. This effort requires mainstreaming environmental, sustainability, and climate change

---

In 2005, the World Bank established the Pilot Program on Institution-Centered SEA (I-SEA) to test a strategic environmental assessment (SEA) approach centered on institutions and governance rather than on impact assessment. As the pilots were evaluated, it became clear that many of the observations and conclusions derived from the six pilot studies were applicable to SEA of policy and sector reform. Consequently, the terms "SEA at the policy level," "policy SEA," and "I-SEA" are used interchangeably in this report.

considerations into policy and sector reform.[1] This idea has been recognized at a high level, for example, in Millennium Development Goal 7, which requires countries to "integrate the principles of sustainable development into country policies and programs and reverse the loss of environmental resources" (http://www. un.org/millenniumgoals/environ.shtml).

Environmental mainstreaming requires consideration of the environment in the earliest stages of the decision-making cycle, when development challenges as well as proposed interventions are framed. In this conception, environmental issues are thought of as a cross-cutting dimension of development. Within European and national policy debates, environmental mainstreaming at the policy level is more often referred to as environmental policy integration. Over the last decade, substantial experience has been gained by both governments and the research community in how to promote such integration, particularly in the making of national and European policy.[2]

Integration of environmental concerns into strategic decision making requires an understanding of the complexities of policy making. Public policies are made by governments within the institutional[3] framework of the public sector. Consequently, attempts to take account of the environment in the making of economic development decisions require attending to the sometimes opaque and messy areas of governance and institutional reform.

There are numerous tools or approaches that can be used to integrate environmental concerns into strategic decision making,[4] and one of the most promising is strategic environmental assessment (SEA). SEA has its roots in environmental impact assessment (EIA) of development projects. In the late 1980s, environmental assessment practitioners began to turn their attention to the environmental impacts of policies, plans, and programs. Many countries began to experiment with the application of strategic environmental assessment to plans and programs, and some jurisdictions produced SEA policies, laws, or regulations (Dalal-Clayton and Sadler 2005). In Europe, this new development was given significant impetus with the coming into law of the European Directive on SEA.[5] International development agencies also began to test SEA in the 1990s, with the World Bank leading the way with a range of sector and regional environmental assessment initiatives.[6]

Environmental assessment of policies began to take hold around the turn of the new millennium. By that time, 30 years of experience with project-level EIA, and with other environmental "safeguarding" approaches to environmental improvement such as end-of-pipe pollution control, had taught that treating the symptoms of existing pollution was not helping enough in the struggle to foster more environmentally benign or sustainable development. Instead, the idea began to grow that the forces driving environmental damage could be most effectively addressed by integrating environmental considerations into the design and adoption of policies in all sectors. The argument was that cumulative environmental change, environmental opportunities, and potential interactions between different sectors could best be considered upstream in the selection and design of development and sector policies, rather than downstream through project management and end-of-pipe solutions.[7] This was a major conclusion of the World Summit on Sustainable Development in Johannesburg in 2002, and the view is also reflected in the Millennium Development Goals and the Paris Declaration on Aid Effectiveness. The corollary of this new way of thinking is that economic efficiency can be improved if environmental and social issues are considered alongside traditional economic concerns when new policies and strategic plans are developed.

Because of this realization, national governments and development agencies have begun to experiment with approaches that attempt to integrate environmental concerns into new and reformed policies. In international development, most notable has been the initiation of environmental mainstreaming programs by agencies such as multilateral development banks, the United Nations Development Programme (UNDP) and United Nations Environment Programme (UNEP), and others. For example, the UNDP-UNEP Poverty-Environment Initiative has done much to promote the idea of environmental mainstreaming in national and sector development policy, plans, and budgets.[8] Similarly, the multiagency network known as the Poverty Environment Partnership is attempting to mainstream environmental concerns into development aid in support of national and sector development planning.[9]

Another notable initiative from the early 2000s was the Organisation for Economic Co-operation and Development (OECD) Development Assistance Committee's SEA Task Team. This was established by the donor community to promote the development and harmonization of SEA approaches, and is made up of most donors and a number of leading nongovernmental organizations, consultants, and academics with an interest in SEA for development cooperation. In 2006, the task team produced *Applying Strategic Environmental Assessment: Good Practice Guidance for Development Co-operation* (OECD DAC 2006), which has been followed by four specific advisory notes. These were a timely response to the 2005 Paris Declaration on Aid Effectiveness, which calls upon donors and partners to work together to "develop and apply common approaches for strategic environmental assessment at sector and national levels" (OECD 2005).

The OECD DAC SEA *Guidance* describes SEA as a "family of approaches which use a variety of tools, rather than a fixed, single and prescriptive approach." It acknowledges that "SEA applied at the policy level requires a particular focus on the political, institutional and governance context underlying decision making processes" (OECD DAC 2006, 17, 18). The *Guidance* also acknowledges the need for different approaches to SEA for plans and programs, on the one hand, and policies, on the other.

The World Bank first pointed to the need for SEA to include institutional and governance dimensions in its 2005 report titled *Integrating Environmental Considerations in Policy Formulation: Lessons from Policy-Based SEA Experience* (World Bank 2005). This report set the groundwork for the World Bank's interest in SEA at the policy level and was, in part, a response to the requirement for upstream analytical work on environmental assessment of the Bank's Environment Strategy (World Bank 2001), and subsequently to the application of Operational Policy 8.60 on development policy lending (World Bank 2004). This policy SEA approach originated in experience accumulated through country environmental analysis of middle-income countries to inform the World Bank's dialogue on environment with borrowing countries (Pillai 2008; Sanchez-Triana, Ahmed, and Awe 2007).

The World Bank suggests that political scientists' insights into policy formation should be brought to bear on policy-level SEA.[10] It points out that policies are the result of competing interests in the political arena that are influenced by the historical, economic, social, cultural, and institutional context present in a given jurisdiction.[11] Further, it suggests that effective policy-level SEA has to be responsive to windows of opportunity and should increase attention to environmental priorities; strengthen stakeholder constituencies; and contribute to enhancing the capacities of institutions to respond to environmental priorities. These ideas are extended in a 2008 World Bank book, titled *Strategic Environmental Assessment for Policies: An Instrument for Good Governance* (Ahmed and Sanchez-Triana 2008), where the analytical foundations for applying SEA in policies are discussed in detail.

Piloting SEA in Policy and Sector Reform

Acknowledging the tentative nature of policy-level SEA, the Bank established a pilot program in 2005 to test this approach and to promote SEA in the Bank's policy-related operations.

The main objective of the program has been to test and validate SEA at the policy level in different sectors, countries, and regions. Ultimately, the pilot program seeks to draw lessons about the effectiveness of SEA in policy and sector reform and to yield tools for its application in development cooperation. The pilot program was planned to be undertaken over a five-year period (fiscal year 2006 to the end of fiscal year 2010).[12] Although the policy SEA approach originated in middle-income countries, the pilot program supported SEAs mostly in low-income developing countries that are the priority of the World Bank Group's objective of poverty alleviation.

There are two components to the pilot program. The first provided grants and specialized assistance to support eight SEA pilots linked to the Bank's activities. Box 1.1 provides a brief summary of each of the six pilots[13] that have been completed and evaluated.[14]

The second component of the policy SEA program consisted of an evaluation of the pilots, conducted in partnership with the Environmental Economics Unit at the University of Gothenburg in Sweden, the Swedish EIA Centre at the Swedish University of Agricultural Sciences, and the Netherlands Commission for Environmental Assessment.

Objectives of the Evaluation

Given the sparse experience with environmental assessment of policies, *the main objective of the evaluation was to draw lessons from the pilot cases to further develop tools and guidance for applying SEA in policy and sector reform, thereby contributing to sustainable development outcomes.*

The specific objectives of the evaluation were the following:

- Assess how SEA was applied in the pilot cases
- Make policy-level SEA more effective from an operational perspective
- Further develop methods and guidance for applying SEA in policy and sector reform (this is a common goal of the program and of the OECD DAC SEA Task Team)
- Allow the donor community and SEA specialists to reflect on the pros and cons of SEA as a tool for enhancing the environmental sustainability of development policies
- Inform the implementation and updating of the OECD DAC SEA *Guidance* as it relates to policy-level SEA
- Inform the preparation of the World Bank's New Environment Strategy as it progresses during 2010.

BOX 1.1

Brief Summary of the Policy SEA Pilots

1. *Strategic Environmental Assessment of the Kenya Forests Act 2005*

   The objectives of the SEA were to inform and influence the implementation of Kenya's Forests Act of 2005 and to inform the policy dialogue between the World Bank and the government of Kenya on sustainable natural resource use. The SEA also fed into the preparation of the Forestry Reform Support component of the World Bank's Natural Resource Management Project.

(continued)

BOX 1.1 *(continued)*

2. *Sierra Leone Mining Sector Reform Strategic Environmental and Social Assessment (SESA)*

   This SEA originated in a policy development loan that was adapted during its implementation to inform the preparation of the Sierra Leone Mining Technical Assistance Project. SESA's main objective was to help promote long-term country development by integrating environmental and social considerations in mining sector reform.

3. *Dhaka Metropolitan Development Plan Strategic Environmental Assessment*

   This SEA aimed at incorporating environmental considerations into Detailed Area Plans, which make up the lowest tier of the Dhaka Metropolitan Development Plan. The SEA was also intended to inform the preparation of the World Bank's Dhaka Integrated Environment and Water Resources Management Program.

4. *Strategic Environmental Assessment for the Hubei Road Network Plan (2002–2020)*

   This pilot assessed the impact of the Hubei Road Network Plan (HRNP) on environmental and social priorities in Hubei Province, China. The HRNP proposed a system of expressways (totaling 5,000 kilometers) and highways (class I and II, totaling 2,500 kilometers), which provided road links between all major cities in the province.

5. *West Africa Minerals Sector Strategic Assessment (WAMSSA)*

   The purpose of this pilot was to identify the regional policy, institutional, and regulatory adjustments required to integrate social and environmental considerations into minerals sector development in the Mano River Union countries. It was undertaken with a view to informing the preparation and implementation of the West Africa Mineral Governance Program, an adjustable program loan for supporting mining reform in West Africa.

6. *Rapid Integrated Strategic Environmental and Social Assessment (SESA) of Malawi Mineral Sector Reform*

   As part of the Malawi Mineral Sector Review that assessed the need for mining reform in Malawi, a rapid integrated SESA was undertaken, whose main purpose was to review the mining sector's environmental and social regulatory framework. The rapid integrated SESA also attempted to incorporate critical environmental and social considerations into the ongoing discussion of Malawi's mines and minerals policy.

The Evaluation Approach

The pilot program evaluation was designed as a three-stage process, and is presented in a schematic form in figure 1.1. The **first stage** (the boxes on the

FIGURE 1.1
The Policy SEA Pilot Program Evaluation Approach

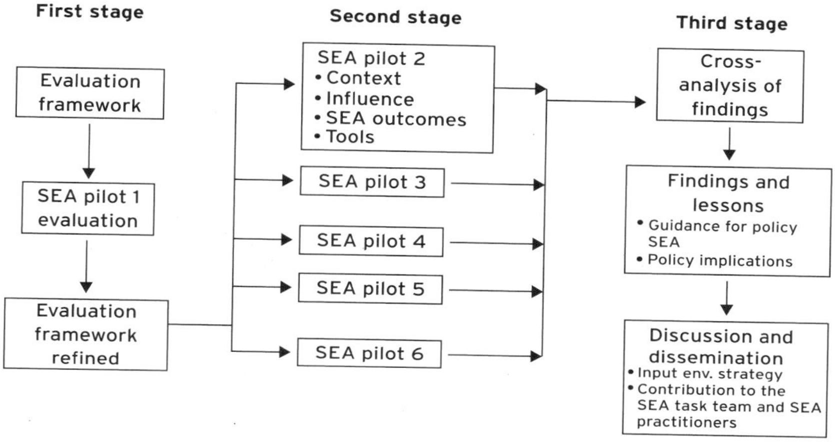

Source: Authors.

left-hand side of figure 1.1) consisted of a detailed literature review, the purpose of which was to strengthen the analytical basis of the evaluation and to provide guidance for the evaluators. The outcome of this literature review is a document titled "Conceptual Analysis and Evaluation Framework for Institution-Centered Strategic Environmental Assessment" (Slunge et al. 2009). This document, referred to as the evaluation framework, is included as appendix B of this report. The objectives of the literature review were to summarize and critically discuss the analytical underpinnings of institution-centered SEA (policy SEA), and to provide an analytical framework for evaluation of the pilot SEAs (appendix B).

Before the second and third stages of the evaluation are described, it is necessary to briefly explain the evaluation framework. The first part of the evaluation framework outlines a proposed conceptual model of policy SEA, which includes process steps, process outcomes, and objectives. This conceptual model is presented in figure 1.2. Its purpose was to guide the evaluations of the pilots and to present an approach for undertaking future policy SEA activity. When this conceptual model was developed, it was expected that lessons learned from the evaluation of the six pilots would lead to refinements of the model.

The second part of the evaluation framework consists of an extensive literature review of policy processes, environmental prioritization, stakeholder representation, institutional capacity, social accountability, and social learning. All these are part of the policy SEA conceptual model. The third and final part of the document proposes an approach for evaluating the policy SEA pilots, which includes a set of generic questions that evaluators can adapt to the context of each pilot and a possible structure for each evaluation report.[15]

FIGURE 1.2
Initial Conceptual Model of Policy SEA: Process Steps, Process Outcomes, and Objective

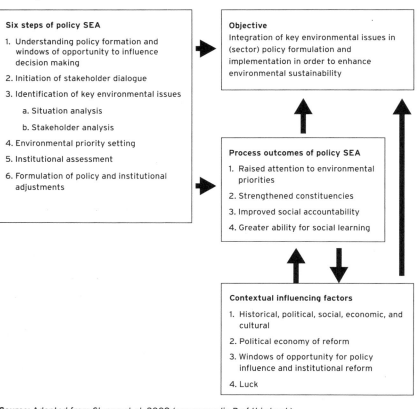

Six steps of policy SEA

1. Understanding policy formation and windows of opportunity to influence decision making
2. Initiation of stakeholder dialogue
3. Identification of key environmental issues
   a. Situation analysis
   b. Stakeholder analysis
4. Environmental priority setting
5. Institutional assessment
6. Formulation of policy and institutional adjustments

Objective
Integration of key environmental issues in (sector) policy formulation and implementation in order to enhance environmental sustainability

Process outcomes of policy SEA

1. Raised attention to environmental priorities
2. Strengthened constituencies
3. Improved social accountability
4. Greater ability for social learning

Contextual influencing factors

1. Historical, political, social, economic, and cultural
2. Political economy of reform
3. Windows of opportunity for policy influence and institutional reform
4. Luck

Source: Adapted from Slunge et al. 2009 (see appendix B of this book).

The **second stage** of the evaluation process consisted of the evaluation of the different SEA pilots (the boxes at the center of figure 1.1). Each evaluation included an initial literature review followed by a period of fieldwork, usually taking from one to three weeks. Stakeholders who had participated in the SEA pilots were interviewed. Interviews were guided by a generic protocol contained in the evaluation framework, which was customized by each evaluator to address the particular context of the pilot to be evaluated. In some of the evaluations, interviews were extensive. For example, the evaluators of the Kenya Forests Act SEA interviewed 45 stakeholders individually and an additional 21 participants in a group meeting. The final outcomes of these six separate evaluations were substantial reports consisting on average of 40 pages of analysis and recommendations. These evaluation reports became the main resource for the final stage of the pilot program evaluation. Summaries of the evaluations are contained in appendix A.

The **third and final stage** of the evaluation was the cross-analysis of the findings from all six pilot cases (as shown by the boxes on the right-hand side of figure 1.1). The cross-analysis was undertaken at two levels. The first level focused on the strengths and weaknesses of the policy SEA approach with regard to influencing policy processes. The second level of analysis drilled down deeper to examine the methods that can be used to make policy SEA effective. The outcomes of both levels of analysis are a refined conceptual model and operational guidance for applying SEA in policy and sector reform.

Preliminary results of the evaluation were discussed, and feedback received, at an international workshop on SEA held on April 7, 2010, in Geneva, jointly organized by the OECD DAC SEA Task Team and the World Bank (see box 1.2 and appendix D.)

BOX 1.2

SEA for Development Cooperation: Taking Stock and Looking Forward

The OECD DAC SEA Task Team and the World Bank held a joint workshop at the 30th International Association for Impact Assessment annual conference in Geneva on April 7, 2010. The workshop was organized to review and discuss the overall progress of policy SEA, and to discuss the relevance of SEA in the New Environment Strategy of the World Bank Group. A process known as "dialogue mapping" was used to focus discussions on four topics:

1. Obstacles and enabling factors for SEA effectiveness in development cooperation and poverty reduction
2. The role of the World Bank in strengthening environmental governance and institutions for sustainable development
3. SEA as a tool for strengthening environmental governance and institutions
4. Main steps for scaling up SEA in development policy

The workshop broadly supported the need for a specific SEA approach for policy and the relevance of further promoting this approach for environmental mainstreaming at the strategic level in developing countries. Much attention was devoted to the importance of country ownership for SEA, including its connection to the role of development agencies and its implications for future interdonor discussions. Furthermore, the workshop highlighted the need to show evidence of the benefits and added value that policy-level SEA brings to existing processes, and to show how such benefits can be sustained in processes that extend beyond the completion of the SEA.

Limitations of the Pilot Program and Evaluations

The evaluation is focused on six completed policy SEA pilots that do not pretend to be representative of specific sectors, regions, or groups of countries. The analytical value of the sample is that each pilot focuses on a different aspect of SEA application at the strategic level. Following accepted principles of case study research strategy, this approach allowed for a systematic comparison of the results of policy SEA application in a variety of contexts and circumstances, thereby enabling generalizations to be made. While the cases and consequent evaluations were carefully designed and undertaken, care should be exercised in making generalizations (see box 1.3).

In addition, although special efforts were made to engage governments in these pilots, the pilots were all "driven" by the World Bank. This fact may limit the applicability of the lessons learned for future policy SEA activity undertaken by developing countries. However, this limitation does not undermine the principles underlying the application of policy SEA. In fact, if policy SEA were driven by developing countries, the effectiveness of the outcomes would likely increase. This issue is further discussed in chapters 2 and 4 of this report.

It is widely understood that policies are rarely implemented as originally defined. During implementation, policies are often reformed as a consequence of contextual influences. Because four of the six policy processes that the pilots attempted to influence had not yet been implemented when the evaluation was carried out, the effect of the pilots during policy implementation could not be fully and conclusively evaluated. The focus of the evaluation was the pilots' influence on policy formulation, and their potential influence on policy implementation.

BOX 1.3

How Can One Generalize from Case Studies?

"The answer is not simple. However, consider for the moment that the same question had been asked about an experiment: How can you generalize from a single experiment? In fact, scientific facts are rarely based on single experiments; they are usually based on a multiple set of experiments that have replicated the same phenomenon under different conditions. The same approach can be used with multiple case studies but requires a different concept of the appropriate research designs. . . . The short answer is that case studies, like experiments, are generalizable to theoretical propositions and not to populations or universes. In this sense, the case study, like the experiment, does not represent a 'sample,' and in doing a case study, [the] goal will be to expand and generalize theories (analytic generalization) and not to enumerate frequencies (statistical generalization)" (Yin 2003, 10).

Finally, the purpose of the pilot program and its evaluation was not to compare the relative effectiveness of policy SEA and other SEA approaches. Consequently, the results of the evaluation presented in this report do not provide evidence for or against the effectiveness of other SEA approaches. The case for policy-level SEA as a particular approach in the family of SEA approaches was made in World Bank (2005, 2008).

Structure of the Report

The remainder of this report presents the outcomes of the cross-analysis of the six pilots. The body of chapter 2 consists of a detailed cross-case analysis. It examines whether the pilots have influenced policy interventions in their jurisdictions, and if so, how. It also examines the extent to which the SEA pilots achieved the four identified outcomes of environmental prioritization, environmental constituency building, improved social accountability, and strengthened social learning. A special attempt is made to examine the contextual factors that either enable or constrain the ability of the SEA pilots to integrate environmental considerations into policy making.

Chapter 3 of the report presents guidance for applying SEA in policy and sector reform. Using the pilot cases as a basis, this chapter describes the policy SEA process steps. The main objective of this section is to provide guidance to practitioners in methods and approaches for undertaking SEA in policy and sector reform.

Chapter 4 of the report summarizes the findings of the evaluation and addresses the practical challenges of scaling up SEA in policy and sector reform. It argues that policy SEA approaches can assist countries in developing more environmentally sustainable policies. This chapter draws out the policy implications of the evaluation for SEA systems in developing countries and for development cooperation.

Notes

1 It is recognized that climate change issues are closely linked with environmental concerns. Throughout this report, the term "environment" will be defined as incorporating climate change concerns.

2 See Jordan and Lenschow (2008) and Nilsson and Eckerberg (2007).

3 The definition of the term "institutions" in this report is a broad one. It is based on the definition provided in the evaluation framework, which is introduced later in the chapter and which supports this evaluation. In the evaluation framework, institutions are defined as being made up of formal constraints such as rules and laws, and informal constraints such as norms of behavior and self-imposed rules of conduct. The evaluation framework makes the point that the concept of institutions is thus much broader than that of organizations. While institutions design and implement rules, organizations are the players. The distinction between institutions and

organizations is important since there is a tendency to equate the two concepts in discussions of institutional capacity building for improved environmental management. A too-limited focus on environment sector organizations (such as environment ministries and agencies) risks diverting attention from other institutions that may be equally or more important for environmentally sustainable development (Slunge et al. 2009).

4 See, for example, Dalal-Clayton and Bass (2009).

5 Directive 2001/42/EC.

6 Kjørven and Lindhjem (2002) review 20 examples of sector and regional environmental assessments undertaken by the World Bank between 1997 and 2001. See Annandale et al. (2001) for examples of SEA initiatives in other multilateral agencies.

7 See, for example, Brown and Tomerini (2009).

8 See http://www.pei.org.

9 The Poverty Environment Partnership is a group of donor agencies, multilaterals, and research-focused international nongovernmental organizations. See http://www.povertyenvironment.net/pep/.

10 Policy formation is the continuous process of policy formulation and implementation. While policy formulation has well-defined boundaries, policy formation does not. See chapter 3 of World Bank (2008).

11 For example, see Cohen, March, and Olsen (1972); Sabatier (1975); Kingdon (1995); and chapter 3 of World Bank (2008).

12 Documentation describing the work undertaken in each of the pilots is available at the World Bank's "SEA Toolkit" Web page: http://web.worldbank.org/WBSITE/EXTERNAL/TOPICS/ENVIRONMENT/0,,contentMDK:21911843~pagePK:148956~piPK:216618~theSitePK:244381,00.html.

13 More-detailed summaries of the six pilot projects are presented in appendix A. Documentation describing the work undertaken in each of the pilots is also available at the World Bank's "SEA Toolkit" Web page, referred to in the previous note.

14 A pilot focused on trade policy was delayed due to the political instability affecting Pakistan, and was therefore not included in the evaluation. Another pilot on climate change in Orissa, India, started when the evaluation of the original pilots was being completed. For this reason, this pilot was not included in this evaluation.

15 The evaluation framework was discussed at two workshops in Europe in late 2008 and at a meeting in Washington, DC, in June 2009.

References

Ahmed, K., and E. Sanchez-Triana, eds. 2008. *Strategic Environmental Assessment for Policies: An Instrument for Good Governance.* Washington, DC: World Bank.

Annandale, D., J. Bailey, E. Ouano, W. Evans, and P. King. 2001. "The Potential Role of Strategic Environmental Assessment in the Activities of Multi-lateral Development Banks." *Environmental Impact Assessment Review* 21 (5): 407–29.

Brown, A. L., and D. Tomerini. 2009. "Environmental Mainstreaming in Developing Countries." Proceedings of the International Association of Impact Assessment Meeting, Accra, Ghana. http://www.iaia.org/iaia09ghana/.

Cohen, M. D., J. G. March, and J. P. Olsen. 1972. "A Garbage Can Model of Organizational Choice." *Administrative Science Quarterly* 17: 1–25

Dalal-Clayton, B., and S. Bass. 2009. *The Challenges of Environmental Mainstreaming: Experience of Integrating Environment into Development Institutions and Decisions.* Environmental Governance 3. London: International Institute for Environment and Development.

Dalal-Clayton, B., and B. Sadler. 2005. *Strategic Environmental Assessment: A Sourcebook and Reference Guide to International Experience.* London: Earthscan.

Jordan, A., and A. Lenschow. 2008. *Innovations in Environmental Policy: Integrating the Environment for Sustainability.* Cheltenham, UK: Edward Elgar.

Kingdon, John. 1995. *Agendas. Alternatives and Public Policies,* 2nd ed. New York: Harper Collins.

Kjørven, O., and H. Lindhjem. 2002. "Strategic Environmental Assessment in World Bank Operations: Experience to Date—Future Potential." Environmental Strategy Paper 4, World Bank Environment Department, Washington, DC.

Nilsson, M., and K. Eckerberg, eds. 2007. *Environmental Policy Integration in Practice: Shaping Institutions for Learning.* London: Earthscan.

OECD (Organisation for Economic Co-operation and Development). 2005. "Paris Declaration on Aid Effectiveness." http://www.oecd.org/dataoecd/11/41/34428351.pdf.

OECD DAC (Organisation for Economic Co-operation and Development, Development Assistance Committee). 2006. *Applying Strategic Environmental Assessment: Good Practice Guidance for Development Co-operation.* Paris: OECD Publishing.

Pillai, Poonam. 2008. "Strengthening Policy Dialogue on Environment: Learning from Five Years of Country Environmental Analysis." Environment Department Paper 114, World Bank Environment Department, Washington, DC.

Sabatier, Paul 1975. "Social Movements and Regulatory Agencies: Toward a More Adequate and Less Pessimistic Theory of Clientele Capture." *Policy Sciences* 6 (1975): 301–42.

Sanchez-Triana E., K. Ahmed, and Y. Awe, eds. 2007. *Environmental Priorities and Poverty Reduction: A Country Environmental Analysis for Colombia.* Washington, DC: World Bank.

Slunge, D., S. Nooteboom, A. Ekstrom, G. Dijkstra, and R. Verheem. 2009. "Conceptual Analysis and Evaluation Framework for Institution-Centered Strategic Environmental Assessment." Working paper, World Bank, Washington, DC. June 23. http://web. worldbank.org/WBSITE/EXTERNAL/TOPICS/ENVIRONMENT/0,,contentMDK: 21913032~pagePK:148956~piPK:216618~theSitePK:244381,00.html.

World Bank. 2001. *Making Sustainable Commitments: An Environment Strategy for the World Bank.* Washington, DC: World Bank.

———. 2004. BP 8.60—Development Policy Lending. World Bank Operational Manual. http://go.worldbank.org/1GPIUNWHW0.

———. 2005. *Integrating Environmental Considerations in Policy Formulation: Lessons from Policy-Based SEA Experience.* Report 32783. Washington, DC: World Bank.

———. 2008. *Environmental Sustainability: An Evaluation of World Bank Group Support.* Independent Evaluation Group. Washington, DC: World Bank.

Yin, Robert K. 2003. *Case Study Research, Design and Methods.* 3rd ed. Los Angeles: Sage.

CHAPTER 2

Influencing Sector Reform
for Sustainability

THE CONCEPTUAL MODEL OF POLICY STRATEGIC ENVIRONMENTAL
assessment (SEA) introduced in figure 1.2 assumes that by following a series of
procedural steps, SEA can result in one or more of four outcomes (raised attention to environmental priorities; strengthened environmental constituencies;
improved social accountability mechanisms for policy implementation; and
greater ability for social learning). The conceptual model also suggests that by
following the procedural steps, the potential for achieving integration of key
environmental issues in policy formulation and implementation can be greatly
enhanced.

Figure 1.2 recognizes that contextual factors in given jurisdictions will likely
influence the ability of SEA to affect outcomes and influence policy formulation.
In this chapter, the impact of the six pilots on policy SEA outcomes is reviewed.
This review is followed by an analysis of the contextual factors that either enable
or constrain the attainment of the four outcomes. The chapter concludes with
suggestions for refinement of the conceptual model for applying SEA on policy
and sector reform.

The Pilots and Policy SEA Outcomes

Each evaluation assessed the influence that the pilot had on the four identified outcomes. This task was not always easy. All evaluations did address the question of outcomes by focusing on changes in behavior, relationships, and activities or actions on the part of people, groups, organizations, and institutions that came into contact with the SEA pilots.

The next four subsections analyze the extent to which the pilots managed to achieve the four outcomes.

Raising Attention to Environmental Priorities

Evaluators were asked to address four questions to determine whether each pilot had succeeded in raising attention to environmental priorities:

1. Are priorities more clearly defined than previously, and how has this change been documented?
2. Have environmental priorities been placed on the policy agenda and linked to growth, poverty reduction, or other key development issues?
3. To what extent are priorities shared among key stakeholders?
4. How has the pilot helped to raise attention to priorities?

This outcome is intimately connected with public participation, as priorities are social choices that ultimately reflect the social preferences of interest groups and communities. Priorities cannot realistically be uncovered without interaction with stakeholders. The process of prioritization involves first identifying key issues through some kind of scoping exercise, and then sorting and possibly ranking the issues in order of importance.

In some cases, the sheer act of awareness raising can have a positive impact on prioritization. In the Hubei pilot, for example, the SEA provided an overall, holistic picture of the possible environmental impacts of planned transport projects. This outcome was sufficient to increase the awareness of senior managers at the Hubei Provincial Communication Department (HPCD) about macro-level environmental implications of the proposed development of road transport. The HPCD management now pays more attention to environmental issues, as evidenced in detailed investigations carried out during the design stage of each road project. The SEA also indirectly contributed to a new circular, issued by the HPCD management, which encourages the enforcement of environmental protection requirements during expressway construction.

All the evaluations showed evidence that the pilots had contributed to improved dialogue over environmental and social issues, although the extent of this dialogue and its potential to influence policy reform varied significantly across the pilots. In one case, the Malawi Rapid SESA (strategic environmental and social assessment) pilot, time restrictions constrained the ability of the SEA specialist to fully examine priorities. The rapid assessment focused on the system and capacities for environmental and social management in the mining sector. The assessment identified major gaps and made it possible to make the case for including environmental and social issues in the reform agenda. It also recommended that a full-fledged policy SEA be undertaken during the formulation of mining sector reforms to properly assess key issues and select priorities in a participatory and well-informed way.[1]

Other pilots, for example the West Africa Minerals Sector Strategic Assessment (WAMSSA) and the Sierra Leone SESA, included quite elaborate techniques for involving stakeholders in the ranking of environmental and social priorities.[2] Perhaps more important than the approach taken to prioritization is the effect that it had on policy dialogue, and the likelihood that it would have a long-term impact on the movement toward environmentally sustainable policies. In two of the cases, WAMSSA and Malawi Rapid SESA, there is evidence that raised attention to environmental priorities may well have moved environmental and social issues upward in the reform agenda and thus broadened mining policy horizons.

For example, WAMSSA has had a substantial impact on how stakeholders view the regional harmonization of mining policy, which is important for addressing transborder environmental and social impacts of mining activities (such as the deforestation of the Upper Guinean forest) as well as migration of miners and people attracted by mining discoveries. This may well be the most important influence that WAMSSA has had on regional mining reform. Before WAMSSA was undertaken, most stakeholders were skeptical about regional approaches. Their negativity tended to be based on the view that minerals are traditionally owned by individual states, which will always assert sovereignty over their valuable resources. This is a difficult viewpoint to challenge. However, by making regionalism and the associated concept of mining "clusters" the focus of the strategic assessment process, the SEA team managed to change the views of most stakeholders. On the whole, stakeholders saw the benefits in reforms that would integrate regulatory frameworks and the provision of infrastructure. This change of perspective tied in with the outcomes of extensive consultation exercises that saw "insufficient transparency and consistency of government decision making" as a highly ranked priority (World Bank 2010, 65). Detailed one-on-one interviews undertaken during the evaluation suggested that underlying this acceptance of regional harmonization and mining cluster development is the belief that harmonization might reduce illegal trade and rent-seeking behavior.

Another example is offered by the Malawi Mineral Sector Review (of which the rapid SESA is a part). This pilot showed specific evidence of environmental issues being pushed onto the political agenda. A longitudinal comparison showed that environmental issues in the mining sector were low on the political agenda some three to five years prior to the review. The current situation is very different, and the change was largely driven by the development of uranium mining and prospective iron ore and rare earth mines. The review provided an opportunity for concerns about environmental hazards to be openly discussed. According to the evaluation, another important indicator of increased attention to environmental priorities is the government of Malawi's explicit ambition to ensure that small-, medium-, and large-scale miners comply with environmental and occupational health and safety standards, as indicated in the national strategic plan (Growth and Development Strategy 2010–2011).[3]

The cases where priority setting was more successful in politicizing environmental and social issues also indicated that priorities are not uniformly shared among stakeholders. In the Malawi case, it became obvious that the various stakeholders did not share the same view of the relevance, magnitude, and risks of the different environmental problems associated with mining. By extension, there were differences of opinion about the relative importance of environmental issues relative to other social and economic issues. In the WAMSSA case, not all stakeholders shared a positive view of regional harmonization. Many pointed out that the governments of the three Mano River Union countries were not driving the regional approach. Government representatives appeared to support the harmonization concept, but skeptical stakeholders claimed that this position was presented for public relations purposes only. Political economy analysis suggests that government agencies susceptible to rent-seeking behavior would want to maintain the status quo.

Even in these successful examples, it is clear that the impact of prioritization can be temporary and punctuated, rather than permanent and sustained. The Malawi evaluation pointed to the need to sustain dialogue among key stakeholders over a considerable period of time. Such dialogue also needs to be based on solid environmental information that is communicated widely across stakeholders to encourage equitable participation.

The cases in which prioritization did not work well also provide useful examples for future practice. The Dhaka case showed that influential groups can be given undue priority in stakeholder analysis, and therefore during the consultation process. The reverse side of this situation is that vulnerable groups are often underrepresented. In the Dhaka case, this imbalance resulted in issues such as vulnerability and health being effectively ignored. Ahmed and Sanchez-Triana (2008) and World Bank (2005) make much of the need for prioritizing activities to include the viewpoints of vulnerable groups, who disproportionately bear the burden of environmental degradation and who have less of a voice in policy formulation.[4]

Even in pilots that expended considerable energy on consultation processes, it was clear that some vulnerable groups were not properly included. For example, despite undertaking 10 separate consultation exercises in mining communities in Guinea, Liberia, and Sierra Leone, WAMSSA still did not find a way to include the artisanal mining sector in what was otherwise a very effective dialogue.

The conclusion from this brief analysis is that *SEA should always include a careful analysis of the obstacles to full representation, and should propose mechanisms by which unorganized stakeholders can be reached.* On the whole, this kind of analysis was not part of the six pilot studies.

Finally, for policy-level SEA to have an impact in the long term, there is a need for local capacity development for environmental priority setting. While some SEA teams used local consultant partners to organize consultation activities, there is not much evidence of determined local capacity development in the pilot studies. This gap is not necessarily the fault of consultant teams. *Terms of reference for policy SEA should include a substantial local capacity-building component.*

Strengthened Constituencies

Another precondition for the development of environmentally sustainable policy is the strengthening of constituencies. The policy SEA approach assumes that a critical force for integrating environmental considerations in the continuum of policy formation are groups organized around a common environmental interest or concern directly or indirectly affected by the policy process. As stated in the evaluation framework (appendix B of this volume), "without strengthened and effective environmental constituencies . . . the [policy SEA] model assumes that environmental mainstreaming in policy making would be short-lived. Laws, presidential decrees, or regulations eventually adopted when policies are formulated risk being partially applied, reverted, distorted, or even ignored during policy implementation."

In their terms of reference, evaluators were asked to address the following questions:

1. Which constituencies have been strengthened (civil society organizations, private sector organizations, networks within the bureaucracy, networks involving many different kinds of actors)?
2. Have stakeholder engagement and networks been maintained after completion of the SEA report?

This SEA outcome is closely connected with the goal of raising attention to environmental priorities. Both require engagement with stakeholders, although this second outcome relates more generally to the building or strengthening of constituencies that can demand accountability.

The pilots varied in the extent to which they were able to actively strengthen constituencies. In some instances, a pilot showed evidence of constituency strengthening, even when other aspects of the policy SEA project were not all that influential. For example, in the Dhaka metropolitan development planning pilot, actions taken by civil society organizations suggest that the SEA may well have contributed to strengthening constituencies. In late 2008, one year after the completion of the policy SEA, a committee was established by an alliance of civil society groups to review the Detailed Area Plans (DAPs) produced by the Capital Development Authority, for which the SEA was undertaken. The review highlighted, among other things, inconsistencies between the higher-level Dhaka Metropolitan Development Plans and the DAPs, for example with regard to the protection of low-lying flood flow zones. When the committee presented its findings, it delayed the approval of the DAPs by at least six months. Several members of the committee also participated in the SEA stakeholder consultation process. It is possible that the SEA consultation process catalyzed the joint action taken on this issue by these civil society organizations.

Another example of strengthened constituencies is evident in the WAMSSA pilot, where the policy SEA appears to have opened up for examination the institutional mechanisms used to deal with regional planning and harmonization. A considerable amount of time was spent in the final validation workshop discussing the proliferation of regional initiatives, which was a source of some concern and confusion. A number of stakeholders were keen to see WAMSSA, or at least its outcomes, carried through beyond the completion of the World Bank project. The argument was that WAMSSA had created a substantial momentum for regional mining policy harmonization that should not be lost. Participants then discussed how best to institutionalize this new policy dialogue.

There was a strong call from the stakeholder group for some kind of permanent, multistakeholder constituency to keep the policy dialogue going. Participants made clear their frustration with the fact that the outcomes and recommendations of many previous reports and consultations seem to have been instantly forgotten once the donor-funded project was completed. Even work that has high-level government support can be stalled or shelved following changes in political leadership. A policy or program may have the backing of a development partner or a particular administration, and then a change of decision makers causes those priorities to shift. An example is the Sierra Leone pilot SESA, which provided useful recommendations, but saw mining reform set aside for around two years when a new government was elected.

The proposal put forward by WAMSSA stakeholders is worthy of brief discussion. Figure 2.1 presents an example of an approach to building long-term environmental and social constituencies by establishing an implementation framework for the proposed World Bank $300 million West Africa Mineral Governance Program (WAMGP). During consultation workshops, stakeholders called for the constituency mechanism established during WAMSSA to be expanded and adapted to become part of an advisory and social accountability

FIGURE 2.1
Example of a Long-Term Constituency Proposal: The West Africa Mineral Governance Program Implementation Framework

Source: World Bank 2010, figure 10.

Note: ECOWAS = Economic Community of West African States; UEMOA = West African Economic and Monetary Union; EITI = Extractive Industries Transparency Initiative; EITI++ = Extractive Industries Transparency Initiative Plus Plus; CBO = community-based organization.

role within the management of the WAMGP. This would be the purpose of the regional multistakeholder steering committee placed in the top right-hand corner of figure 2.1.

WAMSSA's multistakeholder dialogue is one of the few examples from the six case studies of a carefully thought-through attempt to build long-term constituency engagement linked to the task of environmental mainstreaming, which was also supported by a wide array of stakeholders. Other pilots did tackle this issue, but with limited success. For example, the Malawi Mineral Sector Review, and the incorporated rapid SESA, managed to strengthen constituencies through consultations and the stakeholder workshop where the sector review was discussed. According to the evaluation, the rapid SESA workshop created a more level playing field across actors, and encouraged some weaker and more vulnerable communities and nongovernmental organizations to claim larger stakes both in the development of the general mining sector and in specific mining operations. However, the strengthening of constituencies was considered to be temporary and had already tapered off at the time of the evaluation.

Other pilots had relatively little success in strengthening broad-based, long-term constituencies. In the Hubei road transport planning case, for example, consultations involved only government agencies. Recommendations from the SEA team relating to the establishment of a standing committee on environmental management of road networks were not met with enthusiasm by the responsible authority (the HPCD).[5]

Finally, one outstanding and consistent conclusion from the cross-case analysis is that *consultation and constituency building require considerable time and effort if they are to lead to changes in the way policies are developed.* Concerns were often expressed that one-off consultation exercises, where consultants run "single-day-one-room" workshops, may not be the most effective approach for dealing with local people. In the three mining pilots, it was suggested that consultation in mining communities that are remote from cities, and that have a significant proportion of illiterate people, may require more preparation, longer face-to-face time, and less intimidating surroundings. The most frustrating example of poorly designed consultation strategy comes from the Dhaka metropolitan development planning case, where the evaluators found that a number of people who participated in SEA meetings could not remember ever having attended.

Improving Social Accountability

Social accountability is defined in the evaluation framework as "bottom-up" or demand-side accountability. It is the environmental constituencies' task to demand social accountability mechanisms.

Reinforcing social accountability is a key mechanism for improving environmental governance and ensuring that SEA can have an influence beyond a discrete policy intervention. According to World Bank (2005), specific social accountability mechanisms are required in order to ensure that commitments made through policy design are implemented and last over time. The evaluation framework and Ahmed and Sanchez-Triana (2008) make it clear that social accountability can be reinforced by the following methods:

- strengthening underlying legislation and implementation practices on information disclosure, public participation, and access to justice
- establishing institutions that create more transparency, and supporting scrutiny of policy and implementation
- institutionalizing participatory elements in the implementation of policies or management of natural resources
- strengthening long-term constituencies and policy advocacy networks

World Bank (2005) indicates that the mere balancing of stakeholder interests is not enough to guarantee improved social accountability. In order to ensure that commitments made through policy design are implemented and last over time, specific social accountability mechanisms are required.

Evaluators were asked to address improvements in social accountability by posing the following questions:

1. Is there evidence of new or improved legislation on access to information, public participation, or justice in environmental matters?

2. Have institutional mechanisms for the implementation/enforcement of legislation on access rights been strengthened?
3. Have mechanisms been put in place for stakeholder participation or involvement in strategic decision making, particularly by weak and vulnerable stakeholders?
4. Is there evidence of enhanced transparency and media scrutiny of policy decision making?

Given that even the longest pilot was undertaken over a period of just less than two years, it is difficult to claim that the processes had a direct and permanent impact on social accountability. However, it is possible to consider the role of SEA as a *catalyst* within an institutional setting that makes policy makers more accountable for their decisions.

Some of the countries in which the pilots took place have not always been amenable to public pleas for greater social accountability. For example, the evaluation of the Hubei Road Network Plan SEA points out that decision making in China is fundamentally centralized and highly political. According to the evaluation, "all plans prepared depend on political instructions . . . and the leaders of various government departments . . . determine every key aspect of the plan. The ultimate principle is that the leaders determine everything and this creates an unfavorable atmosphere for independent thinking, stakeholder consultations and impartial assessments" (Dusik and Jian 2010).

Other policy SEA pilot countries exhibit different problems that could inhibit attempts to improve conditions of social accountability. Some African countries, especially those recovering from conflict, were described by interviewed participants as being "low-trust" societies (Annandale 2010). It can be very difficult to build social accountability mechanisms in such countries, although on the positive side, there is sometimes considerable public demand for greater accountability, and excitement when it is actually achieved.

Two examples from the pilots show small but significant steps forward in overcoming cynicism in the move toward improved social accountability. In Malawi, against a background of deep mistrust, the efforts to collect and share information on key environmental and social concerns in the rapid SESA helped to advance the accountability agenda of civil society organizations working in the mining sector. Stakeholders also welcomed the recommendation to investigate the possibility of membership for Malawi in the Extractive Industry Transparency Initiative, which was seen as an important way of enhancing accountability.

In the WAMSSA case, stakeholders from Liberia and Sierra Leone appreciated the policy SEA process because it had the potential to "take decisions away from mining companies and governments" (Annandale 2010). It is a matter of fact that large mining companies often work with governments directly, and in secret, in their attempts to negotiate contracts that allow favorable access to mineral deposits. While powerful stakeholders are within their rights to negotiate under their own terms, public commitments to social accountability mechanisms such as multistakeholder processes can make it more embarrassing for mining companies, and possibly governments, to back out and resort to bilateral negotiation.

The literature surrounding social accountability often focuses on the need to build or strengthen institutional mechanisms for ensuring that policy decisions are made in a more transparent fashion. As was the case with constituency building, such mechanisms need to be strong enough to ensure that there is long-term engagement with the idea of mainstreaming environmental concerns into policy development. Figure 2.1 presented a sophisticated proposal for an accountability framework associated with the upcoming WAMGP. This kind of accountability mechanism shows promise, because it would be closely associated with a management system that is internal to the state.[6] As the evaluation framework argues, institutionalization is important as a way of overcoming one-time participation exercises, which can perpetuate the idea that participation is a punctuated process.

While the proposed WAMGP accountability framework is encouraging, there are more simple steps that can be taken to begin the process of improving social accountability. For example, the evaluation of the Dhaka metropolitan development planning pilot made much of the fact that the final SEA report was not disseminated to stakeholders. In failing to provide feedback to the participants in the consultation process, the SEA missed an opportunity to strengthen learning, accountability, and environmental constituencies, and possibly contributed to a sense among participants that their input was not taken seriously. This direct quotation from a civil society representative interviewed during the Dhaka pilot evaluation amplifies this point:

> After [the SEA], they should involve all the parties. . . . Let's make it an issue [for] government . . . and let them know that this is our common analysis. But because of the fact that we were not involved in the [follow-up] activities of this SEA, we don't own it anymore, this is the bad side. We were involved, we were very eager and we were very optimistic, but my involvement was not taken into consideration . . . so that I don't believe [the interviewee's organization] is [a] strong part or strong participant or strong owner of that report. We could not pursue it because we don't have a copy of it . . . .; we thought that this particular report [would] give us a tool for our movement (Axelsson, Cashmore, and Sandstrom 2009).

Somewhat surprisingly, given the amount of money, time, and energy poured into SEA, this problem seems to be quite common. SEA proponents often talk about the importance of consultation and constituency building, but continue to treat participation exercises as discrete, one-off events. A cynic would suggest that all the proponent wants out of consultation is to prove that it has been undertaken, and to show as much in a final SEA report. Clearly, this kind of approach to participation is counterproductive if the goal is to improve social accountability in the long term.

SEA can also indirectly influence social accountability. In the SESA pilot in Sierra Leone, the evaluator discovered that the SEA process had influenced the Justice for the Poor (J4P) initiative. This program is now examining practical interventions for promoting social accountability at the mining community level, such as improving knowledge about interactions between mining companies and local communities and strengthening the institutional arrangements that govern relationships between mining companies and communities. According to the director of the program, "SESA was incredibly useful in providing sound arguments about the importance of developing further research and practical interventions to strengthen the accountability of the mining industry at the local level" (Albarracin-Jordan 2009).

In conclusion, some of the pilots exhibited tentative movement toward greater social accountability, but it is too early for the required institutional mechanisms to be put in place.

Supporting Social Learning

Social learning, the fourth of the key outcomes of policy SEA, relates to the broad processes of changing perceptions, values, and priorities in society. More precisely, SEA attempts to facilitate learning processes among key policy-making actors and stakeholders, either through incremental or technical learning (so-called single-loop learning) or through more transformative and conceptual learning (so-called double-loop learning) (see Ahmed and Sanchez-Triana 2008).

It is inherently difficult to measure the type and extent of social learning through a given intervention because learning occurs slowly (usually over a period of several years). As a result, and as will be seen below, of the four outcomes of policy SEA, social learning has been the most complex one to demonstrate.

Evaluators were asked to address the following questions about the pilots:

1. Who has learned? Is it primarily government officials and policy makers, or a broader set of societal actors?
2. What has been learned? Is it mainly technical learning, or have more fundamental problems and strategies been re-conceptualized?
3. Has the policy SEA pilot initiated or strengthened mechanisms for learning through
   a. intersector or multisector coordination procedures?
   b. dialogue on policy reform that includes environmental and social perspectives and involves multiple stakeholders?

    c. compensating potential losers created by policy changes?

    d. monitoring and evaluation, creating feedback for policy and planning fine tuning?

    e. linking policy making with research communities?

The pilot cases provided some limited answers to these questions. In the Hubei road transport planning pilot, all those interviewed during the evaluation agreed that sharing data from baseline analyses was the most useful aspect of this SEA pilot, and that learning was facilitated through this sharing. Part of the contextual background to this case is that institutional control of decision making in China makes access to data very difficult. Data are often treated as "privately" owned by government agencies, and SEA teams are required to purchase data from the relevant agency. This privatization of data was considered by the Hubei pilot evaluators to be a potentially significant constraint on social learning in China. Consequently, the relatively open sharing of baseline data in the Hubei case was considered unusual, and notably led to technical learning on the part of participating institutional stakeholders.

While institutional analysis was considered controversial in the Hubei pilot,[7] three respondents found it a useful part of SEA. Some stakeholders who participated in workshops indicated that they used aspects of the institutional analysis in their daily work, especially the overview of relevant laws and obligations for environmental management in road planning. A similar response was evident in the Dhaka metropolitan development planning pilot, where the evaluation suggests that the SEA has had an indirect influence on the urban development process. It appears to have contributed to raising some limited awareness within the Capital Development Authority of the need for environmental assessment in order to take a more holistic approach to planning and urban development.

Two of the African cases highlighted the role that SEA can play in enhancing social learning that is already underway. In the evaluation of the Malawi SEA, interviews with government officials indicated that there was an increased understanding of the need for improved coordination between ministries in managing mining sector risks and opportunities; the need to bring civil society organizations into the development process; and the need for benefit-sharing arrangements between the mining industry and local communities. The evaluators make it clear that this is evidence that learning has taken place, although it is difficult to distinguish the precise role played by the rapid SESA.

Interviews with stakeholders during a validation workshop in Sierra Leone provided evidence that WAMSSA had promoted new ways of thinking about the development of high-level policy. For example, institutional stakeholders from Guinea were confident that WAMSSA would provide a methodological approach for dealing with environmental and social issues that go beyond the mineral sector.

This brief summary of the role pilots have played in activating some form of social learning shows that learning is a difficult concept to operationalize, partly because it is broad and abstract. A more tangible concept of what learning means in the context of policy making, and a better understanding of how it can be measured, are needed. This point is elaborated in the following section.

Table 2.1 summarizes the policy SEA pilots' outcomes on raised attention to environmental and social priorities, strengthened constituencies, and improved social accountability. The issue of social learning is redefined in the next section.

Policy Learning

Social learning involves broad societal and collective processes of reframing and developing new understandings, as well as dialogue and reflection. The cross-analysis of the pilot evaluations suggests that social learning in the context of policy SEA is better framed as "policy learning." Policy learning occurs when actors who are engaged as stakeholders in a policy process reflect on and rethink policy-making problems, goals, and strategies. The mechanism of policy learning can be understood as a cumulative process involving at least three stages: knowledge acquisition, knowledge interpretation, and knowledge institutionalization (Huber 1991).

A tangible way of conceptualizing policy learning in relation to SEA is through its influence on policy capacities, policy horizons, and decision regimes. Changes in these underlying conditions of policy processes may be considered as concrete manifestations of policy learning taking place. Reflection and rethinking, for example, will expand policy capacities. Incorporating new ideas in the framing of policy problems will broaden policy horizons, and the evidence that this broadening occurs can be seen in concrete changes in specific decision regimes.[8] Affecting these underlying conditions of policy processes will in the end enable long-term changes in actual policy decisions. Carden (2009, 21) states: "The crucial point about these three categories of influence is that they go well beyond changing particular policies. The most meaningful and lasting influence is less about specific policy change than about building capacity to produce and apply knowledge for better development results. This kind of influence can take years, or even decades, to take effect or become apparent. But it is no less important for that."

This book argues that the main process behind this influence is the learning mechanism. In other words, the policy learning process, involving knowledge acquisition, interpretation, and institutionalization, cumulatively helps to broaden policy horizons, enhance policy capacities, and affect decision regimes. Table 2.2 draws on this conceptualization to tentatively apply these categories, ex post, to the pilots. The pilots show evidence of *expanded policy capacity* in the fostering of interactions across organizations and the consideration of policy

TABLE 2.1
Policy-Level SEA Outcomes (excluding social learning)

Pilot	Raised attention to environmental priorities	Strengthened constituencies	Improved social accountability
Sierra Leone SESA	Environmental and social priorities informed preparation of a loan to support mining reform. Priorities were selected by stakeholders in provincial workshops informed by the results of case studies and interviews. National priorities were drawn from the provincial priorities and validated by stakeholders in a national workshop.	SESA initiated a multistakeholder dialogue on the environmental and social dimensions of mining sector reform. However, involvement of local mining communities and customary authorities in the dialogue was limited.	SESA has influenced the J4P initiative in Sierra Leone. J4P's program has acknowledged SESA's important contribution to its activities, which includes fostering public debate on issues of accountability.
Hubei road transport planning	The pilot produced an overall, holistic picture of the possible environmental impacts of planned transport projects. This outcome increased the awareness of senior managers at the Hubei Provincial Communication Department about macro-level environmental implications of the proposed development of road transport.	There was no substantial impact on constituencies, although the relatively open sharing of baseline data in the Hubei case was considered to be unusual, and led to technical and social learning on the part of participating institutional stakeholders.	There was no substantial impact on social accountability.
WAMSSA	The pilot contributed to better dialogue over environmental and social issues, including elaborate techniques for involving local, national, and regional stakeholders in the ranking of priorities. It built support for a regional approach to addressing environmental and social priorities in the context of mining reform.	SEA process appears to have opened up examination of the institutional mechanisms used to deal with regional planning and harmonization. The process strengthened civil society organizations working in the mining sector by promoting discussion of a regional agenda for mining reform.	Stakeholders proposed a sophisticated ongoing multistakeholder framework that would become a "home" for the policy dialogue begun during WAMSSA consultations. It would include a series of multistakeholder bodies formed at the regional, national, and local level to ensure transparent stakeholder participation and social accountability for mining development decisions.

Dhaka metropolitan development planning	Identification of environmental priorities was based on a combined ranking of the SEA team's analytical assessment and selected stakeholders' ratings of environmental concerns. However, these were not used to guide subsequent consultations and have not been addressed in the DAPs. Vulnerability and health aspects were poorly considered.	The brief consultation initiatives provided little time for individual reflection and mutual understanding to develop. By not providing feedback to participants, the SEA process missed an opportunity to empower constituencies with a tool to demand accountability.	SEA recommendations regarding institutional reform and improved accountability do not appear to have been taken forward by the Capital Development Authority or any other national actor.
Kenya Forests Act SEA	Nationwide stakeholder workshops facilitated ranking of environmental and social issues and priorities, and reinforced the need to adequately address these priorities. SEA fostered consensus on actions to address priorities by formulating the nationwide forest policy action matrix.	By bringing in local and arguably less powerful/influential stakeholders (such as nongovernmental organizations, CBOs, local community representatives), the SEA process created a more level playing field for discussions and prioritization of forest reform actions. It made a marginal contribution to strengthening local constituencies through community forest associations.	Stakeholder workshops and open discussions brought up accountability issues and encouraged development of practices that might improve social accountability. With the formulation of the forest policy action matrix (in which government ministries and agencies commit themselves to a set of actions), the SEA provided stakeholders with a tool to hold government and other stakeholders to account.
Malawi Rapid SESA	Environmental and social priorities were discussed by stakeholders during a workshop, but time restrictions constrained participants' ability to fully examine priorities as part of the rapid SESA. Contributed to move environmental and social issues upward in the reform agenda.	The stakeholder workshop encouraged some weaker stakeholders, notably from civil society, to claim larger stakes in the mining sector reform process and in specific mining operations.	Against a background of deep mistrust, the efforts to collect and share information on key environmental and social concerns in the rapid SESA were small but highly relevant for strengthening social accountability.

Source: Authors.

trade-offs. Evidence of *broadening policy horizons* can be seen in the framing of policy problems in innovative ways (for example, WAMSSA's regional approach); the creation of opportunities for dialogue through public participation processes; and the acknowledgment of policy ideas, values, and perspectives from multiple stakeholders (seen in the establishment of a process through which SEA priorities and recommendations were selected and validated by all stakeholders). One impact of the pilots that remained more potential than actual, mainly because of the short time between the pilots' conclusion and their evaluation, was *affecting decision regimes* (which would be seen through changing incentives and modifying the decision rules that affect behavior). However, significant potential was identified for the WAMSSA and Malawi pilots, moderate potential was identified for the Hubei and Sierra Leone pilots, and moderate actual impacts were identified for the Kenya pilot. Table 2.2 presents a snapshot view of the influence that each of the pilots may have had on these three categories.

Enabling and Constraining Factors for Effectiveness of SEA in Policy and Sector Reform

The analysis presented in the previous section indicates that SEA outcomes varied substantially across the pilots. Understanding why policy SEA appears to have succeeded in some circumstances and not in others requires an analysis of the context within which each pilot took place, and how the pilot adapted to that context.

TABLE 2.2
Influence of SEA Pilots on Policy Capacities, Policy Horizons, and Decision Regimes

Pilot	Expansion of policy capacities	Broadening of policy horizons	Shaping of decision regimes
Sierra Leone SESA	SESA had a significant impact on the design of the proposed World Bank Mining Technical Assistance Project (MTAP), which aims at facilitating the sustainable growth of the sector. The SESA has also provided important data and information to the World Bank's J4P initiative, aimed at strengthening community-level accountability.	Discussions of key environmental and social issues in the context of preparing the mining reform incorporated multiple perspectives—of mining and environmental sector authorities, donors, and civil society stakeholders at provincial and national levels.	SESA may affect decision regimes on access to land and water for mining activities, environmental management, and benefits distribution of mining activities through implementation of the MTAP.

TABLE 2.2 (*continued*)

Pilot	Expansion of policy capacities	Broadening of policy horizons	Shaping of decision regimes
Hubei road transport planning	The SEA helped to strengthen environmental management at the HPCD, which has established new criteria to examine the environmental performance of its various departments. HPCD now also requires developers of various expressway projects to pay more attention to environmental issues. The pilot SEA stimulated more detailed monitoring of the overall development of the road network	Although controversial, the institutional analysis provided suggestions for inter- and intra-institutional coordination, which may influence HPCD organization over time. Data sharing with regard to baseline analyses was the most useful aspect of this SEA pilot, and learning was facilitated through this sharing.	The HPCD management now pays more attention to environmental issues during the design stage of each road project. The SEA also indirectly contributed to a new circular, issued by the HPCD management, which encourages the enforcement of environmental protection requirements during expressway construction.
WAMSSA	The added value of a multistakeholder consultative framework at the local, national, and regional levels has been established. Stakeholders discussed and validated policy recommendations to promote regional harmonization and transborder management of key environmental and socioeconomic issues associated with mining in West Africa.	WAMSSA clarified the link between regional harmonization/coordination and enhancing governance by empowering national and local stakeholders. Stakeholders became committed to a regional cluster-based approach to mining policy in the three Mano River Union countries.	West African governments adopted the WAMSSA proposal for a multistakeholder framework, which is expected to become the WAMGP accountability framework.

(*continued*)

TABLE 2.2 (*continued*)

Pilot	Expansion of policy capacities	Broadening of policy horizons	Shaping of decision regimes
Dhaka metropolitan development planning	The Capital Development Authority did not consider the SEA recommendations relevant. The policy note prepared for policy makers has not yet been approved by the government of Bangladesh.	The World Bank Country Office and the Capital Development Authority now recognize the need for capacity development within the Capital Development Authority through continued technical assistance. No technical assistance has, however, been offered to the Capital Development Authority up to the time when the evaluation was undertaken.	The SEA process highlighted the fact that the Capital Development Authority had a long way to go before it could fulfil its land use planning responsibilities and may thus have helped to narrow the focus of the proposed World Bank intervention.
Kenya Forests Act SEA	The SEA offered stakeholders an opportunity to better understand the possibilities and innovations in the new Forests Act, especially the opportunities for rural communities to take charge of new forest user rights and invest in enhanced forest management.	The SEA helped show the need for stakeholder involvement in planning and implementation of actions identified by key government ministries and agencies addressing forestry issues. It raised awareness of the need for intersectoral/ ministerial collaboration and for implementation of the new Forests Act via implementation of and follow-up to the forest policy action matrix.	The SEA informed implementation of new Forests Act, and gave impetus to finalization of the new national forest policy. It facilitated interpretation and raised awareness of the content of the new Forests Act ("devolution of user rights, investments, forest management for sustainable development," etc.) It supported long-term strengthening of Kenya's ability and capacity to manage and monitor forests sustainably.

TABLE 2.2 *(continued)*

Pilot	Expansion of policy capacities	Broadening of policy horizons	Shaping of decision regimes
Malawi Rapid SESA	There was no substantial impact on policy capacities.	The pilot increased understanding of (i) the need for improved coordination between ministries in managing mining sector risks and opportunities; (ii) the need to bring civil society organizations into the development process; and (iii) the need for benefit-sharing arrangements between the mining industry and local communities.	There were no tangible changes in laws or policies at the time of the evaluation. However, the rapid SESA and the broader mineral sector review are likely to have an influence on subsequent policy developments.

Source: Authors.

The World Bank literature on SEA at the policy level stresses contextual factors as the drivers that either enable or constrain the ability of SEA to influence outcomes. Context also drives outcomes in other SEA approaches. This argument is supported by recent reviews of other attempts to mainstream environmental thinking into development policy. For example, Dalal-Clayton and Bass (2009) undertook an international survey of the use of mainstreaming tools in developing countries. Midway through their work, however, they realized that the "main lesson from the country survey work was that respondents were more exercised on issues of context—the mainstream drivers of change, the constraints to influencing them, and the associated political and institutional challenges— than the technical pros and cons of individual tools" (Dalal-Clayton and Bass 2009, 10). In another recent case study of environmental mainstreaming, Brown and Tomerini (2009) argue that effective environmental mainstreaming within a developing country has to involve understanding both the structure and process of policy and plan making within the country.

The rest of this section focuses on the contextual factors that either enable or constrain achievement of policy SEA outcomes. The cross-case analysis suggests a variety of contextual factors that are worthy of discussion: ownership, windows of opportunity, political economy and power elites, informal or customary institutions, and capacity. These are a mix of historical, political, economic, social, cultural, and institutional determinants.

Ownership

All of the pilot evaluations comment on the importance of ownership of the SEA process in some fashion (see table 2.3). Ownership needs to be addressed in the relationship between the donor/multilateral agency and the partner countries on the one hand, and internally within governments and key constituencies of partner countries on the other. It also needs to be addressed internally within the donor/multilateral agency that promotes SEA.

As pointed out by the evaluators, lack of ownership has made the pilot SEAs less effective in influencing the policy process. The importance of national ownership in the SEA process is highlighted by agreements under the Paris Declaration on Aid Effectiveness (OECD 2005), in which countries commit to "exercise leadership in developing and implementing their national development strategies" (§14), and donors commit to "respect partner country leadership and help strengthen their capacity to exercise it" (§15) and to "increase alignment with partner countries' priorities, systems and procedures" (§3).

The evaluations indicate a continuum of interest in the SEA processes from the partner governments, ranging from polite acceptance at one end to thinly veiled hostility at the other. Unfortunately, in none of the pilot cases was there evidence of strong local ownership, with the possible exception of WAMSSA, where ownership of the policy dialogue opened up by WAMSSA was found in civil society organizations. This leads to the question, what are the prerequisites for good local ownership, and how can they be met?

In the Dhaka metropolitan development planning case, local ownership was clearly missing. This absence led the evaluators to suggest that there are three main preconditions to be met before a country can be considered ready to accept the responsibilities of running effective SEA. These are sufficient capacity and training to understand the concept of SEA, incentives to consider the results and recommendations of SEA, and sufficient capacity to allow for adequate process integration of the SEA in policy and sector reform. These preconditions set a high bar for some of the less robust partner countries, although they do provide donors and multilaterals with direction for targeting capacity-building assistance and determining whether SEA would be the most effective way to achieve environmental mainstreaming objectives.

Sector ownership is a critical condition for policy SEA effectiveness. In the pilots, for example, the Sierra Leone SESA was steered by an intersectoral committee led by the environment agency, National Commission for Environment and Forestry (NACEF). Ownership of SESA by mining authorities was further weakened because the decision to house the SEA in NACEF came from the president's office. WAMSSA, on the other hand, was steered by a committee made up

TABLE 2.3
Contextual Factors that Constrain or Enable Achievement of Policy SEA Goals

Pilot	Country ownership of the policy SEA process	Windows of opportunity	Political economy and power elites	Role of informal institutions	Sustaining of environmental and social mainstreaming
Sierra Leone SESA	Country ownership was limited because the process was led by the World Bank. The change of government after completion of the SESA aggravated this situation.	The SESA was linked to the reform agenda because it informed the preparation of a mining loan. However, the newly elected administration left the mining reform dormant for around two years.	Political economy factors had a major role in delaying mining sector reform.	The role of chiefs in regulating access to and use of land was only partially analyzed. This limited the effectiveness of SESA's recommendations for addressing high-priority social and environmental priority issues.	When the mining reform process became dormant, the J4P program and WAMSSA carried forward the policy dialogue on mining reform and social accountability initiated by the SESA.
Hubei road transport planning	There was ownership by the HPCD.	Prefectural and municipal authorities should have been involved to increase the effectiveness of the SEA.	While the pilot promoted better-than-usual stakeholder engagement, the highly hierarchical power structure prevailing in China limited the effectiveness of the policy components of the SEA.	Informal institutions seem to play no role in SEA in China.	The SEA provided consolidated baseline analyses and general recommendations that are now being used by the HPCD as it continues to make decisions about development of the road network.
WAMSSA	There was strong ownership of the policy dialogue process by civil society organizations and the WAMSSA Steering Committee.	The policy SEA capitalized on a growing recognition that poverty alleviation in West Africa could best be addressed through regional approaches.	Extensive consultations built up a strong case for regional harmonization of minerals policy in Liberia, Guinea, and Sierra Leone, which might help the political economy of the region.	Powerful rent-seeking interests within governments, "middlemen," and informal customary institutions (chieftains) may threaten the long-term success of the proposed reforms.	The proposal of a multistakeholder management framework was accepted by West African governments. This framework will establish a long-term constituency process that has the potential to outlast changes in governments.

(continued)

43

TABLE 2.3 (continued)

Pilot	Country ownership of the policy SEA process	Windows of opportunity	Political economy and power elites	Role of informal institutions	Sustaining of environmental and social mainstreaming
Dhaka metropolitan development planning	Country ownership was initially very weak. The Capital Development Authority staff apparently saw the SEA entirely as a World Bank project.	Because it attempted to use spatial planning as a window for wide-ranging policy reform, the SEA had less opportunity to address some of the underlying causes of urban degradation in Dhaka.	The Capital Development Authority is not accountable to higher administrative levels because it generates much of its own funding through land development, and for the same reason has very little interest in reform or change.	The SEA didn't consider the historically ingrained patron-client behavior that affects the system of checks and balances within the administration.	The SEA report was not disseminated to stakeholders, nor was any other kind of feedback provided. This frustrated stakeholders.
Kenya Forests Act SEA	Country ownership was limited because the process was led by the World Bank. Abolition of the Interim Forest Reform Secretariat further reduced ownership.	The SEA offered an opportunity to reinforce momentum in the practical interpretation and implementation of the new Forests Act.	The SEA addressed underlying political economy issues, such as political pressures on weaker forest stakeholders, which drive use/misuse of Kenya's forest resources.	Informal institutions play only a minor role, if any, in the forest sector.	The impacts of the SEA were mainly temporary and not sustained despite the implementation of the forest policy action matrix.
Malawi Rapid SEA	Country ownership was limited. The exercise was led by World Bank staff.	The rapid SESA was timely and fed into the process of developing new mining sector policy and legislation as well as a new growth and poverty reduction strategy.	Evaluators did not find this issue significant in the rapid SESA.	Customary institutions were not analyzed in the rapid SESA.	A full policy SEA was recommended, and is planned for implementation.

Source: Authors.

44

of mining sector national authorities and sector representatives of regional integration organizations. This arrangement greatly facilitated the support provided by mining authorities in West Africa to the WAMSSA process and recommendations. For example, in a meeting held in Ouagadougou on December 3, 2009, the WAMSSA multistakeholder process was adopted by the West Africa Mineral Governance Program as the social accountability mechanism to support mining reform in West Africa.

Another example of the importance of identifying a suitable "owner" of policy SEA processes is illustrated by the Dhaka pilot. Here, the evaluators claimed that the unwillingness of the Capital Development Authority to fully cooperate with the SEA team was a contributing factor in the reorientation of the SEA process away from its initial impact-centered approach toward a greater focus on planning institutions. The evaluation went on to state that the failure by the World Bank to seek a new local counterpart agency at this stage was a key weakness of the overall policy SEA process. It is important to determine up front in the SEA process that the policy proponent—who should be the owner of the SEA process—has the capacity and commitment to integrate the SEA process and recommendations with the policy formulation process and to take responsibility for uptake and implementation of the recommendations.

Since the policy SEA approach has only recently been conceptualized, the Bank needs to take a careful approach to balancing its interest in promoting policy SEA with its wider alignment objectives. The Bank is at a difficult stage because it wants to advocate for the concept, but not alienate partners by pushing too hard. The fact that benefits of policy SEA are not immediately obvious further merits a cautious approach, which will let partner countries gain experience in the application of the new concept over a considerable period of time (see chapter 4).

Finally, issues of ownership also exist within the World Bank itself. In the pilots, this situation was addressed by linking SEA with proposed Bank interventions. This link has proved a crucial determinant of successful environmental mainstreaming in the medium term, but ongoing success requires that concerned staff are familiar with the expected benefits of SEA and are prepared to take the recommendations emerging from SEA processes into account.

Windows of Opportunity

The idea of windows of opportunity is fundamental to policy SEA. These windows provide entry points for effective policy interventions.

They are, however, not easy to predict, and they can also close unexpectedly. A good example from the pilot studies is offered by the Sierra Leone SESA, which was undertaken at a time when there was extraordinary global demand for minerals and strong interest from foreign investors. Emerging from a long period of impoverished internal conflict, the Sierra Leone government of the day acknowledged this exceptional opportunity and was apparently enthusiastic about mineral sector reform. However, this window did not remain open for long; a new government was elected soon after the completion of the SESA and it ranked agricultural investment as a higher priority than mining. In addition, this change of government coincided with the sharp global economic downturn that began in 2008.

At least the Sierra Leone SESA was originally designed with a window of opportunity in mind. According to the evaluators of the Hubei road transport planning pilot, the SEA team did not seek to—and as a consequence did not—take advantage of windows of opportunity. The Dhaka metropolitan development planning case exhibited a different problem. The evaluation argues that the counterpart agency was not the most appropriate local leader for the policy SEA process because it had a narrow and inappropriate mandate. Hence windows of opportunity were significantly less likely to open.

In conclusion, correctly identifying an appropriate window for influencing policy through SEA is clearly an important enabling factor for achieving policy SEA goals. Predicting when future windows of opportunities might occur is a difficult task, however. One option, presented by the evaluators of the Dhaka case, is to think of policy SEA as a staged process. When a window of opportunity is first recognized, a preliminary institutional analysis should be undertaken to generate an overview of the prevailing institutional circumstances. This initial work could identify a partner with the capacity to take ownership of the SEA process and its recommendations. It could also confirm that the objectives of policy SEA can be achieved through the identified window of opportunity.

Political Economy and Power Elites

For the most part, the literature considers strong public institutions as enabling rather than constraining the achievement of SEA outcomes. On the whole, this is a reasonable conclusion, especially when institutional strengthening means building environmental constituencies that can foster social accountability and policy learning. However, it needs to be borne in mind that public institutions can sometimes be constraining, in particular when they exist to protect power elites and provide cover for rent seeking.

The pilot studies indicate that using SEA to mainstream environmental concerns in policy and sector reform is fundamentally a task of changing attitudes and cultures within organizations and professional disciplines. Carrying out this task will result in structural changes in power relationships inside governments. In conservative government organizations, these kinds of radical reforms will be fought against with intensity.

The pilots provide some examples of how organizational culture in public institutions can be a constraint to the achievement of policy SEA outcomes. In the Hubei road transport planning case, policy SEA ran up against the legal processes prescribed for plan environmental impact assessment (plan EIA) in Chinese law. The evaluators describe these processes as being "very rigid" and with corresponding institutional arrangements that do not necessarily support the flexibility and inclusiveness sought by SEA approaches at the policy level. The SEA team prepared an institutional analysis and action plan for strengthening the management of social and environmental issues in provincial road planning, but according to the evaluators, when these proposals were presented to stakeholders at a workshop, debate was constrained by resistance from the HPCD. The following quotation from the Hubei pilot evaluation further describes what took place: "The final proposals prepared by the SEA team regarding institutional strengthening were appreciated by three important stakeholder groups but they were never fully accepted by the HPCD leaders. On the contrary, the institutional proposals became one of the key reasons for HPCD's hesitation to formally disseminate the SEA report" (Dusik and Jian 2010).

Ahmed and Sanchez-Triana (2008) discuss the related problem of dealing with power elites. They point to the tenacious manner in which elites can hold on to the status quo, and how difficult this tenacity can make institutional change. In the WAMSSA pilot, the SEA team undertook extensive consultations and built up a strong case for regional harmonization of minerals policy in Liberia, Guinea, and Sierra Leone. The SEA team concluded that the majority of stakeholders supported the concept of regional harmonization. However, as the evaluator points out, the minority of stakeholders who did *not* support the idea might well be more powerful (Annandale 2010). Elite interest groups would not see a move to regionalism as being to their advantage. A move toward cluster development and regional harmonization would tend to lead to a more transparent system of governance that would threaten the existing privileges to make discretionary decisions.

In the Dhaka SEA pilot, SEA influence was disadvantaged by the informal power exercised by elites in relation to the responsibilities of the Capital Development Authority. Apparently, the authority has strong links with private sector development companies, which hamper its accountability and its incentives to pay attention to advice concerning institutional reform (Axelsson, Cashmore, and Sandstrom 2009).

One of the most interesting examples of a challenge to elite power is the multistakeholder framework proposed in the WAMSSA pilot and outlined in figure 2.1. If this framework is implemented by the WAMGP, it will establish a long-term constituency-building process that is outside of existing national and regional institutions, and that has the potential to outlast changes in governments. If combined with long-term program loans, it could be all the more influential.

In conclusion, *changing organizational cultures and navigating the currents of political economy in the context of sector reform are major challenges that require sensitivity, long-term engagement, and a great deal of political skill.* Moreover, they require the ability to foster inclusive policy dialogue that indirectly threatens the opaqueness of policy-making regimes prevalent in many countries. These skills and capabilities are not usually present in SEA teams.

The Importance of Informal and Customary Institutions

Much attention was paid in the pilot SEAs to the role of formal institutions, such as laws and regulations, organizations such as government ministries or agencies, and nongovernmental and civil society organizations. Government departments were the policy SEA counterparts, and with some notable exceptions, consultation processes tended to call on government officers and representatives of known civil society organizations and the private sector. This focus on formal organizations was understandable, given the Bank's remit to work directly with governments, and because this approach has been the natural tendency of SEA activity in the past. However, some of the evaluations, particularly of the three African pilots, indicated that informal organizations and institutions were important influences on policy development, implementation, and reform.

For example, the evaluation of the Sierra Leone pilot suggested that the SESA's emphasis on formal institutions had left a "somewhat unbalanced view of what really occurs in everyday life at the local level"(Albarracin-Jordan 2009). The evaluation argued that Sierra Leone's precolonial political administration was dominated by a patrimonialistic system controlled by "paramount chiefs." Chiefdoms continued in parallel with colonial systems of government and are still a powerful influence on the daily politics of all the African countries that were part of the pilot program. Moreover, conservatism also prevails in the local governance system of chiefdoms. For example, public consultation is not free and open. The chiefs have considerable say over who participates in consultation exercises. Clearly this situation would substantially affect the ability of SEA to encourage constituency building and improve social accountability.

While the African pilots did make mention of this informal system of social organization, they tended not to fully engage with it. The evaluators of the Malawi Rapid SESA stated that there was no focus on, or analysis of, informal institutions and the role played by traditional leaders and traditional systems of belief. Policy reform effectiveness is impaired if power and influence of informal institutions are not taken into account.

Capacity

Low capacity for environmental policy integration in developing countries is most definitely a constraining factor in effective SEA. It is a consistent problem, and one that is constantly stressed by the international cooperation community. Commitments are made in the Paris Declaration on Aid Effectiveness to strengthen partner countries' capacity to exercise leadership and build their national development strategies and systems. For policy-level SEA, capacity building is also required for civil society organizations and the media.

An issue that is not often addressed, however, is capacity-building needs within SEA consulting teams, and within donor agencies. While a number of the pilot projects exhibited extraordinary dedication on the part of consulting teams working in very difficult circumstances, the analysis thus far has shown that some SEA teams lacked the appropriate skills to understand the contexts within which they were working. For example, in the Dhaka metropolitan planning pilot, the evaluators pointed out that the SEA team did not recognize the 30 to 40 percent of Dhaka's population that lives in slums and informal settlements as important stakeholders because of their limited political influence. As a result they were not properly included in the consultation process. In addition, as previously noted, the SEA teams responsible for the Sierra Leone SESA and Malawi Rapid SESA did not fully account for the influence of the informal power of chiefs.

It is recognized that these problems are sometimes caused by tight timelines, lack of sufficient budget, and terms of reference that were not well crafted. At the same time, however, it does seem that more thought should be given to the makeup of consulting teams and to their preparation prior to undertaking SEA in policy and sector reform.

SEA consulting has tended to be dominated by people and firms who built their experience in the project EIA arena. These are often environmental professionals, engineers, and technical specialists. While policy SEA requires some of the skills used in project EIA, it also needs to draw on new disciplines in order to make sense of the complex world of policy making, political economy, and institutional analysis. Examples of disciplines that could possibly be drawn on include political economy, anthropology, sociology, and political science. It may also be that donors should turn to policy analysis consulting firms for overall policy SEA project management.

Sustaining Continuous Processes of Environmental and Social Mainstreaming

Probably the strongest and most consistent refrain from participants in the pilot projects was that policy SEA processes should be continuous in some sense. The one-off nature of most SEA activity was considered to constrain the achievement of policy SEA goals and process outcomes. The following quotations from two different policy SEA pilot evaluations strongly support this argument:

> Ideally the engagement of SEA specialists should not be confined to writing an assessment report but also cover communication and dialogue [about] the findings and recommendations of the assessment and preferably also different types of follow-up activities (Slunge and Ekbom 2010).
>
> Many actors ([the] SEA team as well as public sector and civil society representatives) in the SEA process expressed the view that a single study or a few workshops are not enough to address the issues at stake. Rather, they felt that a long-term approach to addressing environmental concerns in urban development in Dhaka is required (Axelsson, Cashmore, and Sandstrom 2009).

Some possible responses are relatively straightforward. For example, the engagement of SEA specialists should cover communication and dissemination of results and recommendations. In some cases SEA teams might also be retained to lead follow-up activities such as monitoring the outcomes of stakeholder action plans. Dissemination of SEA results is an area in which the donor community can be more proactive. As discussed in World Bank (2005), the Bank can help countries transition from one administration to the next by conveying consistent messages, either through policy notes or long-term programmatic loans.

More substantial responses to the problem of lack of continuity depend on the policy SEA process being driven by the partner country government and owned by a suitable national actor. The policy proponent needs to be committed to taking responsibility for the recommendations emanating from the SEA process. The kind of multistakeholder framework proposed by WAMSSA for the West Africa Mineral Governance Program is entirely positive, but requires high-level commitment from a number of national governments and regional organizations if it is to become functional.

The WAMSSA framework is an example of a deliberative institution which may well assist in building semipermanent environmental constituencies that could then lead to improved social accountability and learning. A similar recent example from a developed country is Australia's Resource Assessment Commission (RAC), which was established in the early 1990s by the federal government as a response to intense conflicts over resource development projects such as pulp mills. The RAC was seen by the Australian government as depoliticizing information and scientific data by filtering a wide range of inputs at the evaluative stage, while attempting to reconcile hitherto irreconcilable interest groups on both the development and environment sides of the land use debate. The RAC was supported by an act of Parliament and undertook high-level resource assessments on the request of the prime minister. Public inquiries were staffed by appointed commissioners who were often impartial judges, and who focused on issues such as forests and timber, fisheries, coastal zone management, and mining. While it is recognized that the level of sophistication attained by the RAC would not be appropriate in most developing countries, a politically mandated and open public inquiry process taking place over a long period of time could be possible in some developing countries.

Table 2.3 summarizes the contextual factors that constrain or enable the achievement of policy SEA outcomes.

Refining the Conceptual Model of Policy SEA

The conceptual model for applying SEA to policy summarized in section 2 of Appendix B can be refined based on the evidence provided in this chapter. Adjustments required for this refinement cover SEA outcomes and contextual influencing factors, as discussed below.

Outcomes

The analysis presented above suggests that the "process outcomes" box that is part of figure 1.2 should be refined as indicated in figure 2.2. Process outcomes

FIGURE 2.2
Outcomes and Influence of Policy SEA

Refined outcomes of policy SEA
- Raised attention to environmental priorities
- Strengthened constituencies
- Improved social accountability
- Policy learning

Influence on policy processes
- Expanded policy capacities
- Broadened policy horizons
- Modified decision regimes

Source: Authors.

BOX 2.1
Contextual Influencing Factors

- Ownership
- Windows of opportunity
- Power elites and political economy
- Consideration of informal institutions
- Sustaining continuous process

---

of policy SEA are now defined as raised attention to environmental priorities; strengthened constituencies; improved social accountability; and policy learning. Social learning is thus removed as an outcome and replaced by policy learning. Through these outcomes, SEA influences policy processes by expanding policy capacities, broadening policy horizons, and modifying decision regimes. SEA's long-term expected impact is better policy making that integrates environmental and social issues into policy formulation and implementation.

Contextual Influencing Factors

The analysis of contextual factors presented above suggests that the "contextual influencing factors" box shown in figure 1.2 should be refined as indicated in box 2.1.

In this refinement, the most important constraints emanating from the evaluation of the pilot cases are the way in which ownership of SEA is achieved in a given country; the ability of SEA promoters to seize windows of opportunity; resistance to change presented by conservative organizational culture and other power elites; the role of informal institutions; and the various influences that work against sustaining continuous environmental and social mainstreaming processes. It also needs to be recognized that SEA at the policy level is but one discrete intervention in the chain of environmental and social mainstreaming.

Refined Conceptual Model of Policy SEA

Taking into account these revisions, figure 2.3 presents a new policy SEA model, with refined process outcomes and contextual influencing factors. The right-hand side of the figure summarizes the discussion and findings of the evaluation presented in this section regarding process outcomes of policy SEA contextual influencing factors, and the potential of SEA to influence policy. The left-hand side of the figure is developed in the next chapter. Its aim is to provide guidance for undertaking SEA in policy and sector reform.

FIGURE 2.3

Refined Conceptual Model of Policy SEA: Process Steps, Process Outcomes, and Objective

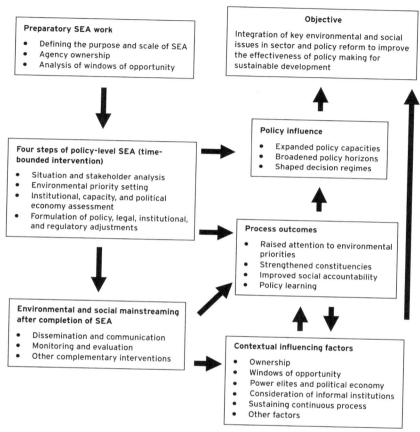

Preparatory SEA work

- Defining the purpose and scale of SEA
- Agency ownership
- Analysis of windows of opportunity

Objective

Integration of key environmental and social issues in sector and policy reform to improve the effectiveness of policy making for sustainable development

Four steps of policy-level SEA (time-bounded intervention)

- Situation and stakeholder analysis
- Environmental priority setting
- Institutional, capacity, and political economy assessment
- Formulation of policy, legal, institutional, and regulatory adjustments

Policy influence

- Expanded policy capacities
- Broadened policy horizons
- Shaped decision regimes

Process outcomes

- Raised attention to environmental priorities
- Strengthened constituencies
- Improved social accountability
- Policy learning

Environmental and social mainstreaming after completion of SEA

- Dissemination and communication
- Monitoring and evaluation
- Other complementary interventions

Contextual influencing factors

- Ownership
- Windows of opportunity
- Power elites and political economy
- Consideration of informal institutions
- Sustaining continuous process
- Other factors

Source: Authors.

Conclusion

This chapter has compared the six evaluated pilots. It shows that the hoped-for outcomes—identified environmental priorities, strengthened constituencies, improved social accountability, and policy learning—varied across the cases. This variety is largely due to contextual factors such as country ownership; windows of opportunity; power elites and political economy; consideration of informal institutions; and sustaining continuous processes.

It is not possible to make substantial claims about impact attribution. To say that applying SEA in policy and sector reform has exerted an influence in a particular case is only to say that it is one of several influences. As Carden (2009, 19) aptly puts it: "The thread between cause and effect in a policy decision invariably gets tangled in the coalitions and contradictions of policy processes in any country. This is transparently true of democratic governments, and less transparently, but no less true, of dictatorships and oligarchies."

This report suggests the use of the revised conceptual model of policy SEA when policy makers and practitioners contemplate undertaking SEA in policy and sector reform. The aim of the next chapter is to provide specific step-by-step guidance to practitioners by focusing on "preparatory policy SEA work," "steps of policy SEA," and "continuous environmental and social mainstreaming after completion of SEA," as outlined in the left-hand box of figure 2.3.

Notes

1 At the time this report was being prepared, the government of Malawi asked the World Bank to help prepare a mining technical assistance project to reform the mining sector. This project will include a full policy SEA (SESA).

2 The techniques used to prioritize issues are discussed in chapter 3.

3 See World Bank 2009.

4 See in particular World Bank (2005, 47–49).

5 The impact of institutional and cultural constraints on SEA will be examined later in the chapter.

6 The evaluation framework argues that social accountability initiatives tend to be most effective if they are combined with accountability mechanisms internal to the state, that is, they are institutionalized and systematically implemented by a civil society, state, or hybrid institution (appendix B).

7 This point is explained more fully later in this chapter.

8 The typology of expanded policy capacities, broadened policy horizons, and affected decision regimes is based on a five-year study (2001–05) by the International Development Research Centre (IDRC) examining how IDRC's support for research influences public policy in developing countries. The results of this study have affected how IDRC research projects are designed and evaluated. See Carden (2009).

References

Ahmed, K., and E. Sanchez-Triana, eds. 2008. *Strategic Environmental Assessment for Policies: An Instrument for Good Governance*. Washington, DC: World Bank.

Albarracin-Jordan, J. 2009. "Evaluation of the World Bank's Pilot Program in Institution-Centered SEA: The Sierra Leone Mining Sector Reform Strategic Environmental and Social Assessment (SESA)." Unpublished report, World Bank, Washington, DC.

Annandale, D. 2010. "Evaluation of the World Bank's Pilot Program on Institution-Centered SEA: The West Africa Minerals Sector Strategic Assessment (WAMSSA)." Unpublished report, World Bank, Washington, DC.

Axelsson, A., M. Cashmore, and U. Sandstrom. 2009. "Evaluation of the Dhaka Metropolitan Development Plan Strategic Environmental Assessment." Unpublished report, Swedish EIA Centre, Department of Urban and Rural Development, Swedish University of Agricultural Sciences, Uppsala.

Brown, A. L., and D. Tomerini. 2009. "Environmental Mainstreaming in Developing Countries." Proceedings of the International Association of Impact Assessment Meeting, Accra, Ghana. http://www.iaia.org.

Carden, F. 2009. *Knowledge to Policy: Making the Most of Development Research.* Ottawa: International Development Research Centre.

Dalal-Clayton, B., and S. Bass. 2009. *The Challenges of Environmental Mainstreaming: Experience of Integrating Environment into Development Institutions and Decisions.* Environmental Governance 3. London: International Institute for Environment and Development.

Dusik, J., and Y. Jian. 2010. "Evaluation of the World Bank's Pilot Program in Institution-Centered SEA: Strategic Environmental Assessment for Hubei Road Network Plan (2002–2020)." Unpublished report, World Bank, Washington, DC.

Huber, George P. 1991. "Organizational Learning: The Contributing Processes and the Literatures." *Organizational Science* 2 (1): 88–115.

OECD (Organisation for Economic Co-operation and Development). 2005. *Paris Declaration on Aid Effectiveness.* http://www.oecd.org/dataoecd/11/41/34428351.pdf.

Slunge, D., and A. Ekbom. 2010. "Evaluation of the Rapid Integrated Strategic Environmental and Social Assessment of Malawi Mineral Sector Reform." Unpublished report, Environmental Economics Unit, Department of Economics, University of Gothenburg, Sweden.

World Bank. 2005. "Integrating Environmental Considerations in Policy Formulation: Lessons from Policy-Based SEA Experience." Report 32783, World Bank, Washington, DC.

———. 2009. "Malawi Mineral Sector Review: Source of Economic Growth and Development." Report 50160-MW, World Bank, Washington, DC.

———. 2010. "West Africa Mineral Sector Strategic Assessment (WAMSSA): Environmental and Social Strategic Assessment for the Development of the Mineral Sector in the Mano River Union." Report 53738-AFR, World Bank, Washington, DC.

CHAPTER 3

Guidance for Applying SEA in Development Policy and Sector Reform

MEETING THE GOALS prescribed for strategic environmental assessment (SEA) in policy and sector reform requires the implementation of a methodology of some kind. Typically, this would entail the following of a series of procedural steps. It is important to point out, however, that because the ultimate goal of SEA is to influence policy and promote institutional change, SEA at the policy level cannot simply be reduced to a consistent formula. Chapter 2 has already made it clear that the success or failure of SEA is context dependent. This means that whatever procedural steps or tools are used to reach the SEA goals must be designed to work with a highly specific set of institutional contexts, entry points, and drivers.

Nevertheless, it is possible to illustrate the basic steps that can be followed to incorporate environmental considerations into policy and sector reform. This incorporation was an important issue for the pilot program and the evaluation because there was a need to compare results across the cases and replicate them in the future. Operational experience accumulated during the pilot program led to the following suggested procedure for policy SEA, consisting of three stages: (i) preparatory work, (ii) implementation, and (iii) environmental and social mainstreaming beyond the completion of SEA.

Preparatory Policy SEA Work

Before implementation of SEA at the policy level can begin, there is a need to understand the context within which SEA will take place. Various questions need to be asked to ensure that the goals and intentions of the specific policy

SEA process are understood by the major stakeholders. The most important questions relate to the purpose of the process (issues, initiatives, or questions to be addressed); the scale of the process; agency ownership; and the assessment of windows of opportunity.

Defining the Purpose and Scale of SEA

There may be a number of reasons why SEA might be applied in a particular context, and different stakeholders may well have different perceptions about the purpose of the exercise. It is important for the success of the initiative that different views about the purpose of SEA be clear. Other important questions that require clarification before SEA is implemented include the following:

- What is the particular policy or sector reform that is being addressed?
- Are there any interventions being planned that the SEA process should influence?
- Why are SEA approaches being applied?
- What is the SEA exercise expected to deliver, and does the answer to this question depend on the perspectives of specific interest groups?

In this preparatory phase of SEA, it is also important for the scale of the exercise to be clear. There is no required template for policy SEA. Inputs of time and resources can vary significantly in different contexts. For example, sometimes a *rapid policy SEA*, such as the Malawi policy SEA pilot, is appropriate (box 3.1). This might require the professional time of one expert for four or five weeks. It is important to note, however, that the main outcomes

---

BOX 3.1
Rapid Policy SEA

Objective The objective of a rapid policy SEA is to include environmental and social issues in the reform agenda and engage key stakeholders in the earliest stages of policy dialogue.

Process Analytically, the focus of a rapid policy SEA is on assessing existing laws, regulations, codes of practice, and institutions connected with the environmental and social management of the sector to be reformed. The stakeholder analysis and consultations are tailored to engage key constituencies in the policy dialogue about the need for sector reform.

Expected outcome There are two expected outcomes. First is the broadening of policy dialogue on sector reform, which occurs when stakeholders' awareness of key environmental and social management issues affecting the sector is raised. Second is the development of a road map of environmental and social actions to be undertaken during formulation of sector reform, including a full SEA.

Source: Adapted from Loayza and Albarracin-Jordan 2010.

and benefits of SEA in policy and sector reform are unlikely to be achieved through a rapid policy SEA. Therefore, this option should be applied only when the alternative is no action. The general rule, and one applied in the case of the Malawi pilot, is that a *full-fledged SEA* should follow a rapid SEA. The point to stress here is that stakeholders should all be aware of the chosen scale and expected outcomes.

Agency Ownership

As the previous chapter showed, identifying a suitable owner for the SEA process is vital. A reluctant lead agency can set back the general development of the approach. Accordingly, a preliminary institutional analysis is warranted to identify a lead agency that has the capacity and incentive to take ownership of the SEA process and recommendations. Securing ownership at an early stage is partly dependent upon the identified partner/policy proponent having the following: sufficient capacity and training to understand the concept of SEA and the specifics of policy SEA; incentives to consider the results and recommendations; and sufficient capacity to allow for adequate integration of the SEA in the policy process. In general, for SEA to be effective, it should be undertaken by sector and planning agencies instead of environmental agencies. The latter should not be operationally active, but should participate through interministerial consultation or steering groups governing the SEA. Box 3.2 presents a case study of a weak sector agency, as faced by the forestry sector in Liberia; the implication is that establishing a multisector approach could be the appropriate response to this situation.

As the SEA process unfolds, new roles and responsibilities will often present themselves, and a strong leader is required to ensure that the process is kept on track. Care needs to be taken to ensure that weak sector agencies are not subject to regulatory capture and the rent-seeking behavior that can accompany conflicts of interest. Methods for ensuring that such problems do not eventuate include the establishment of multistakeholder frameworks as outlined in the West Africa Minerals Sector Strategic Assessment (WAMSSA) pilot. With well-designed institutional support, SEA can help to reconcile different interests (since stakeholders choose policy SEA priorities, as discussed below), and it can deal with regulatory capture by enhancing transparency and social accountability (since legal, regulatory, and capacity gap assessments are validated openly). Equally important is that SEA is able to address issues that are seen as relevant by the policy proponent. Initial and ongoing awareness raising and training about the outputs and benefits of policy SEA may be required if the partner does not have previous experience in addressing environmental and social concerns at strategic levels of decision making. Unless understanding of SEA at the policy level is secured, contributions to policy SEA outcomes and influence on policy processes will likely be limited.

BOX 3.2

The Need for Multisector Ownership of SEA When the Counterpart Sector Agency Is Not Strong

In postconflict Liberia, natural resources are viewed as a means of kick-starting the economic development of the country. The forest sector—historically dominated by commercial forestry—has played an important economic role in Liberia. Due to the connection between forestry and armed conflict, the United Nations Security Council decided in 2003 to impose three years of sanctions on Liberian timber exports. The Liberian government used the sanction period to reform forestry practices and pave the way for restoring the rule of law. Liberia's forest reform involved developing a new forest policy, revising forest legislation, and putting in place a chain-of-custody system governing all commercial log and wood exports. Reforms in the sector recognized that economic and environmental values of forests extend beyond commercial forestry. A new National Forestry Reform Law was passed in 2006, and the next year a forest strategy was developed. In 2007, the World Bank began engagement in Liberia. As part of this engagement, the World Bank financed an SEA of the forest sector, primarily to inform the development of community rights to forest lands, and secondly to assess capacity and institutional adjustments that might be needed in the implementation of the Liberian National Forestry Reform Law of 2006.

The Forest Development Authority was the main counterpart for the SEA team. However, key social and environmental issues associated with community rights to forest lands and the forest strategy often required institutional and capacity measures in other sectors, such as mining, agriculture, and planning. The SEA task force included staff of the Forest Development Authority and the Environmental Protection Agency, but in order to enhance ownership, commitment to reform, and capacity development, the core members of the SEA task force were occasionally supplemented by representatives from other institutions: the Office of the Chairman, House Committee on Agriculture and Forestry; the Ministry of Planning and Economic Affairs; the Ministry of Land, Mines, and Energy; the Ministry of Internal Affairs; and the National Investment Commission. The engagement of additional ministries strengthened information sharing and awareness raising, but it had marginal impact on how committed these ministries were to jointly identified actions to address institutional and capacity needs. This experience pointed to the need to create a multisectoral lead or counterpart for SEA when the sector agency has limited influence on other relevant ministries and issues cut across sector lines.

Source: Diji Chandrasekharan Behr, personal communication.

Within development cooperation agencies, it is important that there is adequate understanding of the results and recommendations that can be expected from the policy SEA at an early stage, so that these can be more widely taken on board and integrated in relevant agency interventions. There is therefore a need for good internal communication, capacity development, and coordination to ensure that SEA for policy and sector reform can be applied effectively.

Assessing Windows of Opportunity

Another consideration at this early stage is assessing windows of opportunity. As discussed in the last chapter, windows of opportunity can be difficult to predict. They can also open and close unexpectedly and at short notice. However, there are some circumstances that seem favorable for applying SEA in sector reform, for example the following:

- There is a change of government to one that is more open to deliberation and to the incorporation of environmental issues in development policy.
- A government's development strategy prioritizes specific sectors for development. Usually this would lead to policy and sector reform of these same sectors. Where these sectors have potentially significant impacts on the environment and natural resources, such as is the case with mining and forestry, SEA is highly recommended to enhance the sustainability of the reform.
- The government has decided that a specific sector should be reformed in response to economic or political pressures.
- Economic conditions change radically to favor improved environmental outcomes. Examples might include steeply rising oil prices that drive the introduction of renewable energy technologies, or economic stimulus packages that favor green jobs.
- Changing market conditions for certain commodities drive regulatory reforms.
- Civil conflicts are resolved and a new desire for development presents itself.
- Civil society organizations are given more freedom to participate and advocate.

Implementing SEA in Policy and Sector Reform

As indicated in figure 2.3, implementing SEA in policy and sector reform generally includes most of the following steps: (i) situation assessment and stakeholder analysis; (ii) environmental priority setting; (iii) institutional, capacity, and political economy assessment; and (iv) formulation of policy, legal, institutional, regulatory, and capacity recommendations. Figure 3.1 outlines these steps, and makes it clear that multistakeholder dialogue is a common touchstone throughout the process. Moreover, it shows that SEA is linked to a discrete policy intervention through influence on its formulation and implementation. Ideally, but not necessarily, the SEA process should be integrated into the policy process.

FIGURE 3.1
Policy SEA Process Steps

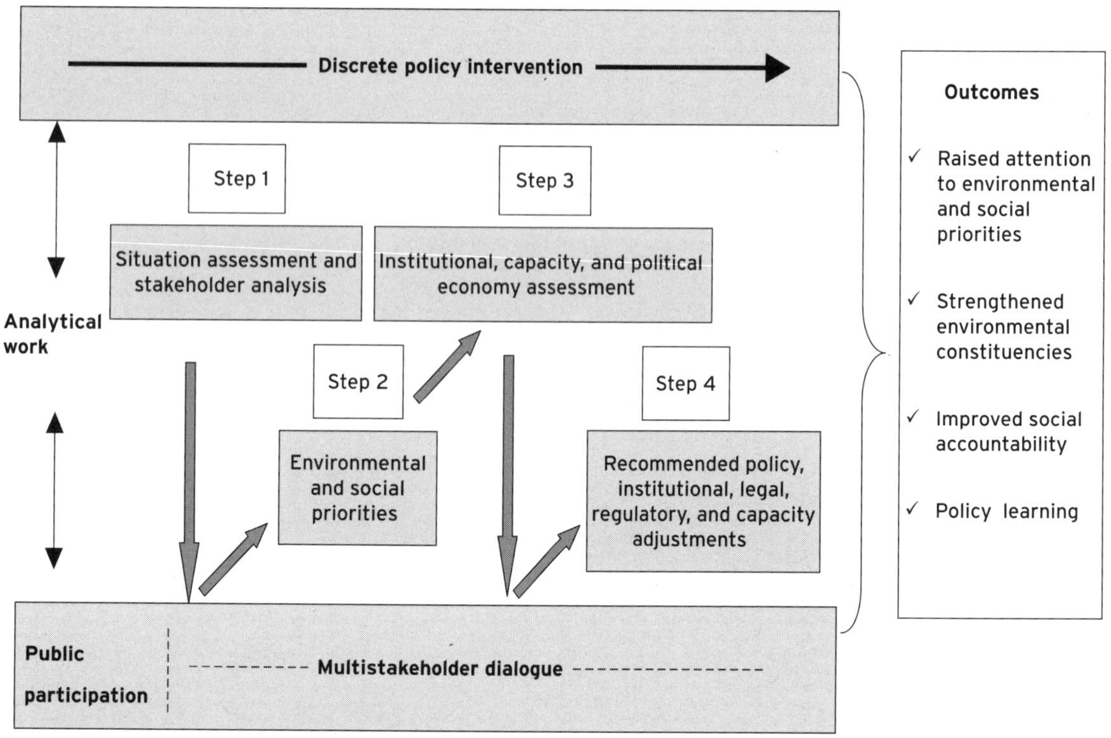

Outcomes

✓ Raised attention to environmental and social priorities

✓ Strengthened environmental constituencies

✓ Improved social accountability

✓ Policy learning

Discrete policy intervention

Analytical work

Step 1

Situation assessment and stakeholder analysis

Step 2

Environmental and social priorities

Step 3

Institutional, capacity, and political economy assessment

Step 4

Recommended policy, institutional, legal, regulatory, and capacity adjustments

Public participation

Multistakeholder dialogue

Source: Adapted from Loayza and Albarracin-Jordan 2010.

These steps are not necessarily followed in a linear fashion. For example, sometimes the SEA process will begin with intensive stakeholder dialogue as a method for undertaking situation, stakeholder, and political economy analysis. In other cases, environmental priority setting will be undertaken in parallel with components of the institutional analysis. For example, in the WAMSSA national workshops, stakeholders combined selection of priorities with a discussion of enabling and blocking factors for addressing these priorities. The point is that there is no single "correct" way in which SEA should proceed. What is important is that the four steps outlined above are undertaken in some fashion.

In what remains of this section, each step is briefly outlined; its objectives, the process to be followed in it, and its expected outcomes are all presented. Details of specific methods that can be applied at each step are contained in appendix C.

Situation Assessment and Stakeholder Analysis

SEA requires a reference scenario of the environmental and social situation in which policy and sector reform will take place. This scenario should assess key environmental and social issues (the situation assessment) that the SEA will focus on, and the key actors (the stakeholder analysis) that should be involved in the SEA process.

Situation Assessment

SEA at the policy level usually begins with an assessment of the key environmental and social issues currently affecting the sector to be reformed.

Objectives

The objective of situation assessment is to account for the key environmental and social issues prevailing in a region, or associated with a sector, so as to inform deliberations on priorities by stakeholders. Most policy SEA views situation assessment as a process that provides an *overview* of the sector or geographic area that is the subject of the SEA, highlighting key environmental and social issues.[1]

Process to Be Followed

Situation assessment does not need to be as detailed as a baseline study. It should be based mainly on information from secondary sources and expert opinion. The depth of the assessment depends on the issues identified and the expected information requirements of the audience. For example, in WAMSSA the situation analysis focused on the notion of three potential mining infrastructure clusters (see box 3.3). Because the clusters affected at least two countries, the situation assessment attempted to make a detailed case for the efficiency of a multicountry approach for mining development. However, key economic and financial information for making a strong case was not available.

BOX 3.3

Approaches to Situation Assessment in the Sierra Leone SESA and the WAMSSA

The Sierra Leone SESA

Mining in Sierra Leone consists of large-scale, small-scale, and artisanal mining. The situation assessment undertaken in the strategic environmental and social assessment (SESA) included an overview of the socioeconomic and environmental situation in the country, which provided the general context for the mining sector. The analysis then focused on the mining subsectors through case studies at the three different levels of scale. These assisted in identifying the most important environmental and social issues. The list of key issues informed the presentations and discussions held at workshops in four regions of the country. The case study approach used in the situation assessment showed that a distinct set of issues was linked to each subsector.

The West Africa Minerals Sector Strategic Assessment

The West Africa Mineral Governance Project proposes to help countries in the Mano River Union (Guinea, Liberia, Sierra Leone, and Côte D'Ivoire) to use their large untapped mineral wealth for promoting sustainable development. A mining infrastructure cluster approach was used by WAMSSA to assess "the common, overlapping environmental, social, economic, and sector governance issues" (World Bank 2010). The following methodology was used to identify the clusters:

1. A base map (layer 1) was constructed using information on geological provinces, operating mines, major mineral occurrences, and potential new mining projects.

2. Geopolitical, infrastructure, environmental, and community features were mapped (layer 2).

3. Proposed road, rail, and electrical projects under investigation or implementation by the African Union and other multilateral agencies were identified (layer 3).

4. Layers 1–3 were cross-examined to help identify potential clusters where new projects would create sustainable opportunities in the region.

5. Economic analysis was undertaken of the differential costs of developing regional facilities versus developing infrastructure on a project-by-project basis. The scope and depth of this analysis was constrained by insufficient information available on planned projects.

Sources: Adapted from Loayza and Albarracin-Jordan 2010.

In some cases, the situation assessment can be viewed as a second phase, one that takes the role of detailed baseline assessment of the kind that is an integral part of traditional project environmental impact assessment (EIA), with the exception that it focuses much more intensely on understanding fundamental political economy issues. This alternative view of situation assessment was followed in the Kenya Forests Act SEA.

The important point here is that the purpose of situation assessment is to sharpen the strategic focus of the SEA by identifying key environmental and social issues associated with the sector to be reformed or with development policies under formulation in a region.

Examples of Situation Assessment from the Pilots

Box 3.3 presents examples of situation assessment taken from the two West African SEA pilots.

Expected Outcomes

The expected outcome of the situation assessment is a clearer understanding of the key environmental and social issues affecting a region or associated with a sector to be reformed. These issues are usually presented in a report that is discussed by the stakeholders when policy SEA priorities are selected.

Stakeholder Analysis

A thorough understanding of the interests, concerns, and power basis of stakeholders is a fundamental part of any SEA process, and is especially important in policy SEA.[2]

Objectives

The purpose of the stakeholder analysis is to identify all key stakeholders having an environmental or social stake in the sector to be reformed, and then engage them in a meaningful policy dialogue. It assists in identifying those vulnerable stakeholders whose voices are not usually heard, and provides information that helps the SEA team to involve them effectively in SEA. It is, therefore, critical to achieving the outcome of strengthened environmental constituencies.

Process to Be Followed

Stakeholder analysis informs almost all SEA stages. With information on stakeholders, their interests, and their capacity to support or oppose reform, the policy SEA team can better involve stakeholders in priority selection; in the assessment of gaps for effectively managing priorities; and in validating policy SEA recommendations. Stakeholder analysis is also a major input into political economy analysis (discussed below) because it provides an idea of the impact of reform on political and social forces; illuminates divergent viewpoints and the potential power struggles among groups and individuals; and helps identify potential strategies for negotiating with opposing stakeholders.

Four major attributes are important for stakeholder analysis: the stakeholders' position on the sector and their attitudes about the reform; the level of influence (power) they hold; the level of interest they have with regard to key issues identified in the situation assessment; and the group or coalition that they belong to or can reasonably be associated with. These attributes are identified through various data collection methods, including interviews with country experts knowledgeable about stakeholders or with the actual stakeholders directly.

Stakeholder analysis identifies the key social actors in the sector who should be engaged in SEA and in the selection of SEA's priorities. The historical, social, political, economic, and cultural factors that influence the web of relationships among stakeholders need to be examined. This examination was clearly a requirement for all the pilots, but particularly those undertaken in Sierra Leone, Dhaka, and Malawi. Stakeholder analysis deepens the understanding of power relations, networks, and interests associated with the proposed policy or sector reform.

Expected Outcomes

The main expected outcomes of stakeholder analysis are the mapping of stakeholder interests, an analysis of the obstacles to stakeholder representation, and a public participation plan for the policy SEA process. This plan should explicitly

FIGURE 3.2
Mapping of Key Stakeholders: Hubei Road Transport Planning SEA Pilot

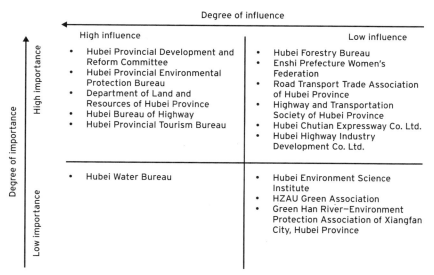

Source: Adapted from World Bank 2009.

consider how vulnerable groups such as women, youth, local communities, and the poor, who have a stake in environmental issues, will be engaged in the SEA. Ultimately, stakeholder analysis is a critical tool in clarifying the micro–political economy of a policy area and can help identify interested parties who should be incorporated in the decision-making process, in addition to establishing the basis for their inclusion.

Examples of Stakeholder Analysis from the Pilots

Two examples from the policy SEA pilots show the mapping of stakeholders. The first can be seen in figure 3.2, which is taken from the stakeholder analysis performed for the Hubei road transport planning pilot. This matrix was produced following a methodology that uses a set of worksheets provided by the World Bank and based on Rietbergen-McCracken and Narayan (1998).[3]

The second example, shown in figure 3.3, is taken from the WAMSSA pilot, and shows the different stakeholder groups' relative influence on and interest in decision making associated with regional mining sector reform. The vertical arrow measures the effect of the reform, and the horizontal arrow measures

FIGURE 3.3

Stakeholder Interest in and Influence over Decision Making: WAMSSA Pilot

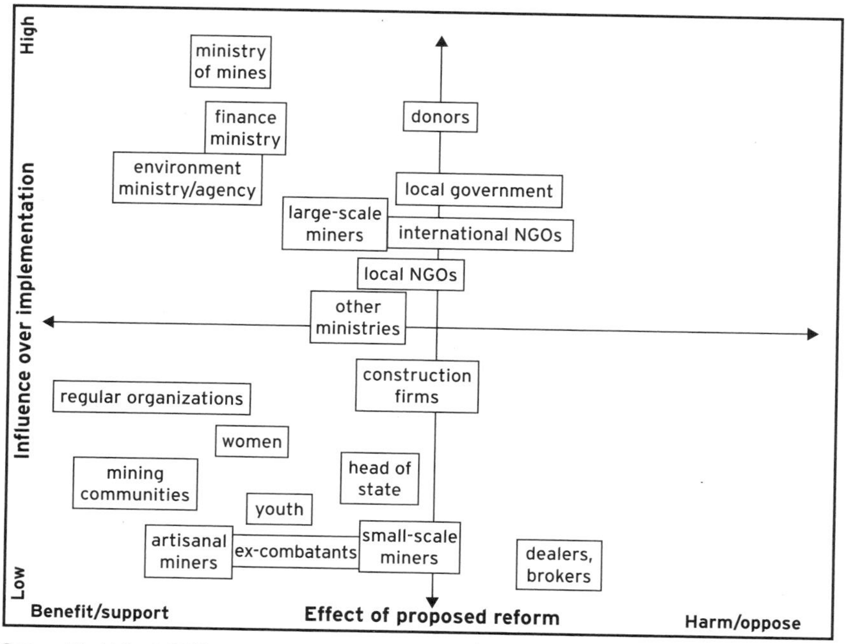

Source: World Bank 2010.
Note: NGO = nongovernmental organization.

the influence over decisions held by the different groups. Groups situated in the bottom right-hand quadrant want to oppose reform, but have relatively little power to do so. Those groups situated in the lower left-hand quadrant view reform more favorably, but are also not that powerful. Stakeholders sitting in the upper left-hand quadrant have more influence, and also happen to be more powerful.

The WAMSSA matrix was built up from a series of characteristics for each group defined through interviews and expert observation:

- Influence: the power a stakeholder has to facilitate or impede the design and implementation of mining subregional and cluster-based policies and approaches
- Interest: the perceived level of interest that each stakeholder has in the cluster-based mineral development, along a continuum from commitment to status quo at one end to openness to change at the other
- Impact: the degree to which the cluster-based mineral development may affect each stakeholder
- Power: the level of coercive power that the stakeholder has to command compliance in the policy process
- Resources: the level of resources that stakeholders possess and are able to bring to bear in the policy process
- Legitimacy: the degree of legitimacy of each stakeholder's interest, that is, the extent to which the stakeholder's claims are seen as appropriate by other stakeholders

The two grids can help SEA teams determine appropriate responsive strategies (for example, which stakeholders to target for negotiations and trade-offs, which to buttress with resources and information, and so on).

Multistakeholder Dialogue

Multistakeholder dialogue is not a separate implementation "step," but rather a necessary support throughout the SEA. In project EIA, and to a certain extent in other SEA approaches, engagement tends to be restricted to discrete events where the point is either to elicit information or to seek stakeholder approval for important decisions. As has already been made amply clear, dialogue in policy SEA ideally takes place on a regular basis and over a long period of time.

Objectives

It is clear from the analysis contained in chapter 2, and from the literature that makes a case for policy SEA, that multistakeholder dialogue is a prerequisite for effective policy SEA. As indicated in figure 3.1, the objective of maintaining a multistakeholder dialogue is involving stakeholders in selection of environmental and social priorities; enriching the gap assessment of systems to manage these priorities; validating the recommendations to address these gaps; and engaging stakeholders in follow-up, monitoring, and evaluation. Consequently, the dialogue should take place throughout SEA implementation.

Process to Be Followed

Multistakeholder dialogue provides a mechanism for stakeholders, especially the vulnerable who are traditionally sidelined from policy decision making, to influence the policy process. This purpose implies the need to establish some kind of institutional structure within which to house dialogue initiatives. It also implies that multistakeholder dialogue has to be structured in a manner that is culturally sensitive. There cannot be a cookie-cutter approach to multistakeholder dialogue; it should be tailored to the cultural and political context in which the SEA is undertaken.

Special thought and effort need to be applied to the issue of how to involve unorganized stakeholders in the SEA dialogue. This was a problem for the WAMSSA and Sierra Leone SESA pilots, where artisanal miners were recognized as an important stakeholder group, but remained not easily accessible, as they had no representative association. Policy SEA can be genuinely effective only if it can find a method for dealing with unorganized stakeholders. This activity will often take time, and it raises the question of whether organizing such interests needs to take place before SEA is initiated.

Expected Outcomes

The expected outcome of multistakeholder dialogue is a robust discussion of key environmental and social issues associated with the sector to be reformed. It opens the policy and reform process to the influence of stakeholders, and particularly to those vulnerable stakeholders who often bear the environmental and social brunt of the reform process. Without a strong multistakeholder dialogue, the preconditions for the SEA outcomes of improved social accountability and policy learning cannot be met.

Examples of Multistakeholder Dialogue from the Pilots

Policy dialogue needs a focus. Proponents should not use participation/dialogue forums merely to talk, or stakeholders will rapidly lose commitment. Figure 3.4 presents an example of how stakeholder dialogue was established in the WAMSSA pilot.

The schematic shows how stakeholders had an input to situation analysis, stakeholder analysis, scenario analysis, and institutional analysis through interviews, focus groups, surveys, and workshops. Worthy of special note is the area below the dotted line in the diagram, which is the process envisaged for

FIGURE 3.4
Interaction with Stakeholders: WAMSSA

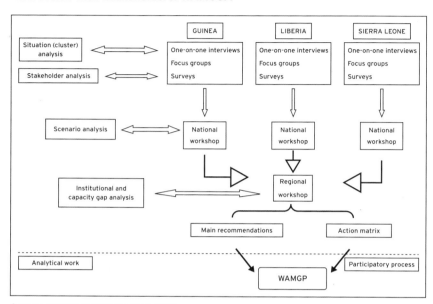

Source: Adapted from World Bank 2010.
Note: WAMGP = West Africa Mineral Governance Program.

continuance of multistakeholder dialogue as part of the development of the West Africa Mineral Governance Program. The proposal for this post-WAMSSA dialogue activity was described in chapter 2 as a long-term, multistakeholder program implementation framework.

Another important part of the multistakeholder dialogue established by SEA is informing and influencing decision makers. Early engagement of policy makers can stimulate ownership, assist in coordinating the timing of the study with regard to the relevant policy dialogue and process, and identify potential windows of opportunity in the policy process for sharing preliminary findings and information. Engaging policy makers early also provides initial insight into areas of concern. In the pilots, SEA steering committees were used as the main mechanism to involve policy makers, with varied degrees of success, as briefly discussed in chapter 2.

Lessons learned from the SEA of the Kenya Forests Act include the following effective approaches for engaging policy makers in SEA:

- The draft concept note and terms of reference for the study should be shared. The concept note must clearly articulate how the SEA will contribute to the reform process.

- Meetings should be arranged to discuss input and key issues such as status of the policy dialogue, mechanisms and timing for including information in the policy dialogue process, other relevant activities (prior, ongoing, and upcoming) with which the SEA should coordinate, and the role and involvement of the key policy makers in the SEA process.
- It is important to work with opportunities and around constraints within the sector. These could be related to or originate in the economic, social, environmental, political, legal, or political economy context of the sector to be reformed (see box 3.4).

In selecting methods for public participation, attention should be paid to power relationships that could suppress the voice of weak and vulnerable segments of society. Consultation with local indigenous groups, for example, may require the use of the local language and local traditional systems for building community consensus. The Las Bambas case, discussed in box 3.5, illustrates good practice in culture-sensitive SEA approaches.

BOX 3.4

Framing the SEA Work in the Context of Forest Sector Reform Priorities

In Kenya, the SEA made a direct contribution to the work of the Forest Sector Reform Committee, which was established by the government of Kenya under the direction of the Ministry of Environment and Natural Resources. This committee was made up of senior representatives from across government, representatives from the forest industry, nongovernmental organizations, conservationists, forest users, and development partners. It was chaired by the permanent secretary of the Ministry of Environment and Natural Resources and was regarded as the main organ for driving the reform process.

The Forest Reform Secretariat was established in the Forest Department to serve this committee and carry out tasks as requested by the committee. One of the first tasks of the secretariat was to develop a roadmap for implementation of the new Forests Act with a clear time frame and outline for budget resource requirements. The SEA team was mandated by the permanent secretary of the Ministry of Environment and Natural Resources to work with the Forest Reform Secretariat. The government of Kenya recognized that these processes were complementary and should seek to strengthen each other. The Ministry of Environment and Natural Resources and the Department of Forestry agreed that the SEA would be able to further strengthen the roadmap and would also help to ensure donor support to the reform process.

Source: Behr and Loayza 2009.

BOX 3.5

Transforming Relationships for Intercultural Dialogue and Sustainable Development: Las Bambas Mining Project in Peru

Mining in the Andean region has a legacy of socioenvironmental conflict. The Apurímac Department, where the Las Bambas project operates, is one of the poorest regions in Peru. The region was also one of the five areas most affected by the armed conflict with Sendero Luminoso (a Maoist guerrilla organization) between 1980 and 1992. Nine indigenous, Quichua-speaking communities are located within the direct area of influence of the Las Bambas copper mining project. With the goal of improving its relationship with local communities and other stakeholders, the project developer (Xstrata) built a regional dialogue around the project.

The construction of dialogue was divided into three phases: (i) awareness raising and diagnosis, (ii) strengthening of capacities, and (iii) follow-up of dialogue mechanisms and processes. The first phase consisted of a series of workshops and interviews with the local communities, performed in Spanish and Quichua (the local language) to gather information about the cultural characteristics of the indigenous actors, as well as their perceptions of power relationships with other stakeholders. Similar workshops and interviews, adapted to the respective cultural contexts, were carried out with other stakeholder groups. The analysis showed that local communities employed internal constituency mechanisms to encourage dialogue, mediated by local authorities, fictive kin, or high-status elders. Following these practices for promoting dialogue and consensus, a culture-sensitive approach to negotiating issues, including the identification of potential environmental and social impacts of the project, was implemented. Similar forums were established to discuss local development programs and a dispute-resolution mechanism that allowed individuals and communities to lodge formal complaints against the mining company. The second phase aimed at strengthening the capacity of negotiation, community organization, environmental management, human rights, leadership, and access to social development opportunities. The expected outcome includes stronger local constituencies, able to demand, implement, and oversee sustainable development interventions.

Sources: Loayza and Albarracin-Jordan 2010.

Finally, it is worth remembering that proposals for policy dialogues are not always openly accepted by governments, especially those with cultures that do not encourage challenging of government authority. In cases such as these, policy dialogue needs to take place within government, first by extending the number of agencies that are included in consultations, and then by gradually encouraging the involvement of nongovernment stakeholders.

Environmental Priority Setting

A useful early focus for policy dialogue is environmental priority setting. Priority setting is a critical stage in policy SEA because it opens up the policy process to the influence of stakeholders. If effective, SEA priorities will inform stakeholders about key environmental and social issues affecting the sector to be reformed and will reflect stakeholders' preferences about which of these issues should be addressed as part of the reform.

Objectives

The purpose of priority setting is to invite stakeholders to react to the situation assessment; raise specific and relevant environmental concerns; and select the SEA priorities. The policy SEA priorities represent a strong demand from the stakeholders that policy makers take sector reform in a specific environmental and social direction.

Process to Be Followed and Examples from the Pilots

Priority setting focuses dispersed environmental and social concerns and presents them as specific policy demands and requests for government intervention supported by constituencies and groups of interest. For this reason, special care is required to ensure that the voices of the vulnerable and weak in society are effectively heard in priority setting. The seeds of social accountability are also sown in this step. Thus priority-setting is critical in strengthening constituencies with environmental stakes in policy and sector reform.

Box 3.6 presents an approach to the ranking of environmental priorities that was used in the Sierra Leone policy SEA pilot.

Expected Outcomes

The expected outcomes from priority setting include a ranked list of environmental and social priorities associated with the sector to be reformed. These represent key issues that stakeholders believe are affecting their lives and need to be addressed by the reform. Another outcome of priority setting is strengthening or building constituencies around these key issues.

Institutional, Capacity, and Political Economy Assessment

Analyzing and helping to strengthen institutions and governance are key features of SEA in policy and sector reform. Strong institutions have increasingly been recognized as critical contributors to sustainable development, particularly as

---

BOX 3.6

Selection of Environmental and Social Priorities: Sierra Leone SESA Ranking Methodology

The ranking methodology for selecting environmental and social priorities in the SESA of the mining sector in Sierra Leone involved horizontal and vertical classification of the issues. Nominal scales and preferred responses were used for cross-comparison of issues. This method aimed at removing some of the potential survey biases and ensured that equal weight was given to the voice of vulnerable groups in the ranking procedure. Horizontal ranking used five dimensions for each of the issues considered. These included (i) health, ecological, and socioeconomic/cultural risk; (ii) number of affected people; (iii) political will; (iv) remediation cost; and (v) technological difficulties. Initially, stakeholders were asked to rank these dimensions in a low-medium-high scale. "Low" scored three points, "medium" received two points, and "high" received one point. The lowest scores corresponded to the potential priorities. In addition, a vertical ranking process involved the selection of 5 issues from a list of between 22 and 25 (depending on the region) that stakeholders thought were the most significant. Each time an issue was included in a person's top-five list, it received one point. Potential priority issues, then, were those that received the highest scores.

A cross-analysis of horizontal and vertical ranking was undertaken in order to identify the SESA priorities. Five cross-regional priorities were established: (i) land and crop compensation and village relocation, (ii) sanitation and water pollution, (iii) deforestation and soil degradation, (iv) child labor, and (v) postclosure reclamation. There were also issues that pertained to specific regions. These regional priorities included (i) mine employment (southern region); (ii) provision of infrastructure, especially paved roads and electricity (southern region); (iii) community development and participation (southern and western regions); and (iv) regulations to mitigate the negative impacts of blasting (eastern region).

Source: Adapted from Loayza and Albarracin-Jordan 2010.

---

they perform three fundamental functions—assessing needs and problems, balancing interests, and implementing solutions (World Bank 2003).

Institutional and Capacity Assessment

The institutional and capacity assessment is focused on the ability of the existing environmental management system to deal with the SEA priorities. Guidance is first provided to undertake this assessment. The analysis of interest groups that seek to protect their interests, which may affect the impact of the policy reform on the environmental management system, is left to the next section.

Objectives

The purpose of institutional and capacity assessment is to consider the policy, institutional, legal, regulatory, and capacity gaps so as to address environmental and social priorities determined in the previous step of policy SEA implementation.

Process to Be Followed

Institutional and capacity assessment consists of the following main stages:

A first step is a thorough review of the formal legal and regulatory framework associated with the management of environmental and social priorities. This is followed by an assessment of why the relevant policies, laws, and regulations have failed to address, or have only partially addressed, the priorities. Mechanisms considered in the assessment include (i) review of procedures for environmental and social assessment, especially focusing on monitoring and compliance mechanisms; (ii) assessment of capacity to enforce compliance with environmental and social regulations and avoid regulatory capture; (iii) assessment of preparedness of relevant ministries/departments/entities, including local governments, to identify and manage environmental and social risks, and to safeguard the interests of affected, vulnerable, and marginalized groups; (iv) assessment of existing systems for handling grievances that stem from environmental damage and social disruption; (v) analysis of interinstitutional links; (vi) analysis of organizational capacity of disadvantaged and vulnerable stakeholders; and (vii) assessment of the role of civil society groups/organizations, media, and other institutions in supporting, facilitating, and monitoring environmental/social safeguards. The assessment's results are the identification of the policy, institutional, legal, regulatory, and capacity gaps affecting the management of the environmental and social priorities.

The next step is to assess the effect of the proposed policy or sector reform on the identified gaps. Finally, an assessment of the potential reaction of stakeholders to this situation is carried out, and identifying the difficulties inherent in addressing these gaps completes the analysis. The assessment should be presented to the stakeholders and validated by them.

Box 3.7 presents a summary example of institutional and capacity assessment identified in the Sierra Leone mining sector SESA.

Expected Outcomes

The expected outcome of this step is the identification of key policy, legal, regulatory, institutional (formal and informal), and capacity *residual gaps*. Residual gaps are those left after factoring the impacts of the proposed policy or sector reform into existing gaps. While identification and assessment of gaps and residual gaps is usually made by the SEA team, involving stakeholders in the analysis not

BOX 3.7

Institutional and Capacity Assessment in the Sierra Leone Mining Sector SESA

The failure of existing policies to effectively address environmental and social priorities in Sierra Leone's mining sector was considered to have arisen from the following conditions:

- Mining legislation and regulations that lacked specificity and left interpretation to be determined on a case-by-case basis
- Insufficient clarity in the environmental and socioeconomic responsibilities of the various ministries and central, provincial, and local authorities
- Lack of monitoring of companies and specific mine sites
- Consistently weak implementation of laws and regulations, which resulted in enforcement having to rely on voluntary initiatives and pressure from civil society

The SESA concluded that some of these shortcomings could be addressed by the proposed mining reform. However, it also found that additional critical institutional and governance adjustments would be needed, outside of the mining sector. These adjustments revolve around land tenure issues and general cross-government concerns about lack of monitoring and enforcement. They include, for example, the following:

- Asymmetries in power among stakeholders (for example chiefs), which are magnified due to lack of transparency and accountability
- Customary relationships that have evolved out of the needs of an agrarian society and are ill-equipped to address temporary and high-risk environmental activities such as mining
- The existence of powerful individuals such as middlemen and traders who could easily take advantage of open, nonexistent, or inconsistent negotiation frameworks

Source: Adapted from Loayza and Albarracin-Jordan 2010.

only refines the assessment, but also exposes stakeholders to the complexities, trade-offs, and dilemmas of policy making, enhancing their capacity to influence policy constructively. Accordingly, another expected outcome of this step is enhancing stakeholders' capacity for contributing to policy formulation and increasing their awareness of the challenges posed by the reform (Loayza and Albarracin-Jordan 2010).

Political Economy Analysis

Sound political economy analysis is critical for policy SEA because it provides information on who benefits from maintaining the status quo, and who loses in the short and medium term as a consequence of adjustments recommended by the SEA. The political economy analysis helps to frame the recommendations in the context of the interplay of political forces shaping policy and sector reform.

Objectives

The main objective of political economy analysis is to assess the political feasibility of the SEA's recommendations. In making this assessment, it takes into account the patterns of incentives and underlying interests that lead political actors to support or resist change.

Process to Be Followed

Common aspects of political economy analysis include the following:

1. Stakeholder analysis
2. Analysis of the political context (focusing on factors that shape the major features of a political system, such as the history of state formation, influence of colonialism, role of social structures, influence of conflict, and patterns of revenue and rents distribution)
3. Analysis of formal and informal institutions (focusing on the nature and extent of political competition, distribution of power, relationship between formal and informal institutions, extent of civil society involvement in politics, role of the media, and the significance of the rule of law)
4. Identification and management of risk (analysis of "winners" and "losers"; relative impacts of reforms on different stakeholder groups; possible triggers of tension and conflict; degree of resistance to change)

As said before, these aspects of political economy analysis should be focused on the residual gaps associated with the management of environmental and social priorities. This focus makes the analysis manageable and useful.

Expected Outcomes and Examples from the Pilots

The outcomes of political economy analysis can be particularly illuminating about the constraints facing sector reform. In the Sierra Leone SESA, for example, two political economy issues were identified as critical for a successful tripartite relationship between the government, the industry, and the mining communities, which would in turn promote sustainable development driven by mining: the land tenure system and the secrecy of mining contracts. The fact that the chiefs could grant access to land that was collectively owned created a major risk for weak stakeholders who were users but not owners of land. Land reclamation was also discouraged because the state makes land accessible to holders of mining rights, and chiefs had little effective power to oppose this entitlement. The result was that many chiefs found themselves accommodating the system in exchange for short-term compensation. The SESA flagged these problems but fell short of suggesting solutions. In addition, land tenure and chiefship are politically sensitive issues in Sierra Leone. In this context, the evaluation of the Sierra Leone SESA pointed to the fact that the SEA had barely touched on the importance of the informal local patrimonial governance system of paramount chiefs. Although sector reform and, particularly, SEA face difficulties in tackling political economy constraints to sustainable and equitable development, it must be acknowledged that this is an area in which policy SEA could be significantly improved.

Policy SEA Recommendations

The outcomes of SEA are meant to influence policy and sector reform design. This means that SEA recommendations need to be organized in a fashion that facilitates action and implementation.

Objectives

The objective of the last step in the implementation phase of policy SEA is to make policy, institutional, legal, regulatory, and capacity-building recommendations for overcoming the gaps and the political economy constraints identified during the institutional and capacity assessment.

Process to Be Followed and Examples from the Pilots

Three of the pilot policy SEAs—the Kenya Forests Act SEA, the SESA for the Sierra Leone Mining Sector Reform, and WAMSSA—used a "policy action matrix" approach to present recommendations and encourage action. Table 3.1 presents a small snapshot taken from the Kenya Forests Act SEA policy action matrix.

The Kenya policy action matrix contained the SEA findings and recommendations to support the implementation of the Kenya Forests Act. Priority areas were broken down into issues identified by stakeholders, which were linked with the actions required to ensure that the issues could be addressed. Milestones, along with an indicative list of stakeholders to be involved in the action, were also identified. The use of a transparent consultative process to reach agreement on action points and milestones meant the policy actions listed in the matrix were identified and prioritized by a broad range of forest sector stakeholders.

Recommendations of SEA should be shared with stakeholders and validated by them. Dialogue, at this stage, builds consensus on what solutions are achievable, as well as effective and sustainable.

Expected Outcomes

The expected outcomes are "validated recommendations and an action matrix that includes monitoring indicators to assess the progress of reform in the short, medium, and long terms. Validation of recommendations and the action matrix by the stakeholders further strengthens constituencies, not only because it enhances ownership but also because it encourages participation of stakeholders in follow-up and monitoring. Ultimately, this increases accountability of policy makers" (Loayza and Albarracin-Jordan 2010, 9).

Environmental and Social Mainstreaming Beyond Policy SEA

The evaluation of the pilots has made it clear that for environmental and social mainstreaming to be achieved, interventions need to follow on from SEA activity to ensure that mainstreaming becomes a continuous process. Thus, to the extent possible, there needs to be agreement up front in the SEA process about who is responsible for taking the SEA recommendations forward. At a minimum, effort needs to be applied to the dissemination and communication of SEA results, and to monitoring and evaluation of outcomes. The objectives, process, and expected outcomes of these two steps are discussed below.

TABLE 3.1
Snapshot from the Policy Action Matrix Produced in the Kenya Forests Act Policy SEA

Harmonization of Kenya forest management legal framework				
Policies/actions	Milestones (including time-based milestones)	Indicative list of stakeholders to be involved	Expected outcomes	Status
The Kenya Forest Service (KFS) should establish an internal working group to ensure that a program for complying with international standards is introduced. This program is important for improving compliance and other initiatives (for example, carbon sequestration and avoidance of invasive species in dry lands).	An internal KFS working group was established by June 2008.	Relevant parties are KFS, the private sector, NGOs, universities.	National forest management standards in conformity with international standards are expected.	Pending.

Source: World Bank 2007.

Dissemination and Communication of SEA Results

It should be acknowledged that dissemination and communication of SEA results is not an area that SEA practitioners or government sponsors of SEA traditionally specialize in. The tendency has been for SEA to be supported only until the completion of the SEA report, with little thought given to the possible benefits of communication and dissemination. This is a major weakness of SEA which, if not addressed, may significantly impair SEA effectiveness in policy and sector reform.

Objectives

A number of the pilot evaluations showed that stakeholders can become frustrated with lack of feedback and follow-up from SEA activities. This is a fairly simple problem to deal with, but ignoring it can create a considerable challenge to the legitimacy of SEA. The main objective of this activity is therefore to disseminate the results of SEA activities as widely as possible.

Process to Be Followed

Terms of reference for SEA in policy and sector reform should include follow-up activities after the SEA report is completed. They should require consulting teams to organize consultation exercises so that stakeholders can see how their views have been addressed.

Communication of SEA results can be more difficult in some jurisdictions than others. For example, lack of media freedom and poor communications infrastructure can inhibit wide dissemination in some developing countries. These problems, and others such as lack of access to funds, mean that communication strategies will probably vary depending on the jurisdiction, the particular political economy context, and the interests and perspectives of stakeholder groups.

A general model for developing a policy SEA communications strategy would consist of the following steps:

1 Identification of the overall objectives of the strategy
2. Refinement of the objectives for each stakeholder group
3. Development of the communication channels and budget
4. Development of communication materials
5. Implementation of the communication activities
6. Monitoring and evaluating of the communication strategy's impact[4]

SEA practitioners who are not schooled in communication strategies tend to choose the form of communication materials and communication channels without thinking about the ultimate purposes of communication, or about the specific needs of different stakeholder groups. In general, there tends to be too great a focus on dissemination in document form at a cost of engagement with multiple stakeholders. The main disadvantage of the document form of dissemination is its limited audience. In order to reach other stakeholders, greater emphasis should be placed on the production of nontechnical reports and nondocumentary modes of dissemination.

Expected Outcomes

Stakeholders are informed of the results of the SEA by using mechanisms appropriate for different audiences. Producing a report on SEA and handing it to the development agency and country partner is only a part of this process. To the extent possible, results should be also disseminated to and discussed with the media.

Monitoring and Evaluation of SEA in Environmental Mainstreaming

SEA is only an initial step for environmental and social mainstreaming in policy and sector reform. However, because policy formation is a continuous and dynamic process, monitoring and evaluation should focus on the extent to which SEA outcomes—raised attention to priorities, strengthened constituencies, enhanced accountability, and greater policy learning—have been achieved, rather than on implementation of the SEA's recommendations. Implementation has to be flexible and adjust to changes in the policy and sector reform as they adapt to the changing economic, political, and social conditions brought about by development.

Objectives

Monitoring and evaluating policy SEA should focus on how policy and sector reform have been influenced by raised attention to environmental and social priorities, strengthened constituencies, enhanced accountability, and policy learning induced by the SEA process and adaptive implementation of SEA recommendations.

Process to Be Followed and Examples from the Pilots

Monitoring of SEA in policy and sector reform should focus on SEA expected outcomes. It should concern itself specifically with availability of information on environmental and social priorities to key stakeholders; vitality of the engagement of stakeholders in environmental and social management; transparency in decision making associated with environmental and social priorities; and the legal, regulatory, and institutional adjustments implemented as part of the reform. This focus was attempted with the policy action matrix of the Kenya Forests Act SEA, which is discussed in box 3.8.

Ultimately, policy SEA contributes to improved policy making if it expands policy capacities, broadens policy horizons, and encourages policy regimes to

---

BOX 3.8

Kenya Forests Act SEA Policy Action Matrix

The policy action matrix was designed to be a key guide and monitoring device for the implementation of the Forests Act.

The SEA findings and recommendations were presented as a policy action matrix to support widespread implementation of the Kenya Forests Act. Endorsed by all the different groups of stakeholders (including permanent secretaries representing both the Ministry of Finance and the Ministry of Environment and Natural Resources), the matrix is an important tool that permits stakeholders to monitor progress on implementation and hold government accountable. According to the evaluation, several interviewees testified that the policy action matrix had provided them with an important lever in their advocacy work. For example, the Kenya Forestry Working Group has published two policy briefs assessing the implementation of the Forests Act through indicators developed for the policy action matrix. The matrix is also accessible via the Internet (http://www.policyactionmatrix.org). However, the dismantling of the Kenya Forest Sector Reform Secretariat and some other contextual factors limited a broader use and influence of the policy action matrix. Moreover, the expectation that the same wide group of stakeholders that was consulted during the SEA should be reconvened at appropriate intervals to review progress against this matrix has not been fulfilled.

Source: Slunge et al. 2010.

---

promote more environmentally and socially friendly behavior. Evaluation should concentrate on how these underlying conditions of policy processes have changed over time. This focus requires finding appropriate indicators. It should also be borne in mind that these effects will be the result of many different causes. Some could be related to the SEA recommendations, others to the reform itself, and there will be effects that originate in external factors. It is suggested that for monitoring and evaluating SEA in policy and sector reform, a useful starting point is the framework developed for this evaluation (see the section of appendix B entitled "Evaluating I-SEA").

Expected Outcomes

The main expected output of the proposed monitoring and evaluation framework would be continuation of the multistakeholder dialogue set up during the policy SEA. This dialogue will allow for reflection on how successfully the SEA and sector reform addressed gaps in managing environmental and social priorities.

Conclusion

Chapter 2 stated that SEA in policy and sector reform is fundamentally focused on changing incentives, attitudes, and cultures inside organizations and social groups so as to foster increased environmental and social awareness. The result of such changes should ultimately allow for strengthened constituencies, more carefully identified environmental priorities, and improved social accountability and policy learning.

This chapter has focused on the methods that can be used at each stage for applying SEA in policy and sector reform. It has provided guidance for policy makers, donors, and practitioners who might want to experiment with introducing SEA at these strategic levels.

Some words of caution are relevant at this point. Policy making is far more fluid than the design and implementation of development projects. As a consequence, the accepted stepwise methodological approach applied in most project EIA is not relevant to policies. While this report attempts to provide some methodological guidance, practitioners should not be wedded to it. Earlier studies that attempted to derive "cookbooks" for environmental mainstreaming have rapidly come to the realization that dealing with institutional and contextual challenges is generally considered by stakeholders to be far more important than choice of technical tools. In fact, in their review of the challenges associated with environmental mainstreaming, Dalal-Clayton and Bass (2009) point to indications that an exclusive focus on tools is part of the problem—technical safeguards and conditionalities "pushed" by environment interests on development interests—rather than a strategy to link mutual interests.

The final word on this issue is perhaps best left to the evaluators of the Hubei road transport planning pilot SEA: "Terms of Reference for such processes (i.e., policy SEA) should stipulate only basic requirements for analytical approach, leave the actual choice of specific methodology to those who undertake the SEA, and require SEA consultants/facilitators to duly consider stakeholders' needs and preferences when choosing or developing the actual methodology used in the SEA" (Dusik and Jian 2010).

Notes

1   Hence the use of the term "assessment"; "analysis" would imply something more careful and detailed.

2   This material is partially adapted from the World Bank Web site dealing with stakeholder analysis as part of anticorruption work. See http://www1.worldbank.org/publicsector/anticorrupt/PoliticalEconomy/stakeholderanalysis.htm.

3 The worksheets are part of the World Bank Labor Toolkit, and are available at http://
web.worldbank.org/WBSITE/EXTERNAL/TOPICS/ENVIRONMENT/0,,contentMD
K:21324896~menuPK:5065940~pagePK:148956~piPK:216618~theSitePK:244381~is
CURL:Y,00.html.

4 Steps are adapted from UNDP (2008).

References

Behr, Diji Chandrasekharan, and Fernando Loayza. 2009. "Guidance Note on Mainstreaming Environment in Forest Sector Reform." Environment Notes 2, World Bank, Washington, DC.

Dalal-Clayton, B., and S. Bass. 2009. *The Challenges of Environmental Mainstreaming: Experience of Integrating Environment into Development Institutions and Decisions.* Environmental Governance 3. London: International Institute for Environment and Development.

Dusik, J., and Y. Jian. 2010. "Evaluation of the World Bank's Pilot Program in Institution-Centered SEA: Strategic Environmental Assessment for Hubei Road Network Plan (2002–2020)." Unpublished report, World Bank, Washington, DC.

Loayza, Fernando, and Juan Albarracin-Jordan. 2010. "Mining Sector Strategic Environmental and Social Assessment (SESA)." Environment Notes 4, World Bank, Washington, DC.

Rietbergen-McCracken, J., and D. Narayan. 1998. *Participation and Social Assessment: Tools and Techniques.* Washington, DC: World Bank.

Slunge, D., A. Ekbom, W. Nyangena, and P. Guthiga. 2010. "Evaluation of the Strategic Environmental Assessment of the Kenya Forests Act." Unpublished report, World Bank, Washington, DC.

UNDP (United National Development Programme). 2008. *Generic Guidelines for Mainstreaming Drylands Issues into National Development Frameworks.* Nairobi: UNDP.

World Bank. 2003. *Sustainable Development in a Dynamic World: Transforming Institutions, Growth, and Quality of Life.* Washington, DC: World Bank.

———. 2007. "Strategic Environmental Assessment of the Kenya Forests Act 2005." Report No. 40659-KE, World Bank, Washington, DC.

———. 2009. "Strategic Environmental Assessment for Hubei Road Network Plan (2002–2020)." Unpublished SEA report, World Bank, Washington, DC.

———. 2010. "West Africa Mineral Sector Strategic Assessment (WAMSSA): Environmental and Social Strategic Assessment for the Development of the Mineral Sector in the Mano River Union." Report 53738-AFR, World Bank, Washington, DC.

C H A P T E R   4

Conclusions and Recommendations for Ways Forward

THIS REPORT HAS DRAWN LESSONS FROM THE LITERATURE on strategic environmental assessment (SEA) applied to policy, from the six SEA pilots and their evaluations, and finally from the cross-analysis of the evaluations presented in chapter 2. This concluding chapter first presents the key findings, messages, and recommendations from the pilot program. In particular, it reviews the main benefits and added value of carrying out SEA in policy and sector reform (derived from the cross-analysis of the evaluations). Finally, it goes on to consider how a wider application of SEA in policy formulation and implementation could be promoted, and what particular issues should be considered for this purpose, both by partner countries and the development cooperation community.

Main Findings of the Evaluation

As discussed in chapter 1, SEA is a family of approaches whose common purpose is to mainstream environmental considerations in strategic decision making. These approaches are not in competition, so the argument in favor of an expanded use of policy SEA does not in any way preclude the continued use of traditional (impact-centered) SEA approaches. There is, however, a need for more integrative use of analytical and participatory approaches such as policy SEA to provide knowledge for environmental mainstreaming in sector reform.

The lessons drawn from the pilots largely support this need for knowledge, and suggest that *SEA can, under conducive conditions, help to improve formulation and implementation of policy and sector reform.* In different ways and to differing extents, the pilots contributed to raising attention to environmental and social priorities, strengthening environmental constituencies, and enriching policy learning. The evaluation also found that the pilots contributed to the expansion of *policy capacities*, the broadening of *policy horizons*, and the modification of *decision regimes*. By influencing these three underlying conditions of policy making, SEA can enable long-term changes in actual formulation and implementation of sector reform.

Specific tools that assist in reaching these outcomes already exist, and were presented as guidance in chapter 3. Taking account of environmental concerns in sector reform requires a different emphasis for SEA, and draws upon the use of specific tools grounded in economics, political science, sociology, and adaptive decision making.

It is important to note that experiences with environmental mainstreaming in the World Bank's SEA pilot program have led to conclusions similar to those reached by other researchers, both in the context of development cooperation and in Organisation for Economic Co-operation and Development (OECD) policy processes.[1]

In addition, it was found that *ownership, capacity, and trust are necessary conditions for effective environmental mainstreaming at the policy level.*

Strong evidence was found that SEA has positive outcomes only if it promotes *ownership* of the SEA process by governments, civil society organizations, and local communities. The evaluation confirmed that country ownership has several dimensions. There is government ownership, which involves both a mandate to control the reform, including SEA, and accountability for results. When national agencies are put in charge of designing sustainable policies, they are equipped to deliver much more powerful measures than those that the World Bank or other agencies would be able to induce. It is important to note, however, that when weak sector ministries take ownership of policy SEA, there is a risk of regulatory capture and associated rent seeking. The West Africa Minerals Sector Strategic Assessment (WAMSSA) pilot showed that institutions such as multistakeholder frameworks can guard against this eventuality. Another dimension of ownership is linked to civil society and to potentially affected stakeholders. With well-designed institutional support and multistakeholder frameworks for addressing policy and development decisions in sector reform, SEA can help to reconcile different interests and to discourage regulatory capture by enhancing transparency and social accountability.

Effective environmental mainstreaming requires *capacities* to engage in dissemination, assimilation, and interpretation of knowledge; in strategic thinking; and in interactions with different stakeholders. These tasks take time and require qualified staff. Presently, day-to-day affairs often absorb existing staff capacities.

Finally, environmental mainstreaming requires *trust* because it requires that different stakeholders within and outside government engage in a policy learning process. This learning involves taking risks—accepting that one's arguments might not be robust and might require a change of position—and opening up the policy process to a broad array of stakeholders from the local to the national levels. Hence stakeholders need to have full trust in the process and in the process leadership. Moreover, trust among key stakeholders is required for policy makers to be more receptive to the needs and concerns of weak and vulnerable stakeholders, and their decisions accountable to wider constituencies.

Another important finding emanating from the pilot projects is that *long-term constituency building is needed*. SEA is but a small and bounded intervention in the continuous process flow of policy formation. To sustain outcomes over the long term, it is necessary to build constituencies that can sustain policy influence and institutional changes, since these can take a long time to realize. Constituency building requires considerable time and effort. Therefore, SEA can provide only the first push for long-term constituency building as an ongoing and continuous process. Some aspects of constituency building are relatively easy to address, such as ensuring follow-up activities that keep things going after the SEA process has been completed. Other aspects will be more difficult, especially when they challenge the way established power elites usually make decisions.

Given the amount of time it can take for SEA to influence changes in incentives, attitudes, organizational cultures, professional disciplines, and power relationships within government, effective environmental constituencies have the potential to outlast changes in government. Governments will therefore need demonstrable benefits from the establishment of constituencies as well as supporting structures and processes such as long-term stakeholder engagement. One model presented in chapter 2 was the multistakeholder framework proposed during the WAMSSA pilot. While this is a potentially excellent model, it focuses only on one sector and relates to a specific intervention. A more general, politically mandated, and open public inquiry process, one capable of dealing with a range of natural resource management conflicts, could be a more appropriate model for deliberative institutions that would support continuous environmental mainstreaming. This kind of institutional model would also help to guard against regulatory capture, which is a distinct possibility in countries where sector ministries may be weak, and where rent seeking is prevalent. This kind of approach, however, depends on country-specific conditions such as the existence of well-developed democratic institutions, or a culture of involving stakeholders in natural resource management.

Constituencies need to be strengthened across sectoral agencies and interests. This process requires trust building and the perception that problems are shared. Under conducive conditions, as stakeholders start to deal with the complex problems and responses to sustainable development issues and share policy dilemmas and trade-offs that emerge, joint-problem perceptions and trust in each others' intentions may surface. This change may result in breakthroughs in understanding between people from opposing organizations. As a corollary, the evaluation showed that when constituency building was weak in the pilots, the take-up of the policy SEA recommendations was limited.

A final main finding of the pilots is that *contextual factors are of overriding importance in determining whether the main benefits of SEA are attained.* Chapter 2 highlighted one set of contextual factors identified through the pilots. In some cases, these factors may be aligned in such a way that pursuing policy SEA is not meaningful. This can happen when social tensions are extreme, or—as in the case of the Sierra Leone pilot—when a newly elected government decides to postpone reform processes initiated by a previous administration. In all cases, however, preparation and planning must make sure to adapt and adjust the SEA process in view of contextual factors. Some could be very difficult to influence through SEA, so different types of intervention would have to be sought. Others are easier to influence, such as ownership, cultures and traditions of organizational coordination in the administration, and the capacity to engage in the SEA process. Yet others can be shaped through how the SEA is conducted, such as building trust among different stakeholders in the process, or establishing follow-up measures to sustain outcomes past the duration of the SEA. In some cases contextual factors may be identified through proper initial scoping, but political and social events, such as elections, may drastically change situations in unforeseen ways.

A related lesson is that *the potential benefits of policy SEA need to be clearly articulated.* Developers of policy SEA must recognize that incumbent actors have certain interests when engaging in SEA activities. Their participation will be driven by the extent to which benefits from engaging are greater than the risks and costs. First and foremost, SEA of policy and sector reform must be understood as a strategic decision support that will enable governments to put in motion better policy making, and not as an environmental safeguard. Speaking directly to the development priorities of the country, policy SEA not only works toward improving policy making from an environmental mainstreaming perspective, but also supports better planning and policy making from an overarching development point of view. The sector review's analysis of the potential economic and growth impact of sector reform could be complemented by SEA's exploration of the economic and growth implications of environmental and social priorities. This perspective makes it much easier to establish country ownership (further discussed below).

This framing of SEA also requires a different kind of professional expertise than that associated with SEA generally. To date, SEA practitioners have tended to come from a background in environmental impact assessment (EIA), with

> **Recommendations:**
>
> 1. SEA of policy and sector reform, rather than a mechanism for safeguarding the environment, enables countries to perform better policy making and strategic planning. Dialogues in preparing for policy SEA should focus strongly on the benefits for the decision maker of addressing the concerns and interests of key stakeholders, including the weak and most vulnerable.
>
> 2. The preparation and scoping of SEA at the policy level must carefully consider contextual factors, including economic and political conditions, organizational cultures and traditions, ownership of the SEA process, access to environmental and social information by civil society, and baseline capacities in the government organization. Terms of reference for policy SEA should include requirements for expertise in policy analysis, grounded in disciplines such as economics, sociology, stakeholder engagement, and political science.
>
> 3. Trust and constituency building/strengthening are critical for successful SEA of policy and sector reform. Resources and time should be applied to this task whenever policy SEA is undertaken. The aim is to create communities of practice that go beyond particular policy processes, projects, or personalities and that can exist over long periods of time.
>
> 4. Sustaining the contribution of SEA to environmental mainstreaming should be built into the implementation of policy and sector reform, and into the broader policy environment likely to affect this implementation. This task includes providing detailed feedback to participants on the recommendations and follow-up activities included in the SEA.

technical skills associated with EIA tasks and environmental safeguards. As a consequence, they tend to treat SEA in a similar way. Given the strong focus of policy level SEA on institutions, governance, political economy, and policy issues, their skill background is not the most appropriate. SEA teams working on policy and sector reform need to include expertise in policy-related disciplines such as economics, sociology, and political science.

Promoting Policy SEA: A Phased Approach

Given the potential benefits that SEA could bring to policy and sector reform—and indirectly to growth, climate change adaptation and mitigation, and poverty alleviation—*the main recommendation of this report is to move forward with further testing and scaling up of SEA at the policy level.*

Since this scaling up involves attaining commitment from a wide group of donor agencies and partner/client countries, the case needs to be based on a firm footing. Unfortunately, in both the North and South, systematic studies of the relative effectiveness of different environmental mainstreaming activities are lacking. Yet developing countries are increasingly adopting SEA legislation.[2] Moreover, the policy SEA approach lends itself to the incorporation of climate change considerations in sector reform because it can include climate change concerns in priority setting, or may prioritize activities that are vulnerable to climate change or significantly affect emissions of greenhouse gases. It is suggested nevertheless that a pragmatic, cautious, and phased approach is needed to ensure successful scaling up of SEA in policy and sector reform. The last policy SEA pilot completed under the program (WAMSSA) benefited from the learning accumulated by the pilot program as a whole, and suggests the potential for learning that arises when policy SEA approaches are applied in an incremental fashion.

It is suggested that scaling up be undertaken in three main phases over approximately 10 years (see table 4.1). The main expected outcomes of the three phases are these: in participating countries, where better policy making and successful environmental and social mainstreaming could be featured, key stakeholders will be more interested in and have greater capacity for undertaking policy SEA; trust among stakeholders will grow; and country ownership will be strengthened. The expected development impacts are stronger economic growth, poverty alleviation, and improved environmental and social management of key sectors in participating countries. During scaling up of SEA in policy and sector reform, there is

TABLE 4.1
Phased Approach to Scaling Up of SEA in Policy and Sector Reform (10 years)

Preparation phase (years 1-2)	Implementation phase 1 (years 2-6)	Implementation phase 2 (years 7-10)
1. Preparing technical guidelines and awareness-raising materials for scaling up	5. Preparing SEA of policy and sector reform by initiating constituency building and multistakeholder dialogue in selected partner countries	8. Country-driven institutionalization of SEA at the policy level
2. Establishing donor alliances and partnerships; raising awareness	6. Undertaking SEA processes in 2-4 strategic economic sectors in selected partner countries	9. Situating SEA within national and sector development policy
3. Assessment of windows of opportunity and selection of 8-10 partner countries	7. Evaluation and lessons learned	10. Development of a follow-up and learning system for continuous improvement of policy making and environmental and social mainstreaming
4. Building partner country commitment and ownership for implementation		

Source: Authors.

a need to identify, monitor, analyze, and follow up sector-specific indicators of successful outcomes.

The preparation phase would focus on awareness raising and capacity building for applying SEA in sector reform in participating developing countries, as well as on donor coordination and alliance building. This phase would focus on assessing the preconditions for successful introduction of policy SEA in a country; identifying partners who have the capacity and will to take on ownership of ("champion") the SEA process; and assessing possible windows of opportunity. More specific criteria for selecting countries need to be developed, but would likely include good governance aspects; willingness of countries to participate and to reform their policy processes; and basic public administration capacities. In participating countries the focus of awareness raising and capacity building could be in the most strategic sectors for environmental sustainability, economic development, and climate change adaptation and mitigation. Examples would include forestry, mining, energy, industrial development, or agriculture.

The first implementation phase would consist of participating countries undertaking specific and detailed analytical work and then developing and applying SEA in policy processes. It is suggested that between 8 and 10 self-selected countries would carry out between two and four SEAs in key development sectors to reach a critical mass of experience and capacity for environmental, social, and climate change mainstreaming in sector reform. This phase would be completed by an evaluation and "lessons learned" exercise.

The second implementation phase would consist of a country-driven process with gradual institutionalization of applying SEA in policy making, thereby positioning SEA among the key tools used for sound policy making at the sector level.

As countries continue testing SEA, they will need to keep in the forefront the idea that the purpose of SEA is not to meet some regulatory requirement, but instead to improve policy making in order to promote sustainable development. In particular, SEA should be seen as an approach for strengthening institutions and making governance changes that enable governments to enhance integration of environmental, climate change, and social considerations in sector reform.

If this proposal for scaling up is not fully realized, SEA could still enhance sector reform. Based on the evidence provided by this evaluation, it is suggested that donors and partner countries join efforts to foster SEA in policy and sector reform under the following conditions:

- Country ownership is ensured
- SEA is undertaken along with sector reform design and not as an isolated assessment
- Follow-on activities recommended by the SEA can be supported during sector reform implementation

---

Recommendations:

5. During scaling up, SEA should be applied in a more strategic way than was the case in the pilot program. The scaling up could focus on a set of key sectors within a country that are critical/strategic for growth, poverty alleviation, and climate change adaptation and mitigation. Undertaking SEAs in these sectors will contribute to the building of a critical mass of capacity for economic reform that is environmentally and socially sustainable. It is suggested that support be prioritized to countries that show an interest in ownership through a self-selection process.

Promoting Policy SEA: Issues to Consider in the Partner Country Context

The outcomes of the comparative analysis of the SEA pilots indicated that the scaling up of policy SEA in developing countries needs to focus on conveying the benefits of SEA, boosting sector ownership of the SEA process, and dealing with capacity constraints. These issues are discussed in more detail below.

Conveying Benefits of Policy SEA

In all countries, established authority and elite interests can seriously constrain the uptake of new ideas. This situation can be even more problematic in cultural contexts where challenging authority is traditionally discouraged. In such places, SEA at the policy level promoted by development agencies on a test basis could be tolerated. But scaling up might be considered a threat to the policy-making power of established authority, in particular when the SEA addresses strategic economic development sectors. There is then a risk that SEA could be seen by powerful ministries as being a brake on development championed by external interest groups and donors, and a threat to strategic development interests. There is evidence that this kind of situation existed in Hubei; box 4.1 presents a brief summary.

This situation could be approached in two ways. One strategy is to attempt to structure the policy dialogue to ensure that SEA is not seen as just another regulatory hurdle. The benefits and added value of incorporating environmental and social dimensions in sector reform through SEA should be spelled out. These benefits include, but are not limited to, enhancing risk management in the sectors, enhancing policy capacities, and broadening policy horizons. As has been mentioned, the main challenge is to ensure that potential benefits of SEA are continually stressed and constituencies built around them. Champions of policy SEA are advised to seek out ways to align the environmental agenda with

BOX 4.1
Scaling Up and Threats to Established Authority: The Hubei Transport Planning Pilot

In the Hubei road transport planning case, the SEA approach for policy was not fully consistent with the legal processes prescribed for plan EIA in Chinese law. The evaluators described these processes as being "very rigid" and with corresponding institutional arrangements that do not necessarily support the flexibility and inclusiveness sought by policy SEA approaches. For example, the evaluators observed that if SEA pointed to flaws in plans, the outcome was often rejection of the SEA report, rather than redrafting or rejection of the plan itself.

Another example is evident in the response to the SEA team's institutional analysis and action plan for strengthening the management of social and environmental issues in provincial road planning. Even though this plan was appreciated by three important stakeholder groups, it was never fully accepted by the Hubei Provincial Communication Department, because it proposed changes to authority structures that had not been earlier discussed with and agreed upon by the department.

Source: Adapted from Dusik and Jian 2010.

---

other key development themes higher up on the political agenda (economic growth, poverty reduction, health, employment, etc.) and with the dominant existing perceptions and interests. Often, stakeholders are indeed willing and able to mainstream environmental issues, but will be supported in political decision making only if they align, or create alliances, with important shorter-term interests within the sector.

Another complementary strategy could be to use regulation and guidelines in overarching (long-term) development plans as a lever. Many developing countries still use five-year or ten-year national development plans as the main focus for prioritizing investment decisions and channeling donor funds. In these countries, the plans become a strong focus for sector ministry activity, and considerable effort is put into compiling them, implementing them, and evaluating their outcomes. Incorporating policy SEA requirements into guidance for national and sector planning documents could favorably influence environmental mainstreaming. However, adoption of SEA requirements for sector and policy reform should result from the SEA's own merits as contributing to better policy making.

Boosting Ownership in Strategic Sectors

The evaluations of the SEA pilots have made it clear that country ownership of SEA is a necessary precondition for successful implementation. When SEA is applied in a specific sector reform, then care also needs to be taken in the choice of an appropriate counterpart agency. In at least one of the SEA pilots, the Dhaka urban development planning SEA, a reluctant counterpart agency resulted in a problematic outcome. Insights about the importance of sector ownership and responsibility are also reinforced by the work on impact assessment and policy integration in OECD countries.

SEA is an approach, among others, that sector planners and policy makers could use in formulating and implementing policies. The importance of sector agencies/ministries as actors in the process of moving toward sustainable development cannot be overestimated. As was clearly articulated by the Brundtland Commission in 1987 and at the Rio Summit in 1992, sustainable development that attempts to integrate economic, environmental, and social goals cannot logically be championed by environment agencies, but must occur in the sectors where economic, industrial, and development activities are being decided and implemented. However, as discussed above, care needs to be taken to ensure that sector agencies that accept responsibility for ownership of SEA have the strength and support to resist regulatory capture. With well-designed institutional support and multistakeholder frameworks for addressing policy and development decisions (like those proposed in the WAMSSA pilot), SEA can help to reconcile different interests, and can discourage regulatory capture by enhancing transparency and social accountability.

Sector ownership should not be interpreted narrowly. It includes sector authorities and public agencies, but, as illustrated by the pilots, it should also involve civil society, the private sector, and the media. The pilots have shown the importance of involving all key stakeholders in the SEA process, particularly the vulnerable and weak. The role of the private sector and the media must not be underestimated. Their participation enhances the legitimacy of the contributions of SEA to sector or policy reform, helps to prevent misunderstandings that could be costly during policy implementation, and assists in guarding against regulatory capture.

It should also be noted that sector ownership implies a different role for the environmental agency: in SEA of policy and sector reform there is no operational role for environmental agencies beyond contributing expertise; guarding consistency with environmental policy, regulation, and commitments; and participating in interministerial consultation groups or steering committees. However, the results of policy SEA may well lead to specific changes in environmental regulation, law, or policy, the further preparation of which involves environmental agencies.

Dealing with Capacity Constraints

Lack of adequate capacity has long been discussed as a constraint to development in general. This problem can be even starker in developing countries when it comes to the introduction of a new concept, practice, or analytical approach, such as SEA of policy and sector reform. Concerns about lack of capacity were raised on a number of occasions in the pilots, sometimes implying that it might be unwise to establish SEA systems in countries that are still coming to terms with EIA. The skills required for policy SEA, however, are quite different from those needed in EIA. Capacity constraints are related to skills in policy analysis and stakeholder engagement rather than EIA technical skill gaps.

The pilot evaluations indicated that for SEA to have an impact in the long term, there is a need for local capacity development in governments and civil society. While some SEA teams used local consultant partners to organize consultation activities, there was not much evidence of local capacity development in the pilot studies. To remedy this, SEA of policy and sector reform should include a substantial local capacity-building component. In addition, one of the aims of SEA is to put environmental concerns on the policy agenda. Evidence from the pilots indicated that agenda setting is facilitated when communities of practice are established to work over long periods of time. Communities of practice require strengthening capacities for policy analysis and representation in the policy dialogue of civil society. Otherwise, environmental prioritization and follow-up of SEA recommendations during policy implementation tend to be temporary and punctuated, rather than permanent and sustained.

Important issues for scaling up and dealing with capacity constraints are the identification and nurturing of both SEA champions and ongoing institutions for assisting with SEA capacity building. In resource-scarce developing countries, much momentum for policy SEA can be obtained by encouraging individual policy entrepreneurship. A good model could be the "poverty and environment champions" system being tested by the Poverty-Environment Initiative (PEI). It selects people in its pilot countries who take on the role of advocate for the integration of poverty-environment considerations into development planning at national, sector, and subnational levels. In return for taking on this role, the chosen champions receive high-level recognition and other benefits such as training and membership in an international community of practice.

There may also be a role for some kind of SEA help desk that could provide resources, technical assistance, and capacity-building support to ensure that momentum is maintained after donors leave. One possibility, in some countries, could be for SEA follow-on and monitoring to be incorporated into secretariats such as EITI (Extractive Industries Transparency Initiative) or EITI++ to further promote transparency and social accountability in countries relying on extractive industries to jump-start development.

Recommendations:

6. Governments need to be proactive in their search for the right "owner" of SEA. There needs to be clarity about the criteria for choosing counterpart agencies. For effective SEA, agencies and ministries in charge of planning and sector reform, rather than environmental agencies, should be in charge of undertaking SEA. Environmental agencies and ministries should not be operationally active but should participate through interministerial consultation groups or steering groups governing SEA. To ensure that weak sector agencies are not exposed to regulatory capture and associated rent seeking, it is important to involve stakeholders in sector reform through multi-stakeholder approaches for planning and decision making.

7. When regulatory requirements for SEA exist—for instance, in guidelines for national development planning—they can be used as "levers" to implement SEA in policy and sector reform. However, SEA should be adopted on its own merits as contributing to better policy making. Making policy SEA mandatory during the scaling-up phase risks casting the process in a negative light, as a potential regulatory hurdle. Whether or not SEA of policy and sector reform at some point is made mandatory is a question that can be answered only in view of the specific legal and institutional context at the national level.

8. Substantial investment in local capacity building within governments, civil society organizations, the media, and to some extent the private sector is required to ensure that SEA champions, government officials, and stakeholders can apply SEA effectively in policy formulation and implementation.

Promoting Policy SEA: Issues for Consideration by Development Agencies

Another crucial aspect of scaling up SEA in policy and sector reform is to create an international constituency, through strategic alliances and network building in the development cooperation community, that can further develop and explore the potential of SEA in strategic decision making. Many synergies can be realized through such coordination efforts. Results from the World Bank's SEA pilot program have many commonalities with the agenda of both the OECD Development Assistance Committee (DAC) SEA Task Team and the PEI program of the United Nations Development Programme (UNDP)–United Nations Environment Programme (UNEP). This section discusses issues and identifies possible ways forward under a coordinated approach to scaling up among multilateral and bilateral donors. It focuses on alliance building, the building of awareness and harmonization in the donor community, and funding.

Alliance Building and Harmonization for Fostering Environmental Mainstreaming

Key questions regarding alliance building for promoting SEA at the policy level are these: what are the most effective networks and alliances for scaling up SEA of policy and sector reform, and how can they be most efficiently mobilized and organized? A critical issue here is that with the development of the World Bank Group's New Environment Strategy and the scaling up of the UNDP-UNEP PEI, a window of opportunity seems to be opening for fostering SEA at the most strategic level.

PEI supports capacity building in environmental mainstreaming in developing countries by providing technical assistance to planning, finance, and environmental ministries. Given the lessons learned by PEI about environmental mainstreaming, other development agencies promoting this agenda could benefit from a partnership. The OECD SEA Task Team plays an active role as a broad-based SEA support network. It has been recognized as such in the international development community since the publication of *Applying Strategic Environmental Assessment: Good Practice Guidance for Development Co-operation.* (OECD DAC 2006). Since publication of that document, the task team has been refocusing its efforts on supporting implementation and capacity building.

Other development agencies are also active in the areas of environmental mainstreaming and SEA at the policy level. For example, a number of the so-called like-minded bilateral agencies, such as DfID (Department for International Development, United Kingdom), GTZ (German Agency for Technical Cooperation), and Sida (Swedish International Development Cooperation Agency), have actively investigated the potential for mainstreaming in their aid programs, and multilateral agencies such as the Asian Development Bank and the Inter-American Development Bank have incorporated environmental mainstreaming processes into their program cycles. It is clear that a critical mass of experience in the linked areas of SEA of policies and environmental mainstreaming, emanating from a range of bilateral and multilateral development agencies, now exists. It seems that the time is ripe for the establishment of a broad environmental mainstreaming alliance. This entity would clarify the roles and niches of the different interested parties.

Alliance building not only requires donors to team up and bring added value to the implementation process according to their comparative advantages, but also requires involvement of partner countries and the formation of an alliance across countries engaging in SEA for reform in strategic sectors. Such an alliance would enable exchanges of experiences across countries and render SEA implementation globally more efficient.

The World Bank could add its specialized experience in sector reform to a potentially influential alliance. The World Bank has more than 20 years of experience assisting developing countries in sector reform in agriculture, forestry, mining, oil, water, energy, transport, rural development, and other areas. It also has significant experience in assisting countries in using SEA, and has taken a pioneering role in applying SEA to policies. SEA to support sector reform is being applied in mining and forestry[3] and—less widely—in the water, transport, agriculture, and tourism sectors.

Funding of Policy SEA

Scaling up of policy SEA will require alignment and mobilization of resources. What human, institutional, and financial resources will be needed to support the process of "going to scale," and what needs to be done to ensure that these resources are available? There is no question that scaling up of SEA in general, and policy SEA in particular, will require a substantial commitment in resources from both development agencies and partner countries. For example, prior to the scaling up of the UNDP-UNEP PEI, the two UN agencies undertook an analysis of scaling-up requirements (UNDP-UNEP Poverty-Environment Initiative 2007; UNDP-UNEP 2009). They found that because environmental mainstreaming is relatively new, seeks to change priorities, and involves a number of ministries, it requires a great deal of staff time, as well as technical and political support at different levels, to succeed. The joint program funded focal points in environment, planning, and finance ministries; a national project manager in each country; a technical advisor; a finance assistant; and specialized teams for integrated ecosystem assessments and economic analyses.

Until countries are able to take over SEA as part of regular policy making, the World Bank, together with international and bilateral development agencies, will need to continue to fund such work. Although country ownership should be expressed with country resources directed to policy SEA, external funding is still required for several purposes. One is to support governments of low-income countries to enhance capacities that allow them to fully own and adopt the approach. A second purpose is to provide support to enable stakeholders within civil society, academia and other groups, and the media to become involved in SEA processes of policies, in both low- and middle-income countries.

Awareness Raising and Ownership in the Donor Community

The issue of capacity building in developing countries has been discussed. A precondition for successful scaling up is that additional capacity development and awareness raising occur also within the donor community, including inside the World Bank. There is a need for awareness raising beyond environment departments within donor groups. Operational departments are responsible for designing interventions and activities. The outcomes of policy SEA will likely not be taken into account unless managers responsible for designing interventions are fully cognizant of the purpose of SEA work.

The benefits of applying SEA in policy and sector reform therefore need to be clearly articulated and discussed in relation to the objectives and goals of the donor community and of partner countries. As discussed earlier, the ultimate development impact associated with SEA is stronger and more robust economic development in conjunction with reduced environmental and social pressures. The immediate impact is better policy making, which is achieved through four key outcomes: better priority setting; constituency building; enhanced accountability; and policy learning. The effectiveness of SEA in achieving these outcomes needs to be carefully evaluated during the scaling-up process. To this end, the preparation phase, and awareness raising within it, need to include the development of a framework with operational indicators for follow-up.

As is always the case with new initiatives, applying SEA in sector reform requires champions to advocate its case. Ideally, these would be both individual policy entrepreneurs and government agencies prepared to argue in its favor. Sometimes, positive movements toward ownership do take place in developing countries, as agencies see the benefits of new policy innovations. Similarly, within donor organizations, it is necessary to establish policy SEA champions, potentially linked together in some kind of international network arrangement, possibly under the umbrella of the OECD DAC SEA Task Team.

Conclusion

There is no question that SEA of policy and sector reform has evolved significantly in the past few years, but it is in its early days yet. The evaluations of the six pilots, and related recent environmental mainstreaming activity, suggest that the SEA approach at the policy level has the potential to contribute to better policy making and strengthened governance overall, efficient allocation of resources, and decoupling of economic growth from resource degradation and climate change. Moreover, the tools and methods that can assist with reaching these outcomes already exist, especially within the realms of policy analysis and public participation.

As is the case with most development activities, it is likely that SEA will develop deeper roots if it is championed by developing countries. The building of local ownership will take time and will require constant reiteration of the benefits of the approach, but also trust, constituency building, financial support, and capacity building. Furthermore, it is suggested that promoting the use of SEA in policy making needs to be addressed through an international alliance involving developing countries and the development cooperation community.

However, scaling up of policy SEA needs to occur in a cautious and stepwise fashion, and supported by evidence that preconditions have been met.

Scaling up of new approaches such as SEA of policy and sector reform should be through leveraging alliances and partnerships with other development agencies. Development agencies can continue to build capacity for SEA in many different ways, and their involvement will be necessary for some time to come. The World Bank, multilateral regional development banks, UN agencies, and many bilateral donors have all accumulated significant experience in helping countries to develop capacity for sector reform, including mainstreaming and institutional strengthening on environmental issues. Learning from and building upon this kind of experience is critical for the further development of SEA, because doing so both brings added legitimacy and meets the requirements of aid effectiveness as expressed in the Paris Declaration on Aid Effectiveness and the Accra Agenda for Action.

This report has attempted to draw analytical and operational lessons from the pilot testing of applying SEA in policy and sector reform and to sketch a way forward for scaling up this approach. As countries embrace the imperative of addressing climate change and greening growth, the objective of decoupling growth from fossil fuel—and natural resource—intensive production processes is urgent. While the role of technological and market innovation in sustainable development cannot be denied, sector reform, in sectors critical for economic growth, is also unavoidable. Thus, the overall conclusion of this evaluation is that SEA can support countries in moving along a path toward sustainable development by contributing to greening policy and sector reform.

Notes

1   See for example Nilsson and Eckerberg (2007).
2   See for example Ahmed and Fiadjoe (2006).
3   Guidance for undertaking policy SEA at the sector level is available for these sectors. See Behr and Loayza (2009) and Loayza and Albarracin-Jordan (2010).

References

Ahmed, K., and Y. Fiadjoe. 2006. "A Selective Review of SEA Legislation: Results from a Nine-Country Review." Environment Strategy Paper 13, World Bank, Washington, DC.

Behr, Diji Chandrasekharan, and Fernando Loayza. 2009. "Guidance Note on Mainstreaming Environment in Forest Sector Reform." Environment Notes 2, World Bank, Washington, DC.

Dusik, J., and Y. Jian. 2010. "Evaluation of the World Bank's Pilot Program in Institution-Centered SEA: Strategic Environmental Assessment for Hubei Road Network Plan (2002–2020)." Unpublished report, World Bank, Washington, DC.

Loayza, Fernando, and Juan Albarracin-Jordan. 2010. "Mining Sector Strategic Environmental and Social Assessment (SESA)." Environment Notes 4, World Bank, Washington, DC.

Nilsson, M., and K. Eckerberg, eds. 2007. *Environmental Policy Integration in Practice: Shaping Institutions for Learning*. London: Earthscan.

OECD DAC (Organisation for Economic Co-operation and Development, Development Assistance Committee). 2006. *Applying Strategic Environmental Assessment: Good Practice Guidance for Development Co-operation*. Paris: OECD Publishing.

UNDP-UNEP (United Nations Development Programme–United Nations Environment Programme). Poverty-Environment Initiative. 2007. "Mainstreaming Environment for Poverty Reduction and Pro-poor Growth: Proposal for Scaling-up the Poverty-Environment Initiative." http://www.unpei.org/PDF/PEI-Scaling-up-Proposal-Final.pdf.

———. 2009. "Scaling-up the UNDP-UNEP Poverty-Environment Initiative: Annual Progress Report 2008." http://www.unpei.org/PDF/PEI-annualprogress-report2008.pdf.

Summaries of the Policy SEA Pilots

THE WORLD BANK'S SEA PILOT PROGRAM comprised eight pilots. Six pilots were completed by early 2010 and evaluated. This appendix summarizes the pilots and the findings of the pilot evaluations. It introduces the pilots linked to the country operations that were supported by the Bank. The appendix discusses the outcomes attained by each pilot analyzing the enabling and constraining factors that affected achievement of outcomes. Each pilot summary concludes by drawing some general observations or lessons for policy SEA.

The Sierra Leone Mining Sector Reform Strategic Environmental and Social Assessment

The strategic environmental and social assessment (SESA) of the mining sector in Sierra Leone stands out as a strategic environmental assessment (SEA) originating in a policy development loan (the World Bank's Programmatic Governance Reform and Growth Grant series). The SESA's main objective was to help assist with long-term country development by integrating environmental and social considerations into mining sector reform. This goal was supported by a loan meant to establish the Mining Technical Assistance Project (MTAP). The SESA was undertaken in 2006–07 along with the preparation of the MTAP, which under the original plan was to be approved by the Board of the World Bank by the end of 2007. However, in 2007 a newly elected Sierra Leonean government put mining reform on hold and left the MTAP dormant for approximately two years.

Brief Description of the Pilot

The SESA process consisted of three stages. The first of these included a situation analysis that examined general environmental and social issues in Sierra Leone as a whole and in each of the mining subsectors (large scale, artisanal, and small scale). The analysis was aided by three case studies in each of the subsectors. The situation analysis informed a first round of workshops, held in all four provinces of Sierra Leone, to select environmental and social priorities in the mining sector by applying a ranking methodology. The ranking procedure aimed at removing some of the potential biases and ensured that equal weight was given to vulnerable groups in selecting environmental and social priorities.

The second stage of the process involved the analysis of the institutional, governance, and political economy issues that influence the way policies translate into stakeholder behaviors and development outcomes. The first analytic undertaking involved the review of the legal and regulatory framework for managing environmental and social priorities. The second analytic task involved the assessment of the transmission mechanisms from new mining policies to environmental and social priorities. Mechanisms considered in the analysis included (i) institutional and organizational capacity and coordination; (ii) potential influence of stakeholders on the reform; and (iii) coordination among stakeholders. In the second round of regional workshops, stakeholders were exposed to the preliminary results of this analysis and were given the chance to discuss and comment on them.

A series of recommendations composed the third stage of the SESA. The recommendations aimed at transforming a situation of weak institutional capacity and weak governance. SESA's recommendations, which were validated in a national workshop that included representatives from provincial workshops, encompassed institutional and organizational adjustments to consolidate a policy framework designed to induce sustainable development in the mining sector, and in the country at large.

SEA Outcomes

At the provincial level, environmental and social priorities included mine employment, provision of infrastructure, community development and participation, and mitigation of the negative impacts of blasting. At the national level, stakeholders prioritized land and crop compensation and village relocation, sanitation and water pollution, deforestation and soil degradation, child labor, and post-closure reclamation.

In choosing the SESA's priorities and validating the institutional analysis and recommendations, vulnerable segments of society were given an opportunity to voice their concerns. Attention was paid to the situation of poor and vulnerable stakeholders, such as mining communities generally and women and children in some mining areas. Thus, the SESA helped expand and deepen the dialogue on mining sector reform that informed the preparation of the MTAP, particularly in relation to the project's institutional and governance components. However, because the scope of public participation was limited to provincial and national workshops, involvement of local mining communities and traditional authorities in this dialogue was limited.

The SESA also influenced the Justice for the Poor initiative in Sierra Leone. The initiative's examination of more practical interventions at the local level is based to some extent on SESA's analysis and recommendations. The initiative has acknowledged SESA's important contribution to its approach, which will foster public debate on issues of accountability to inform and help shape mining reform. In addition, important methodological and analytical components of the SESA were introduced into the West Africa Minerals Sector Strategic Assessment (WAMSSA), another policy SEA pilot (see below). SESA has also served as a stimulus for incorporating policy SEA processes into other World Bank–sponsored mining policy projects around the world.

Whereas SESA's contribution to policy dialogue has been significant, its influence on the existing mining policy of Sierra Leone—specifically policy's incorporation of environmental and social considerations—has yet to materialize. This outcome, however, cannot be attributed directly to factors inherent in the SESA process. External political and institutional factors played a significant role in attenuating the short-term impact of the SESA. A newly elected government that took over shortly after the completion of the SESA considered that some sort of diversification of the economy was necessary. The new administration prioritized the review of existing mining contracts and left broader issues of mining sector reform dormant for approximately two years.

Constraining or Enabling Factors

Of the six identified enabling or constraining factors discussed in chapter 2, three were especially evident in the Sierra Leone SESA: windows of opportunity, the role of power elites, and the sustaining of environmental and social mainstreaming beyond the completion of the policy SEA report.

The literature puts windows of opportunity at the heart of a process in which policies might be influenced. However, they are not easy to predict, and they can also close unexpectedly. When the SESA was undertaken, there was extraordinary global demand for minerals and strong interest in them from foreign investors. With the country emerging from a long period of impoverishment and internal conflict, the Sierra Leone government acknowledged this exceptional opportunity and was apparently enthusiastic about mineral sector reform. However, this window did not remain open for long, as a new government was elected soon after the completion of the SESA, and it made agricultural investment and review of mining contracts a higher priority than mining sector reform. In addition, this change of government coincided with the sharp global economic downturn that began in 2008.

While the SESA's analysis of formal institutions and the country's political economy was undoubtedly comprehensive, customary institutions, such as the chiefdom, were given less attention. While numerous opportunities for successful mining reform might open in the future, overlooking the underlying principles of customary institutions, and the extension of informal codes over more than three-quarters of Sierra Leone's ethnic landscape, could lead to a limited understanding of the potential challenges of reform. The institution of the chiefdom has implications for access to land, compensation, and reclamation associated with mining activities that were captured only partially by the SESA, and hence did not fully inform the preparation of the MTAP.

The SESA report included a risk analysis that incorporated latent threats to the proposed actions. This constitutes a distinguishing SESA feature that is not typical of the SEA archetype. In this analysis, the economic and political power that particular interest groups may employ to interfere with the reform process—thus distorting the sought-after outcomes—was examined. In the national workshop, this analysis and the corresponding recommendations were validated. However, dissemination of the SESA's findings and recommendations was not extensive. It could have expanded the dissemination process in order to highlight the importance of environmental and social issues in mining sector reform. A more concrete account of the process, broadly and effectively disseminated, would have had a more enduring effect on the collective memory of stakeholders, as well as on the strengthening of environmental constituencies and on policy learning.

Conclusion

Even though the SESA accomplished its objective of informing mining sector reform on key institutional and political economy concerns, the issue of transferring ownership of the process to specific constituencies raises some important questions. The following recommendations derive from the evaluation of the SESA; however, they may also have implications for the general policy SEA model.

1. Adapt the consultation format to the stakeholders and to the local cultural scenario (for example, the one day/one room consultation format may not be appropriate for consulting with indigenous constituencies, for whom longer consultation periods and focus groups are likely to be required).
2. Establish mechanisms, on the basis of a culture-sensitive approach to dialogue, to transfer the ownership of the process to stakeholders, including vulnerable social segments.
3. In the analytic component, explore the possibility of considering alternative scenarios, such as best-case and worst-case, and how these might influence institutional reforms and their interrelations.
4. Incorporate an analysis of customary institutions, particularly if indigenous constituencies are part of or have a role in the policy process.
5. Ensure that the evaluation results and recommendations are effectively disseminated among all stakeholders.

Strategic Environmental Assessment for the Hubei Road Network Plan (2002-2020)

In 2007, the World Bank and the Hubei Provincial Communication Department (HPCD) embarked on an ambitious project to assess impacts of the Hubei Road Network Plan (HRNP) on environmental and social priorities in Hubei province. The HRNP proposed a system of 5,000 kilometers of expressways and 2,500 kilometers of highways to provide road links between all major cities in the province. This plan was approved by the Hubei provincial government in 2004 but it was not subject to formal plan environmental impact assessment (EIA), which has been required in China since 2003 by the EIA Law.

The HPCD requested the Bank's support to conduct a strategic environmental assessment for the HRNP, and the World Bank agreed to this request. Since the HRNP was already under implementation, the assessment aimed to incorporate environmental considerations into the 2020 long-term road transport plan. It also aimed to help by building the capacity of the HPCD for mainstreaming environmental and social considerations into infrastructure plans and programs, and by facilitating interinstitutional coordination among agencies associated with transport development.

Brief Description of the Pilot

This pilot project was the first SEA for a provincial transport sector plan supported by the World Bank in China. As such, it combined SEA approaches promoted by the Bank with contemporary SEA practice in China. It also tried to combine assessment approaches used in EIA of plans with selected elements of policy SEA. This pilot hence offers lessons that may be of interest for similar processes undertaken in the future, in China or other countries.

The SEA was undertaken by a team of experts from a highly reputed think tank dealing with SEA in China, which was assisted by international consultants. The SEA team operated under a comprehensive terms of reference document elaborated by the World Bank and HPCD, and undertook work in Hubei Province for a period exceeding one year. Specifically, the team (i) identified and engaged the relevant stakeholders, (ii) gathered information related to the environmental baseline, (iii) analyzed consistency of the HRNP with relevant plans and policies, (iv) elaborated scenarios for future development of road transport in the province and assessed their implications for environmental and social priorities, and (v) evaluated existing policies and arrangements for managing environmental and social effects of roads and proposed relevant institutional strengthening measures.

Within this process the SEA team held numerous meetings with relevant provincial government stakeholders, prepared multiple working documents summarizing their findings, and undertook three rounds of consultations to obtain stakeholder feedback on the draft conclusions and recommendations. Since some of the team's findings were still under discussion when this SEA was evaluated, the entire assessment process has not yet been formally concluded with public dissemination of the final SEA report by HPCD.

SEA Outcomes

The SEA provided an overall, holistic picture of the possible environmental impacts of planned transport projects. This outcome was sufficient to increase the awareness of senior managers at the HPCD about macro-level environmental implications of the proposed development of road transport. The HPCD management now pays more attention to environmental issues, as evidenced in detailed investigations carried out during the design stage of each road project. The SEA also indirectly contributed to a new circular, issued by the HPCD management, which encourages the enforcement of environmental protection requirements during expressway construction.

With respect to social learning, all those interviewed during the evaluation agreed that sharing data from baseline analyses was the most useful aspect of this SEA pilot, and that learning was facilitated through this sharing. Part of the contextual background to this case is that institutional control of decision making in China makes access to data very difficult. Data are often treated as "privately" owned by government agencies, and SEA teams are required to purchase data from the relevant agency. This privatization of data was considered by the Hubei pilot evaluators to be a potentially significant constraint on social learning in China. Consequently, the relatively open sharing of baseline data in the Hubei case was considered unusual, and led to technical and social learning on the part of participating institutional stakeholders.

With respect to the building of constituencies, however, the Hubei road transport planning case was less successful. Recommendations from the SEA team relating to the establishment of a standing committee on environmental management of road networks were not met with enthusiasm by the responsible authority (the HPCD). It appears that the institutional strengthening proposals, and especially those that challenged current internal arrangements within the responsible authority, were the most sensitive topics that arose during this SEA.

Constraining or Enabling Factors

The most obvious constraining factors in this case related to the organizational culture of government authorities. For example, while the pilot promoted better-than-usual stakeholder engagement, the evaluation indicated that these consultations—which were appreciated by all the relevant agencies—could have been enhanced by involving the relevant local (prefectural or municipal) authorities in the assessment process. These authorities exercise significant influence on decisions related to road network development and also control detailed environmental data that could be used in the assessment process. However, such consultations may not have been achievable within the scope of this specific assignment and its implementation modalities.

The evaluation makes it clear that policy SEA approaches ran up against the legal processes prescribed for plan EIA in Chinese law. The evaluators describe these processes as being very rigid and with corresponding institutional arrangements that do not necessarily support the flexibility and inclusiveness sought by policy SEA approaches.

The SEA team prepared an institutional analysis and action plan for strengthening the management of social and environmental issues in provincial road planning, but when their proposals were presented to stakeholders at workshops, debate was constrained by resistance from the HPCD. The following quotation from the Hubei pilot evaluation further describes this situation: "The final proposals prepared by the SEA team regarding institutional strengthening were appreciated by three important stakeholder groups but they were never fully accepted by the HPCD leaders. On the contrary, the institutional proposals became one of the key reasons for HPCD's hesitation to formally disseminate the SEA report" (Dusik and Jian 2010).

Conclusion

Overall, it can be concluded that despite the lack of its formal closure, the SEA process has positively influenced wider decision making in road planning in Hubei Province. While the pilot has not triggered any formal changes in the HRNP, it has increased awareness among leaders at the HPCD and other authorities about the major environmental issues associated with the development of the road system in the province. It has also provided a consolidated baseline analysis and general recommendations that are now being used by the HPCD in the continuous process of making decisions about road network development.

The SEA has also helped to strengthen environmental management at the HPCD, which established new criteria to examine the environmental performance of its various departments. HPCD now also reportedly requires developers of various expressway projects to pay more attention to environmental issues. The pilot SEA stimulated more-detailed monitoring of the overall development of the road network. It also helped to establish new contacts between the HPCD and the relevant provincial authorities. Some respondents believe that recommendations of the assessment process indirectly triggered improvements in consultations with stakeholders during the detailed planning of individual roads and also enhanced compensation schemes for those adversely affected by these projects.

A concluding observation made by the evaluators is that the SEA process needs to focus on the key decision-making dilemmas and concerns of the relevant stakeholders. It should use a methodology that allows those taking part to provide their data and jointly undertake the analysis, or at least thoroughly debate the draft findings prepared by the assessment team. The recommendations arising from the assessment should not create direct opposition to their implementation or to the continuation of the SEA process. If the SEA needs to formulate ambitious recommendations, it should determine immediate priorities that can be realistically implemented in the near future and supplement these with a proposed agenda for improvements that can be made in the middle and long term. The effort to achieve very ambitious goals right away could endanger the overall success of the entire process.

The West Africa Minerals Sector Strategic Assessment

The West Africa Minerals Sector Strategic Assessment aimed at informing the preparation of a West African initiative to support mining reform. This initiative, known as the West Africa Mineral Governance Program (WAMGP), initially attempted to help West African countries catalyze development opportunities from mining sector growth by (i) enhancing donor coordination; (ii) harmonizing policies, laws, and regulatory frameworks; and (iii) strengthening regional capacity to negotiate contracts with mining companies. The WAMGP and WAMSSA were endorsed by Mano River Union governments, West African regional integration organizations, and donors at the West Africa Mining Forum held in Conakry, Guinea, on February 11–12, 2008.

Currently, the WAMGP proposes a $300 million adaptable program loan made up of a number of smaller such loans designed for individual countries and focused on good governance, information systems and investment promotion, and value addition to national and regional economies. The intention of WAMSSA has been to influence whatever large-scale regional mining governance project or program is finally adopted by the West African governments.

Brief Description of the Pilot

WAMSSA has its origins in the period of rising commodity prices immediately prior to the economic collapse of late 2008. A combination of resource availability, rising commodity prices, and mining sector experience suggested that minerals and oil were among the few options for jump-starting development, especially in Sierra Leone and Liberia, both of which had been ravaged by civil war during the 1990s.

WAMSSA consisted of four phases:

- Phase 1 was a West African conference on mining and sustainable development in 2008. The conference resulted in an inception report that outlined the approach and methodologies to be employed in the study.
- Phase 2 focused on the collection of background information (through stakeholder engagement and desktop-level data collection) and aimed to identify key opportunities for, and constraints on, environmentally and socially sustainable regional mineral sector development through a mineral clustering approach.
- Phase 3 presented the findings of phase 2 to national-level stakeholders with a view to ensuring that the outcomes were in line with expectations and that a regional approach to mining and infrastructure development made logical sense.
- Phase 4 convened a final round of consultations, including a regional validation meeting and final meeting of the WAMSSA Steering Committee to provide input into the final WAMSSA report.

WAMSSA as a policy dialogue involved an extensive and detailed consultation process. It consisted of focus group meetings in all three national capitals, community surveys undertaken in 10 mining communities in the three countries; national workshops to select and rank environmental and social priorities, as well as to identify key policy and institutional adjustments to be incorporated in mining reform; and a final regional validation workshop.

SEA Outcomes

WAMSSA showed evidence that it had contributed to improved dialogue about environmental and social issues, partly because it used quite elaborate techniques for involving stakeholders in the ranking of priorities. The highest-ranked priorities were "insufficient transparency/consistency of decision-making," "deforestation and loss of biodiversity," and "poverty in mining areas" (World Bank 2010).

Perhaps more important than the approach taken to prioritization is the effect that it had on development issues and the likelihood that it would produce a long-term impact on the movement toward environmentally sustainable policies. There is evidence that raised attention to environmental priorities may well have placed environmental and social priorities in the policy reform agenda, and by extension, may in the future lead to better final outcomes. For example, it is clear that WAMSSA has had a substantial impact on how stakeholders view regional harmonization of mining policy. This may well be the most important influence that WAMSSA has had on regional mining reform.

There is also evidence that the WAMSSA pilot led to environmental constituency building, partly because the SEA process appears to have opened up to examination the institutional mechanisms used to deal with regional planning and harmonization. A considerable amount of time was spent in final validation workshops discussing the proliferation of regional initiatives. This was a source of some concern and confusion. A number of stakeholders were keen to see WAMSSA, or at least its outcomes, carried through beyond its completion.

Workshop participants discussed how best to institutionalize this new policy dialogue. There was a strong call from the stakeholder group for some kind of permanent, multistakeholder constituency to keep the policy dialogue going. Participants made clear their frustration with the fact that the outcomes and recommendations of many previous reports and consultations seem to have been instantly forgotten once the donor-funded project was completed. Even work that has high-level government support can be stalled or shelved with changes in political leadership. A policy or program may have the backing of a development partner or a particular administration, and then a change of decision makers causes those priorities to shift.

The stakeholders proposed a sophisticated, ongoing multistakeholder framework that would become a "home" for the policy dialogue begun during WAMSSA consultations. It would include a series of multistakeholder bodies formed at the regional, national, and local level to ensure transparent stakeholder participation and social accountability for mining development decisions.

Regarding improved social accountability, WAMSSA presents an example of small but significant steps forward in overcoming cynicism. Stakeholders from Liberia and Sierra Leone appreciated the SEA process because it had the potential to "take decisions away from mining companies and governments" (World Bank 2010). It is a matter of fact that large mining companies often work directly, and in secret, with governments in their attempts to negotiate contracts that allow favorable access to mineral deposits. While powerful stakeholders are within their rights to negotiate under their own terms, public commitments to social accountability mechanisms such as multistakeholder processes can make it more embarrassing for mining companies, and possibly governments, to resort to bilateral negotiation.

With regard to policy learning, many interviewed stakeholders agreed that data sharing was a useful aspect of the policy SEA process and that learning was facilitated through this sharing. In addition, interviews with stakeholders during the validation workshop in Sierra Leone provided evidence that WAMSSA had promoted new ways of thinking about the development of high-level policy. For example, institutional stakeholders from Guinea were confident that WAMSSA would provide a methodological approach for dealing with environmental and social issues in that country that go beyond the mineral sector.

Constraining or Enabling Factors

Three of the six identified constraining or enabling factors discussed in chapter 2 were evident in WAMSSA. First, this pilot was one of the few in which strong ownership of the policy dialogue process was found in civil society organizations.

Second, with regard to power elites, the SEA team undertook extensive consultation and built up a strong case for regional harmonization of minerals policy in Guinea, Liberia, and Sierra Leone. The consultants concluded that the majority of stakeholders supported the concept of regional harmonization. However, as the evaluator pointed out, the minority of stakeholders who did not support the idea might well be more powerful. At least four elite interest groups would not see a move to regionalism as being to their advantage. Senior politicians and senior mines ministry bureaucrats in the three countries have often been accused of rent-seeking behavior. A move toward cluster development and regional harmonization would tend to lead to a more transparent system of governance that would threaten existing privileges to make discretionary decisions.

Finally, one of the most interesting examples of a challenge to elite power is offered by the multistakeholder framework proposed in the WAMSSA pilot. If this framework is accepted by the WAMGP intervention, then it will establish a long-term constituency process that is outside of existing national and regional institutions, giving it the potential to outlast changes in governments. In a consultation meeting of the WAMGP held in Ouagadougou on December 3, 2009, countries supported WAMSSA's multistakeholder framework as the basis for the accountability framework of the WAMGP.

Conclusion

The engineering of the existing links between the WAMGP and WAMSSA is one of WAMSSA's strengths. Other benefits of WAMSSA include the extensive process of policy dialogue developed through the consultation program, which led to general acceptance of the concept of regional harmonization; the solid work produced on mining sector development opportunities, which supported the idea of a mining infrastructure cluster; and the establishment of groundwork for enhancing transparency and accountability in managing mineral resources.

However, there are some limitations that are worthy of note. First, the reports may have overplayed the support for the idea of regional harmonization. Entrenched interests, especially those associated with rent-seeking behavior, are quite likely to oppose regional cluster development when they fully understand that it might make mining policy more transparent and hence threaten their illegal profit making.

Second, while WAMSSA does discuss the problems of artisanal mining, the chosen reform option of tying mining clusters to regional harmonization is clearly focused more on large- and small-scale mines. Artisanal mining is essentially left out of this new equation. Because the approaches needed for dealing with artisanal mining problems are so different, it may be that this sector should not have been included in the WAMSSA process, and a separate, parallel study should have been commissioned.

Third, large mining companies will always be tempted to enter into bilateral arrangements with governments. This kind of activity tends not to provide the best outcomes for local communities and the disenfranchised. While WAMSSA did attempt to involve mining companies in the policy dialogue, not many participated. This limitation could possibly have been overcome with greater effort.

Dhaka Metropolitan Development Plan Strategic Environmental Assessment

Dhaka is one of 10 megacities in the world. Growing at a very fast rate, the population of the Dhaka urban area is predicted to increase to about 21 million by 2015. Dhaka's rapid development, its fast-changing urban landscape, and associated critical environmental challenges call for holistic urban planning and the strengthening of institutions responsible for urban development and good governance. In this context in 2006, the Dhaka Capital Development Authority (RAJUK) was preparing what are called Detailed Area Plans (DAPs), which make up the lowest tier of the Dhaka Metropolitan Development Plan (DMDP).

A strategic environmental assessment was commissioned by the World Bank and RAJUK to incorporate environmental considerations into and provide strategic direction for the DAPs. The SEA was also intended to inform the preparation of the World Bank Dhaka Integrated Environment and Water Resources Management Program (DIEWRMP), which supports integrated pollution management and reduction of industrial pollution in the watershed of Greater Dhaka. It was expected that the DIEWRMP design would draw on SEA findings about institutional responsibilities and regulations connected to industrial developments in the watershed.

Brief Description of the Pilot

The SEA was understood by the government of Bangladesh to add value to the technically oriented output of the ongoing local-level planning (DAPs). Therefore, the SEA attempted to provide a platform for dialogue and interaction between policy makers, planners, stakeholders, and civil society at large on environmental priorities, and on how these priorities could be affected by the implementation of urban development plans. The SEA study was launched in 2006 and completed in 2007. It was initially intended to be a conventional impact-centered assessment with some elements of institutional analysis. In the face of constraining factors in the institutional framework for DAP preparation, the analytical focus of the SEA was changed. The higher-level plans of the DMDP planning framework did not provide the strategic guidance needed for the DAPs, and the urban development framework was highly fragmented, with responsibilities divided among a multitude of government agencies. The objectives were revised to focus on institutions and governance conditions, and to provide overall direction to the DAP preparation process.

The analytical component of the SEA was constituted according to the following three areas of concentration:

1. an analysis of the key environmental problems in the DMDP area based on secondary information available in various published studies and documents, and an analysis of their links to policies, legislation, and plans
2. an assessment of the adequacy of existing urban plans and the planning process at the strategic level in order to make recommendations for improved planning and governance
3. an assessment of the efficacy of the ongoing DAP formulation process, review of the design and technical planning capacity in RAJUK, and identification of the areas and needs in RAJUK where interventions for capacity development would be beneficial to overall urban management

Political economy issues and historical aspects of urban development were only indirectly addressed and superficially covered in the institutional analysis. The analysis did not address, for example, the driving forces behind rural to urban migration, and the consequent increase in informal settlements in the urban area, where people live under extremely harsh conditions. The findings of the

SEA addressed two main themes: the weaknesses in the overarching plans and organizational set-up of the strategic-level planning framework; and problems at the implementation level. The recommendations focus on improving the DAP planning process.

The participatory component of the SEA involved one-on-one meetings, an initial stakeholder workshop, a sensitization meeting with the DAP technical management committee, a sectoral stakeholder workshop, six DAP area meetings, and a final consultation workshop. Many of the stakeholders interviewed for the purpose of the evaluation in 2009 had only vague recollections of the SEA process and their participation in it. Those who did remember participating argued, among other things, that insufficient information was provided in the workshops; the purposes of consultation exercises were not adequately explained; workshops were not very interactive; and the consultation exercises were too short.

SEA Outcomes

Due to constraining factors related primarily to a lack of ownership, the Dhaka pilot did not substantially achieve expected policy SEA outcomes. The identification of environmental priorities was based on a combined ranking of the SEA team's analytical assessment and ratings of environmental concerns by selected stakeholders (government and civil society organizations). Vulnerability and health aspects were not considered in the analytical ranking, and identified environmental priorities were not reflected in changes to the DAPs.

The SEA appears to have contributed to raising some limited awareness within RAJUK of the need for environmental assessment in order to take a more holistic approach to planning and urban development. The World Bank Country Office and RAJUK now recognize the need for capacity development within RAJUK through continued technical assistance.

Finally, the results of the SEA informed the preparation of a policy note that had not been decided on by the government when this pilot was evaluated in 2009.

Constraining or Enabling Factors

The main constraining and enabling factors for effective SEA identified in this pilot are briefly discussed below.

Windows of Opportunity

The evaluators suggested that, due to contextual factors, the DAP preparation process did not offer an appropriate window of opportunity for policy SEA. First, attempting to use spatial planning as a window for wide-ranging policy reform made it harder for the SEA to address some of the underlying causes of urban degradation in Dhaka. Second, the role of RAJUK proved complicated.

As a seller of plots, RAJUK generates its own revenues and is not dependent on government funds; thus it is less accountable to higher administrative levels than it would otherwise be. RAJUK has strong links with private sector development companies, which also hamper its accountability and incentive to pay attention to advice concerning institutional reform. The urban (as well as national) governance context in Bangladesh is highly politicized. This situation had implications for the local ownership of the SEA and resulted in a lack of integration with the DAP preparation process.

Ownership and Understanding of Policy SEA Risks and Benefits

Evidence from the Dhaka pilot suggested that securing ownership at an early stage is partly dependent upon the identified partner or policy proponent having the following: sufficient capacity and training to understand the concept of SEA, incentives to consider the results and recommendations of the SEA, and sufficient capacity to allow for adequate process integration of the SEA in the policy formation process. If the partner lacks previous experience addressing environmental and social concerns at the strategic level of decision making, the partner may need to be made aware of the outputs and benefits of SEA. The evidence further suggests that the development cooperation agency beyond the SEA team should understand the potential political economy risks associated with the expected results and recommendations of a policy SEA, in order to ensure that these can be effectively taken into account in the agency's recommendations and actions. In the case of the Dhaka SEA, recommendations have influenced World Bank program and policy to a very limited extent.

Consulting Stakeholders

The failure of the SEA to pay particular attention to the interests of vulnerable groups highlights the need for a careful and thorough stakeholder analysis—one that is sensitive to various types of vulnerabilities—in order to meet the objectives of policy SEA. It also highlights the need to clearly communicate the purposes of policy SEA to the consultants, provide them with clear terms of reference, and give them adequate methodological guidance and training.

Civil society organizations with an interest in urban development in Dhaka are limited in number, but appear reasonably vibrant and influential. They have strong connections with one another and with the media, and several seem to have links with politicians. They appear to have been aware for some time of the importance of environmental issues and of the need for an integrated approach to urban development.

The SEA consultation process certainly provided another venue for these constituent groups to get together to discuss urban environmental issues, and also an opportunity to present their views to decision makers. On the other hand, for some, the SEA consultations probably represented just one workshop among many.

Underestimating the role that civil society and government representatives could play in the SEA process, and neglecting to provide feedback to participants in consultations, compromised the potential of the SEA to contribute to improving accountability and strengthening environmental constituencies.

Follow-Up

With regard to strengthened constituencies, limited consultation provided little time for individual reflection and the development of mutual understanding. In addition, the final SEA report was not disseminated to stakeholders, and so an opportunity was missed to strengthen environmental constituencies by providing them with a tool for learning, advocacy, and accountability.

Conclusion

In a national context where a politicized and weak governance system is the main constraint to effective environmental management, institutional reform is key for addressing the causes of environmental degradation. It is important to recognize that the lack of incentive and capacity to regulate natural resources and polluting activities, and to enforce existing regulations, are the underlying causes of environmental degradation, not overexploitation and pollution per se. Given this fact, the objectives of policy SEA are relevant.

Policy SEA, or elements thereof, could be used by a development cooperation agency as a tool to scope out the strategic direction for support to national or sectoral development. To ensure that development cooperation contributes to sustainable development, however, requires that there are systems in place to pick up the recommendations of the policy SEA and incorporate them in a timely manner into relevant processes and strategic documents. This requirement applies to both the national context in which the SEA is undertaken and the development agency's systems. It further requires that an appropriate window of opportunity in the national/sectoral policy-making context is used as an entry point for the SEA, that there is ownership by a national partner as well as within the development cooperation agency, and that the SEA exercise is seen as a starting point for a long-term commitment to support for environmental mainstreaming.

Strategic Environmental Assessment of the Kenya Forests Act

For many years forest legislation and practice in Kenya failed to protect the country's indigenous forests or ensure sustainable use of plantations and other areas of forests and woodlands. Most forest communities felt disadvantaged in being excluded from forest management, and there was a history of poor management and abuse of power by the state. In 2005, a new act received parliamentary approval and endorsement from the president. The Forests Act contains many innovative provisions to correct previous shortcomings, including strong emphasis on partnership, devolution of forest user rights, organizational and institutional changes at the national and local level, the engagement of local communities, and promotion of private investment. It also extends the concepts of timber management to farm forestry and dryland forests. The adoption of new legislation and establishment of a semiautonomous Kenya Forest Service (KFS) provided a major opportunity to address the inequalities of the past and to improve the quality and sustainability of Kenya's forests, trees, and woodlands.

The role of the SEA carried out for the Kenya Forests Act between 2006 and 2007 was to highlight areas where the reform process should concentrate its activities in order to achieve real and lasting social and environmental benefits. The SEA also aimed at informing the policy dialogue between the World Bank and the government of Kenya on sustainable natural resource use by feeding into the preparation of the World Bank's Natural Resource Management Project.

Brief Description of the Pilot

The SEA team worked closely with the Forest Reform Committee and Secretariat established by the Ministry of Environment and Physical Planning. A crucial element of the SEA was its reliance on the active participation of a wide range of stakeholders, through workshops and one-on-one discussions. This dialogue was essential in identifying key issues and priorities for action. The SEA also examined conditions within two forest areas: Hombe Forest and Rumuruti Forest.

The SEA responded to local circumstances through a rapid appraisal of the political economy and through other situation assessments. The main sequence of activities took place in four phases:

1. *Screening and scoping*, the initial phase, entailed a rapid assessment of the political economy relating to the forest sector in Kenya. It also involved determining who should be approached as a stakeholder, and it identified the environmental and social considerations that would need to be taken into account in later phases of the work.
2. *Situation assessments* provided a baseline description of the governance and institutional, economic, financial, social, and environmental factors that had to be taken into account in implementing the Forests Act.
3. *Setting of environmental policy priorities* was done by the stakeholders in two workshops. Key forest issues related to the implementation of the act were discussed in the first workshop. In the second workshop, findings from the

various assessments were brought together for discussion, and workshop participants agreed on priorities for action.

4. *The preparation of a policy action matrix (PAM)* was the final stage of the SEA. The PAM captured policy issues and priority areas and set out an action plan that clearly indicated timetables, milestones, stakeholders, expected outcomes, status of progress, and responsibilities for action. These actions were discussed at the third workshop, with the intention of obtaining commitments from key stakeholders to take forward the various initiatives.

SEA Outcomes

A clear message from the evaluation was that the SEA process raised attention to environmental priorities and reinforced the need to adequately address these priorities. Examples of key environmental priorities included protection of watersheds and biodiversity; sustainable forest management (in particular, arid and moist forests); and payment for environmental services provided by forests and forest ecosystems. However, the environmental assessment itself was rather shallow and did not address in detail the complexity of Kenya's forest resources.

The evaluation also found that the SEA contributed to strengthening of constituencies. By involving local and arguably less powerful or influential stakeholders in the SEA process (such as nongovernmental organizations, community-based organizations, local community representatives), the process created a more level playing field for the discussion and prioritization of actions. Besides some likely effects of the SEA, a larger and arguably much more important impact on strengthening constituencies was achieved by the adoption and implementation of the Forests Act. The act has called attention to and raised expectations for involving local communities in forest management, and it has encouraged civil society and nongovernmental organizations to support formation of community forest associations and to embrace the view that local communities should take more responsibility for local forests.

Given Kenya's historical record of mismanagement of forestry resources there is a need to strengthen mechanisms for holding government and other stakeholders to account regarding their forest use. The SEA process, including its stakeholder workshops and open discussions, discussed accountability issues as well as encouraged development of practices to improve social accountability. The most tangible and operational evidence of the efforts to enhance social accountability, within the context of the SEA, was the formulation of the PAM. This tool is updated regularly and published on the Internet (http://www.policyactionmatrix.org). It offers a comprehensive, flexible, and easily accessible framework that provides stakeholders with a method for holding government and other stakeholders to account.

A majority of stakeholders interviewed during the evaluation acknowledged *individual* learning from their participation in the SEA. They also learned about SEA from discussions with a broad range of actors and stakeholders. However, the evaluation showed that the SEA exercise was too limited in time and in the number of participants to initiate broad-based policy learning. The interest expressed by local communities in forest use, and the rapid increase in registration of community forest associations, indicate that new information and knowledge ("policy learning") was generated on policy change related to forest management.

As a result of the SEA, the World Bank's Natural Resource Management Project, which was developed in parallel, developed a stronger emphasis on governance issues and community engagement in forest management. However, due to lack of financial and human resources set aside for follow-up of the SEA, and due to staff changes within the World Bank and government of Kenya, the Natural Resource Management Project has not met Kenyan stakeholders' expectations of substantial engagement by the World Bank in forest sector reform. The SEA did influence World Bank activities outside Kenya, including the design of other forest sector–related SEAs and the drafting of guidelines for undertaking strategic environmental and social assessments in relation to the Forest Carbon Partnership Facility.

Constraining or Enabling Factors

Timing

Although evaluation interviewees differed in their opinions about the timing of the SEA, it was clearly conducted when there was a window of opportunity for policy change. However, the SEA would most likely have been more influential if it had been conducted during (instead of after) the process of formulating the Forests Act and if it had provided for clear follow-up support for the implementation of the act.

Ownership

The SEA was initiated and financed by the World Bank. Although serious attempts were made to link the SEA to the government's planning process for the implementation of the Forests Act, the ownership of the SEA remained firmly with the World Bank. Many stakeholders consider that the World Bank has not fulfilled the expectations generated by the SEA process. They expected increased World Bank support to the forest sector reform process and greater follow-up to the PAM and recommendations of the SEA. There were also important factors outside the control of the World Bank and the SEA team that decreased the Kenyan government's ownership of the SEA process. Notably, the dismantling of the Forest Reform Committee and Secretariat just after the SEA was completed led to changes in staff and loss of SEA champions.

Resources

The limited human and financial resources for follow-up to and communication of the SEA findings and recommendations have severely constrained the effectiveness of the SEA. A broader contextual factor is the political history of the Forest Department, which was replaced by the KFS. The history of political interference in the Forest Department has made it difficult for the KFS to generate funds to adequately follow up on the PAM and implement the Forests Act. Since most KFS staff are former staff of the Forest Department, KFS has not been able to change the public image of inefficiency and mismanagement associated with the Forest Department. This situation partly explains why financial support from the treasury and donors has been low. It is also one reason for the political resistance to lifting the ban on logging, which could generate resources for the KFS.

Political Commitment

Forest sector reform in Kenya is highly politicized and involves entrenched vested interests at high political levels. Successive governments have used forest land for political rewards, as a form of patronage. The ambition of the SEA to integrate environmental and social concerns in such a reform context is clearly challenging. Obvious factors beyond the control of the SEA team, but with implications for the implementation of the Forests Act, include the post-election violence of early 2008 and associated government restructuring, and the more recent high-level political attention to the Mau Forest.

To succeed against this contextual background, it would have been vital for the SEA to foster a more sustained change process (through ownership, resources, follow-up, and other means). Many stakeholders stated that the SEA became a too-punctuated intervention. After its completion there was a need for ongoing long-term engagement and swift follow-up on the findings and conclusions; instead there was a void.

Conclusion

The SEA of the Kenya Forests Act was influential in several ways: it spread knowledge about the Forests Act and its intentions from planners to a broader audience; it consolidated knowledge that had been scattered across agencies, ministries, and other key stakeholders; and it created a lever for civil society advocacy to implement the Forests Act. The SEA also showed the need for guidelines for, and promotion of, participatory forest management, and it helped in the formation of community forestry associations and in the preparation of a manual on forest management plans. For some stakeholders, particularly among civil society organizations, the workshops provided important forums for articulating their concerns. The SEA contributed to an understanding of many of the complexities, challenges, and opportunities embodied in the new Forests Act. It also emphasized the need to rethink forest management in Kenya and highlighted the new, innovative tools for sustainable forest management available through the new act. Generally, the SEA facilitated broad but not full stakeholder participation, environmental priority setting, and strengthening of some constituencies. According to some stakeholders, the SEA contributed to improved (government) accountability on forest reform and to learning across key stakeholders. However, these impacts have been insufficiently sustained largely due to limited political support for the forest reform process and to lack of follow-up activities associated with the SEA.

Rapid Integrated Strategic Environmental and Social Assessment of Malawi Mineral Sector Reform

In July 2009, the World Bank completed a mineral sector review (MSR) for Malawi in order to inform the mineral sector reform process in Malawi and to help determine the World Bank's level of engagement in the sector. Between 2008 and 2009, as part of this review, a rapid integrated strategic environmental and social assessment (rapid SESA) was undertaken with the main purpose of reviewing the environmental and social regulatory framework for the mining sector. The rapid SESA also attempted to incorporate critical environmental and social considerations into the ongoing discussion of Malawi's mines and minerals policy and the dialogue between the World Bank and the government of Malawi for reforming the mining sector.

Brief Description of the Pilot

Mining has historically been of limited importance in Malawi. However, large-scale mining, including uranium mining, has recently been initiated, and the potential for future investment in the sector is significant. This development has strained the very limited capacity in Malawi for managing the environmental and social risks and opportunities associated with large-scale mining.

The objective of the rapid SESA was to include environmental and social issues in the initial dialogue between the government of Malawi and the World Bank on mining sector reform. Also, the rapid SESA aimed at opening this dialogue to civil society stakeholders and the mining industry in order to build trust among key policy players. The rapid SESA had two phases. During the first phase— undertaken through a desk review, one-on-one interviews with representatives of stakeholders, and fieldwork in Lilongwe—an assessment of existing systems to manage environmental and social issues in mining activities was drafted. In the second phase, the preliminary results of the first phase of the SESA and the draft MSR were discussed and validated with stakeholders in a workshop held in Lilongwe on March 17–18, 2009.

It is expected that the rapid SESA will be followed by a full SESA during the mining sector reform preparation project to be supported by the World Bank. The rapid SESA was undertaken by a policy SEA specialist in approximately 20 working days.

SEA Outcomes

In line with its limited scope, the outcomes of the rapid SESA are punctuated rather than lasting, and much more thorough approaches are needed in order to substantially strengthen institutions and governance capacity. Nevertheless, the evaluation found that the rapid SESA made relevant contributions toward several broader outcomes.

Environmental and social priorities related to mining sector development in Malawi have been very high on the political agenda during the past few years. In particular, the first large-scale mining development in Malawi, the Kayelekere uranium mine, ignited a confrontational dialogue about social and environmental risks associated with uranium mining between civil society organizations, government, and the mining company. Based on stakeholder interviews, the evaluation found that the rapid SESA contributed to raising attention to environmental priorities. Without ranking or rating the various environmental priorities cited by the interviewees, key environmental priorities included (i) water pollution from uranium mining as well as small-scale coal mining; (ii) occupational health and safety in uranium, coal, and limestone mining; (iii) air pollution from coal and limestone mining; and (iv) risk of losing biodiversity and degradation of ecosystem services, and risk of water draining from uranium mining into river systems and eventually into Lake Malawi. However, it was clear that stakeholders did not share the same view of the relevance of, magnitude of, and risks associated with the different environmental priorities related to mining.

The MSR and the rapid SESA reportedly managed to strengthen constituencies relevant to specific mining sites or specific mining operations. However, this impact was mainly temporary and had already tapered off at the time of the evaluation. The strengthening of some constituencies also started from a very low level. Nevertheless, the consultation conducted as part of the MSR, and the stakeholder workshop in particular, contributed to the strengthening of some constituencies. Reportedly, the workshop created a more level playing field across actors and encouraged some weaker and more vulnerable communities or nongovernmental organizations to claim larger stakes in the development of the mining sector generally as well as in specific mining operations (for example, the Kayelekere uranium mine). However, if this impact is to be sustained, there is a need to (i) review the tools and interventions necessary to strengthen constituencies and (ii) reinforce the efforts to achieve targeted and broad-based strengthening of constituencies.

Against a background of deep mistrust, the efforts to collect and share information on key environmental and social concerns in the rapid SESA played an important role in improving accountability. Civil society representatives interviewed said they welcomed the opportunity to dialogue with government and private sector representatives provided through the stakeholder workshop and would welcome further initiatives in this direction. They also welcomed the recommendation to investigate possible membership for Malawi in the Extractive Industry Transparency Initiative, which was seen as an important way of enhancing accountability.

Finally, the rapid increase in mining activity has generated a lot of new knowledge and learning among individuals and organizations. Interviews with government officials indicate that there is an increased understanding of (i) the need for improved coordination between ministries in order to manage mining sector risks and opportunities, (ii) the need to bring civil society organizations into the development process, and (iii) the need for mechanisms for sharing of benefits from mining with local communities. In this process of learning, it is difficult to distinguish the role of the MSR. It is clear, however, that the MSR and the rapid SESA were an impetus to the learning process because they provided an overview of international good practice and also identified key opportunities and challenges for mining sector reform in Malawi. In a situation of mistrust and value conflicts between stakeholders, dialogue and deliberation may be as important for learning as new information. The stakeholder workshop represented an important but limited platform for dialogue and learning in this respect.

Constraining or Enabling Factors

The rapid SESA was timely and capitalized on windows of opportunity—that is, the process of developing new mining sector legislation and policy, as well as a revised growth and poverty reduction strategy.

The SESA formed a part of the broader MSR. Thus, environmental and social concerns formed part of the overall assessment of, and dialogue on, key mining sector reform priorities. Arguably, this integrated approach lessened the risk of marginalizing the findings of the environmental assessment. However, because the Ministry of Natural Resources, Energy, and Environment is in charge of both mineral sector development and environmental protection, there is a risk that during the ongoing reform process, it will favor activities promoting mineral sector growth and will disregard SESA recommendations for strengthening environmental and social management practices.

Certain political economy factors (for example, vested interests in the mining sector) were identified as constraining the development of environmentally safe mining operations, broad-based sharing of benefits, and securing the rights of local communities. It is also worth noting that the rapid SESA focused entirely on formal institutions, and not at all on informal institutions. There is a need to better understand the role and perspectives of traditional leaders and local communities.

Finally, while the rapid SESA put forward many pertinent recommendations, a key concern is that these recommendations were not properly communicated to stakeholders. Another concern is the punctuated nature of the MSR and the rapid SESA. If the rapid SESA is followed by a more thorough assessment, it could be viewed as an important stepping-stone, or agenda-setting device, for the integration of social and environmental concerns in mining sector development. Currently, the government of Malawi has requested World Bank support for a mining technical assistance project to support mining reform. Among other activities for the preparation of the MTAP, the government intends to undertake a full SESA of the mining sector.

Conclusion

In summary, the rapid SESA was timely, was integrated into the MSR, and highlighted key concerns to be addressed in order to promote sustainable mining development. However, a more substantive environmental and social assessment should follow to generate a deeper understanding of the environmental and social concerns related to mining sector development. A deeper stakeholder analysis and more thorough consultation process might be more likely to bring about the envisioned process outcomes of policy SEA. If, on the other hand, the rapid SESA encourages policy makers (within the government of Malawi or the World Bank) to consider that environmental and social concerns have already been properly addressed, then the rapid assessment runs the risk of being used as a "green alibi" for the sector-reform process.

References

Dusik, J., and Y. Jian. 2010. "Evaluation of the World Bank's Pilot Program in Institution-Centered SEA: Strategic Environmental Assessment for Hubei Road Network Plan (2002–2020)." Unpublished report, World Bank, Washington, DC.

World Bank. 2010. "West Africa Minerals Sector Strategic Assessment (WAMSSA): Environmental and Social Strategic Assessment for the Development of the Mineral Sector in the Mano River Union." Report 53738-AFR, World Bank, Washington, DC.

Conceptual Analysis and Evaluation Framework for Institution-Centered Strategic Environmental Assessment

By

Daniel Slunge[1]
Sibout Nooteboom[2]
Anders Ekbom[3]
Geske Dijkstra[4]
Rob Verheem[5]

In 2005, the World Bank established the Pilot Program on Institution-Centered SEA (I-SEA) to test a strategic environmental assessment (SEA) approach centered on institutions and governance rather than on impact assessment. As the pilots were evaluated, it became clear that many of the observations and conclusions derived from the six pilot studies were applicable to SEA of policy and sector reform. Consequently, the terms "SEA at the policy level," "policy SEA," and "I-SEA" are used interchangeably in this publication.

Acknowledgments

This document has greatly benefited from discussions at three different workshops. The first workshop, which took place in Rotterdam on September 8, 2008, identified key issues and literature to be included in the conceptual analysis. It was arranged by the Department of Public Administration, Erasmus University, with the following participants: Joachim Blatter (University of Lucerne), Jan Kees van Donge and Lorenzo Pelligrini (Institute of Social Studies), Fernando Loayza (World Bank), Rob Verheem (Netherlands Commission for Environmental Assessment), Anders Ekbom and Daniel Slunge (University of Gothenburg), and Arwin van Buuren, Steven van der Walle, Geske Dijkstra, and Sibout Nooteboom (Erasmus University).

The second workshop, in Gothenburg, October 27–28, 2008, discussed a first draft report and identified key gaps to be addressed. It was arranged by the Department of Economics at the University of Gothenburg and included the following participants: Kulsum Ahmed and Fernando Loayza (World Bank), Maria Partidario (University of Lisbon), Neil Bird and John Young (Overseas Development Institute), Måns Nilsson (Stockholm Environment Institute), Anna Axelsson and Mat Cashmore (Swedish EIA Centre), Rob Verheem (Netherlands Commission for Environmental Assessment), Sibout Nooteboom (Erasmus University), and Anders Ekbom and Daniel Slunge (University of Gothenburg).

The third workshop, arranged by the World Bank in Washington, DC, June 12–13, 2009, focused on presenting and discussing the report with the evaluators and revising the proposed evaluation methodology. It included the following participants: Fred Carden (International Development Research Centre), Ineke Steinhauer (Netherlands Commission for Environmental Assessment), Anna Axelsson and Ulf Sandström (Swedish EIA Centre), Anders Ekbom and Daniel Slunge (University of Gothenburg), David Annandale and Juan Albarracin-Jordan (consultants), and Kulsum Ahmed, Fernando Loayza, Dora N. Cudjoe, Setsuko O. Masaki, and Sunanda Kishore (World Bank).

Valuable comments during the workshops as well as on several draft versions have greatly assisted in developing the content of the document.

Financial support from the Swedish International Development Cooperation Agency and Dutch Development Cooperation (through the Netherlands Commission for Environmental Assessment) is gratefully acknowledged.

Contents

Executive Summary

The objectives of this report are to summarize and critically discuss the analytical underpinnings of institution-centered strategic environmental assessment (I-SEA), and to provide an analytical framework for evaluation of pilot I-SEAs conducted in a World Bank program in several developing countries. The analysis mainly focuses on the policy level, but findings are also expected to be of relevance for SEA at the plan and program level.

As outlined in World Bank (2005) and Ahmed and Sánchez-Triana (2008), the principal objective of I-SEA is to integrate key environmental issues in (sector) policy formulation and implementation. In order to successfully integrate key environmental issues in policies, the World Bank assumes that it is vital to put a particular focus on the role of institutions while performing an SEA.

This report is structured in three parts. In part A of the report, a conceptual model of I-SEA is outlined comprising six steps:

- The first step calls for *understanding formation and formulation of policies* for a certain sector or theme in a specific country or region. It is assumed that *policy formation* takes place along a continuum without start or an end. *Policy formulation* may take place as a discrete (time-bounded) intervention along the policy formation continuum. Arguably, policy formulation offers a rare opportunity to exert specific influence on a policy. Consequently, I-SEA aims at incorporating environmental concerns during this "window of opportunity."

- The creation of a *dialogue* is the second step of the I-SEA approach. It aims at bringing all relevant stakeholders together in a discussion of the environmental issues relevant to the proposed policy.

- To inform this dialogue, the third step is the identification of key environmental issues facilitated by a *situation analysis* and a *stakeholder analysis*. The stakeholder analysis should inform the identification of the legitimate stakeholders about the key environmental issues in the sector identified through the situation analysis.

- The fourth step calls for *environmental priority setting*, which implies that the legitimate stakeholders are invited to react to the situation analysis, raise specific and relevant environmental priority concerns, and choose the I-SEA priorities.

- *Institutional analysis* of the strengths and weaknesses, constraints and opportunities, to address these environmental priorities is the kernel of the fifth I-SEA step.
- Finally, in the sixth step, *adjustments* to the proposed policy and the underlying institutional conditions are suggested and recommended.

Part B of the report covers strands of research literature that are relevant to the I-SEA steps outlined above:

On *understanding policy processes* the report presents various metaphors of policy processes, e.g., policy making as rational linear planning, a cyclic process, networking; and policy making as action-flow. It is critical to adjust the I-SEA approach to the particular policy process it is trying to influence. I-SEA can facilitate the solution to complex societal problems through organizing interaction and dialogue between stakeholders and by bringing a greater variety of perspectives into the policy process.

On *identifying environmental priorities* the report presents perspectives on environmental priority setting, and emphasizes the need to understand that environmental priorities are a subset of a larger set of other (political, social, economic, etc.) priorities in society, and must be identified in relation to them. A key message in this section is that priority setting should not be the exclusive domain of experts, nor of public opinion, but rather of both. The report emphasizes the need for an I-SEA team to address key questions: What are the political economy aspects related to environmental priority setting? Who sets the priorities for environmental management? Who sets the environmental agenda?

Strengthening stakeholder representation is presented as a key component of integration of environmental and social concerns in policy formulation. Variety in stakes and preferences in society, and complex policy processes, require that many contrasting stakes and views are represented in planning and decision making as well as in implementation. Of particular importance is the need to promote and ensure representation of weak and marginalized groups in society in policy formulation processes. At a general level, this is promoted by strengthening social constituencies and institutions for good governance and transparency. Specifically, I-SEA can facilitate strengthened stakeholder representation by ensuring broad and multiple stakeholder involvement in planning and implementation of policies.

Conducting institution-centered SEA also requires *analyzing institutional capacities and constraints*, as well as measures to strengthen institutions' capacity to integrate environment in policy planning and implementation. Following North (1994), institutions may be made up of formal constraints (e.g., rules, laws, constitutions) and informal constraints (e.g., norms of behavior, conventions, codes of conduct); they are slow to change, distinct from organizations, and influenced by social capital such as trust, shared values, and religious beliefs. Key institutional features to be assessed are the ability of institutions to pick up signals about social and environmental issues, to give citizens a voice, to foster social learning and public responsiveness, to balance competing interests by negotiating change and forging agreements, and to execute and implement solutions by credibly following through on agreements. In order to ensure integration of environment in policy formulation, it is argued that SEA needs to identify and understand the role of key institutions, and assess needs and possibilities for institutional strengthening and change.

Strengthening social accountability includes ensuring public participation in policy formulation and promoting voice and rights to access to information and justice (especially among weak and vulnerable groups), and social inclusion in key planning and decision-making fora. Key to strengthening social accountability in general, and in I-SEA in particular, is the need to create iterative processes (between the state and the public) in which implementation is assessed by the public in order to ensure accountability of the state vis-à-vis society and its stakeholders, and facilitate adaptive planning, which is sensitive to the preferences and needs of the public.

Ensuring social learning presupposes that the state and the public bureaucracy learn from experiences and modify present actions on the basis of the results of previous actions. It is emphasized that social learning is a subset of learning which also includes e.g. technical, conceptual, and political learning. Social learning builds on both technical and conceptual learning but focuses on interaction and communication among actors. In ensuring social learning in the integration of environment in policies, it is necessary to understand and utilize (the role of) research and science-based evidence. In promoting social learning an I-SEA should (i) "politicize" environmental issues, by linking them to broader development issues and integrating agendas of environmental ministries with those of more influential ministries; (ii) strengthen policy advocacy networks and create public forums for policy debate to ensure that diverse perspectives are repeatedly placed on policy makers' agendas; and (iii) put effective transparency mechanisms in place and support media scrutiny of policy formulation and implementation (Ahmed and Sánchez-Triana 2008).

Based on this conceptual analysis, a *framework for evaluating the SEA pilots* is also proposed as part C of this report. This framework aims at (i) establishing joint objectives and a joint methodology for the pilot evaluations; (ii) forming a shared understanding of the objectives, concepts, and methodologies used in institution-centered SEA; and (iii) facilitating the cross-analysis of the results of the different pilot evaluations. It proposes a specific evaluation methodology, comprising objectives, process steps, evaluation questions, and report narrative.

Instead of providing a benchmark to assess success or failure of specific I-SEA cases or experiences, the purpose of the evaluation framework is to assist the evaluators in studying concrete attempts to influence policy for environmental sustainability. Ultimately, the objective is learning from the cases in order to enrich the I-SEA framework and improve the integration of environment in policy formation. The value of this report therefore depends on its effectiveness to convey clear guidance for the evaluators to achieve this learning objective through an analysis as comprehensive and objective as possible.

A. Institution-Centered SEA

1. INTRODUCTION

Strategic environmental assessment (SEA) originated as an extension of project-level environmental impact assessments (EIA) to the plan, program, and policy level. Many of the SEAs being conducted today are still largely focused on assessing impacts and are based on EIA-type methodologies. Limitations to using this approach, especially at the policy level, have however been identified and have been the focus of much debate (Ahmed and Sánchez-Triana 2008; Fischer 2007; Partidario 2000). A range of alternative approaches have been proposed and used, and there is an ongoing debate among scholars about their respective limitations and merits. For example, Partidario (2000) distinguishes between a "decision-centered model of SEA" and an EIA-based SEA model, and Fischer (2007) distinguishes between "administration-led SEA" and "cabinet SEA."

Based on experiences with integrating environmental considerations in development policy, the World Bank has put forward an institution-centered approach to SEA (I-SEA) (World Bank 2005; Ahmed and Sánchez-Triana 2008). Initiating analytical as well as practical work on I-SEA stems mainly from two sources: it is a response to the World Bank's broadening of lending focus from projects to development policy loans (World Bank 2004) and to its Environment Strategy mandate to focus work on strategic environmental assessment (World Bank 2001). It also stems from the Organisation for Economic Co-operation and Development (OECD) Development Assisstance Committee (DAC) *Guidance* on SEA in development cooperation (OECD DAC 2006), which suggests I-SEA as an approach for assessing the complex interactions between political, social, and environmental factors in policies. Central to the I-SEA approach is that in order for SEA to be effective at the policy level, it should be centered on assessing institutions and governance systems that underlie environmental and social management rather than on predicting impacts of alternative policy actions. However, in line with the OECD DAC SEA *Guidance*, it is recognized that approaches to conducting SEA are varied, and lie on a continuum. While at the policy level a particular focus on institutions may generally be an appropriate

SEA approach, in other circumstances, more impact-oriented SEA approaches may be appropriate.

Acknowledging the tentative nature of I-SEA as well as the limitations of traditional SEA approaches, the World Bank has launched a pilot program on SEA. The main objective of this program has been twofold: (i) to support mainstreaming of environmental and social considerations in the Bank's activities supporting policies and sector reform, and (ii) to test and validate the I-SEA approach in different sectors, countries, and regions.

Scope: The conceptual analysis and evaluation framework outlined in this report are part of the broader World Bank pilot program on SEA. The World Bank coordinates the evaluation of the SEA pilot program with the Environmental Economics Unit at the Department of Economics of the University of Gothenburg (EEU), the Swedish EIA Centre at the Swedish University of Agricultural Sciences, and the Netherlands Commission for Environmental Assessment (NCEA). The report has been developed in a process based on collaborative work among the authors, and has been subject to peer review by the program partners outlined above and external resource persons. The peer review has been facilitated by discussions in workshops held in Rotterdam (September 8, 2008) and Gothenburg, Sweden (October 27–28, 2008), respectively.

This conceptual analysis and evaluation framework will guide the evaluation of the SEA pilots. In order to optimize the dissemination of the evaluation's results to a broader audience, a steering committee of international resource persons and practitioners (e.g., from the development and SEA community, developing country partners, etc.) would be established. This committee would provide feedback on the evaluation design and the draft report and assist the evaluation team in the dissemination of the evaluation results.

Objectives: This report has the following objectives: (i) to summarize and critically discuss the analytical underpinnings of institution-centered SEA; and (ii) to provide an analytical framework for the evaluation of the pilot SEAs of the World Bank program on institution-centered SEA.

The analysis mainly focuses on the policy level, but findings are expected to be of relevance for SEA at the plan and program level as well. The report does not intend to cover all issues pertaining to the broad subject of SEA and institutions. Rather, it covers strands of research literature relevant to institution-centered SEA and issues relevant to guide the evaluation of the pilot I-SEAs.

Report structure: The report is structured in three parts. In part A of the report, a conceptual model of I-SEA comprising six steps is outlined. Part B of the report contains a conceptual analysis of the issues and aspects relevant to the I-SEA steps outlined in part A. The following issues are analyzed: policy processes, environmental priority setting, stakeholder representation, institutional capacities and constraints, social accountability, and social learning. Perspectives on each issue, as well as links to SEA, are presented and discussed. The framework for evaluating the SEA pilots constitutes part C of the report.

2. INSTITUTION-CENTERED SEA–A CONCEPTUAL MODEL

Integrating the environment in strategic planning and decision making implies that key environmental issues are taken up in formation of policies in general and in policy formulation in particular. Arguably, formulation of a new policy implies a window of opportunity over a specific time period during which key environmental issues and concerns have extraordinary possibilities to be addressed and considered. Once a policy is formally adopted, the possibilities to integrate environmental concerns are considerably smaller (Cohen, March, and Olson 1972; Kingdon 1995).

In order to successfully integrate key environmental issues in policies, the World Bank (2005) suggests that it is vital to focus on the role of institutions while performing an SEA. In addition, some other key issues also warrant specific focus to ensure environmentally and (to some extent) socially sustainable outcomes. These issues include understanding the policy process, identifying environmental priorities, strengthening stakeholder representation, analyzing and strengthening institutional capacities, analyzing and mitigating institutional constraints, strengthening social accountability, and ensuring social learning. In order to be effective, the actual application of I-SEA for a certain (sector) policy needs to be adjusted to the location-specific context.

The World Bank's approach to assess and strengthen institutions in integrating environment in policies—planning as well as implementation—builds on six steps:

1. **Understanding policy formation and potential windows of opportunity for influencing decision making:** The first step calls for analyzing and understanding formation as well as formulation of policies for a certain sector or theme in a specific country or region. As illustrated in figure 1, it is assumed that *policy formation* takes place along a continuum without a start or an end. However, *policy formulation* may take place as a discrete (time-bounded) intervention along the policy formation continuum. Such an intervention is an act of power, which may be associated with a policy paper that justifies that act. An act of power can also be a public announcement about the way power will be used in the future (e.g., giving permits, allocation of property rights, environmental entitlements, etc.). The time period in which policy formulation takes place implies a rare opportunity to exert specific and arguably additional influence on a policy compared to other times along the policy formation continuum. Hence, I-SEA has as its goal to incorporate

FIGURE 1
Schematic Representation of I-SEA in Policy Formation

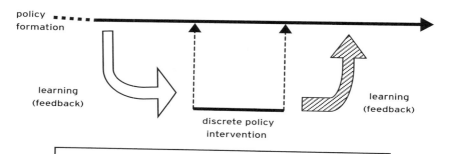

The purpose of I-SEA is to integrate environmental considerations in **continuous policy formation.**

policy formation

learning (feedback)

discrete policy intervention

learning (feedback)

I-SEA entry point is the opportunity to integrate environmental considerations in **discrete (time-bounded) policy interventions.**

Source: World Bank 2008.

environmental concerns in policy formation in general, and focuses its attention on influencing the policy formulation process in particular.

2. **Initiation of stakeholder dialogue:** The second step in the I-SEA approach calls for creation of a dialogue. The dialogue aims at bringing all relevant stakeholders together in a discussion of the environmental issues relevant to the proposed policy. "Relevant stakeholders" implies actors in society who claim a stake in the policy, its implementation, and the associated environmental issues. The dialogue may be facilitated and coordinated by a (formal/informal) intersectoral SEA steering committee. The ultimate objective of the dialogue is to seize the opportunity to incorporate environmental considerations in the continuum of policy formation created by the commitment to formulate a new or reform an existing policy (a discrete policy intervention).

3. **Identification of key environmental issues:** The third step calls for identification of the key environmental issues upon which the dialogue, assessment, and I-SEA recommendations will be focused. The identification builds on two components: a situation analysis and a stakeholder analysis. The purpose of the *situation analysis* is to identify the key environmental issues relevant to the sector or policy process under consideration. Rather than assessing the potential impacts of the proposed policy or plan, the situation analysis focuses on identifying the key environmental issues currently affecting the

sector or region that will be influenced by the proposed discrete intervention. The key question guiding the situation analysis is, what are the existing key environmental issues affecting the sector or region? Likewise, the aim of the *stakeholder analysis* is the identification of the legitimate stakeholders to these key environmental issues in the sector or policy process. The I-SEA model assumes that it is critical for environmental sustainability that these voices be identified and heard during policy formation and planning. It requires therefore that the following questions are addressed: who are the legitimate stakeholders ("are those claiming stakes jointly perceived as legitimate stakeholders?"), and what are their interests and motivation?

4. **Environmental priority setting:** The fourth step calls for identification and selection of environmental priorities. This implies that the legitimate stakeholders are invited to react to the situation analysis and have a leading role in the final environmental priority setting, raising in the process their environmental-priority concerns. This is a critical stage of I-SEA because, on the one hand, it attempts to promote a process by which social and environmental preferences are brought into the policy dialogue, aiming at influencing policy and planning formulation and implementation. On the other hand, it also attempts to facilitate or assist in the creation or strengthening of constituencies with an environmental stake in the policy process. Following recent thinking on political science (e.g., Blair 2008), the I-SEA model assumes that a critical force for integrating environmental considerations in the continuum of policy formation is groups organized around a common environmental interest or concern directly or indirectly affected by the policy process. Without strengthened and effective environmental constituencies, therefore, the I-SEA model assumes that environmental mainstreaming in policy making would be short-lived. Laws, presidential decrees, or regulations eventually adopted when policies are formulated risk being partially applied, reverted, distorted, or even ignored during policy implementation.

5. **Institutional assessment:** The fifth step calls for an institutional analysis of *strengths and weaknesses, constraints and opportunities*, to address the key environmental issues and priorities identified in the fourth step. The scope of the institutional assessment covers sector and environmental organizations that are responsible for the formulation and implementation of the policy under consideration. It also covers the prevailing formal and informal rules that shape conditions affecting or constraining the behavior of social actors affected by the policy, such as property and customary rights, check and balance mechanisms for decision making, access to information and justice, etc. Important questions to address in this part of the I-SEA approach are these: How do existing systems, organizations, and institutions in the country, region, or sector manage the environmental priorities identified by the I-SEA?

Is there adequate capacity to identify and address environmental priorities? Are there underlying rules that constrain or reinforce the effective implementation of the policy changes under consideration?

6. **Formulation of policy and institution adjustments:** Lastly, in the sixth step, adjustments to the proposed policy and the underlying institutional conditions affecting the formulation and implementation of the policy are suggested and recommended. The adjustments aim at complementing the policy under consideration to promote or improve environmental mainstreaming, and at addressing institutional gaps—i.e., making appropriate adjustments based on the strengths and weaknesses, constraints and opportunities, of the existing institutions. Proposed adjustments are taken back to the stakeholders for review and assessment in a *validation analysis*.

As outlined in figure 2 (next page), the World Bank's model assumes that by following the six steps discussed above, the possibilities to achieve the objective of integrating environmental considerations in policy formulation and implementation can be greatly enhanced. Important process outcomes of the I-SEA approach are assumed to be (i) raised attention to environmental priorities, (ii) strengthened environmental constituencies, (iii) enhanced accountability mechanisms for policy implementation, and (iv) greater ability for social learning. Admittedly, however, contextual factors would influence goal achievement.

Although the steps outlined above are suggested for inclusion in practical applications of I-SEA, there is no blueprint for how each step should be undertaken. Conducting I-SEA implies an ability to take advantage of windows of opportunity for influencing policy, flexibility to adapt to circumstances beyond the control of the I-SEA team, and a great dose of common sense. The I-SEA approach is a theoretical construction based on a dearth of practical experience. The validity of this model needs empirical testing and evaluation. That is the purpose of the World Bank's SEA pilot program, based on the methodological framework for evaluating the SEA pilots outlined in this document.

FIGURE 2

Conceptual Model of I-SEA: Process Steps, Process Outcomes, and Objective

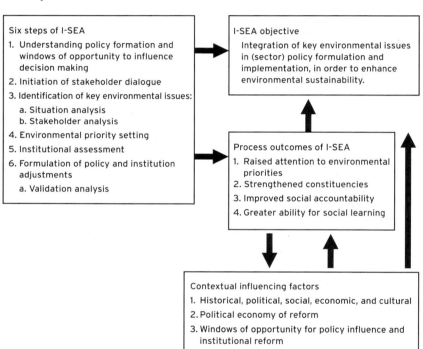

Six steps of I-SEA

1. Understanding policy formation and windows of opportunity to influence decision making
2. Initiation of stakeholder dialogue
3. Identification of key environmental issues:
   a. Situation analysis
   b. Stakeholder analysis
4. Environmental priority setting
5. Institutional assessment
6. Formulation of policy and institution adjustments
   a. Validation analysis

I-SEA objective

Integration of key environmental issues in (sector) policy formulation and implementation, in order to enhance environmental sustainability.

Process outcomes of I-SEA

1. Raised attention to environmental priorities
2. Strengthened constituencies
3. Improved social accountability
4. Greater ability for social learning

Contextual influencing factors

1. Historical, political, social, economic, and cultural
2. Political economy of reform
3. Windows of opportunity for policy influence and institutional reform
4. Luck

Source: Authors.

B. Key Issues in I-SEA

This part of the report elaborates on issues of key importance in I-SEA, including some of the steps and process outcomes outlined in the conceptual model of I-SEA (figure 2). Different perspectives on each key issue are presented before factors to be taken into account when doing an I-SEA are discussed.

3. UNDERSTANDING POLICY PROCESSES

An important prerequisite for influencing policies through I-SEA is to understand policy formation and adjust the I-SEA approach to the particular policy process it is trying to influence. This section discusses critical aspects of policy processes and outlines key factors that need to be taken into account when trying to influence policy formation through an I-SEA.

3.1 Perspectives on Policy Processes

A policy may be defined as a course of action, based on some declared and respected principle or set of principles. Public policies can be defined as the use of state power to change organizational or individual behavior in order to effectuate their national responsibilities and objectives (see Hill [2005] for a discussion of various definitions). However, policy making is multifaceted and subject to considerable debate and analysis. Partly contesting perceptions and definitions is suggested to explain what policy making is, and how policy changes can be explained (Hill 2005). So instead of one comprehensive and exclusive description, policy making is currently best explained in terms of metaphors.

Key metaphors of policy making include (i) policy making as rational linear planning, (ii) policy making as a cyclic process, (iii) policy making as networking, and (iv) policy making as action flow:

(i) *Policy making as rational planning* describes policy planning in terms of a "linear model" with certain "stages," like problem definition, policy formulation, decision making, and implementation. Many impact assessment manuals are structured according to the rational planning perspective.

(ii) *Policy making as a cyclic process*: A policy paper is prepared, implemented, evaluated, and updated. This is closely related to the political process, where the elected government leaders answer to parliament. The need to periodically evaluate and review policy papers may be required by law.

(iii) *Policy making as networking* postulates that decisions about the use of resources emerge in multiactor policy networks (e.g., Kickert, Klijn, and Koppenjan 1997) at multiple levels and scales.

(iv) *Policy making as action flow*: social streams of problem owners (complainers), proponents of a solution (builders), and political parties (selectors), which, if they coincide, form windows of opportunity for policy entrepreneurs (e.g., Kingdon 1995). In a way, problems, possible solutions, and parties find themselves in a "garbage can" from which real solutions may or may not emerge (Cohen, March, and Olson 1972). Although governments cannot fully control policy processes, they can play an important role in them by stimulating the emergence of windows of opportunity for the social streams of actors to interact and find solutions. Facilitating factors for this to happen include skills of social learning and building of trust (e.g., Nooteboom 2006).

The ambiguity of policy processes: Complex policy processes may be ambiguous, largely because of contradictions between existing legislation and political aspirations and objectives (Ritter and Webber 1973; Schön and Rein 1994). Clearly, uncertainties and risk also create (or aggravate existing) ambiguities. Moreover, conflicts between short-term and long-term objectives tend to introduce ambiguities in the policy process, as well as trade-offs between incompatible objectives (such as hydropower investments and sustained ecosystem functions in a watershed). Ambiguities may also occur as a result of different lock-ins. Such lock-ins may be of institutional character (power relations, vested interests) or of physical character (e.g., energy systems which cannot be easily changed within the short term). Such lock-ins constrain the range of opportunities and introduce ambiguities between political objectives (e.g., ecologically sustainable energy production) and practices (ecologically *unsustainable* energy production) (Beck 1992).

Tension caused by ambiguities in the policy-making process may have profound repercussions on the possibility to pursue some sort of rational policy planning and use technical analytical tools for priority setting. Ambiguities have to be identified and sorted out, usually in a process of intensified stakeholder participation with a focus on social issues (preferences, constraints, opportunities) rather than technical issues only (e.g., Feldman and Khademian 2008; Kornov and Thissen 2000).

The risk of a technocratic approach: The metaphors above are not necessarily inconsistent with each other; in fact, they symbolize different aspects of policy processes. However, it is important to understand that the nature of complex policy processes depends deeply on how the system reacts to the limited understanding of individual policy makers (Herbert Simon's [1957, 1991] bounded rationality). Policy makers may either be primarily led by limited one-sided understanding (or rationality), or acknowledge the complexities of policy making and try to merge their own knowledge with that of others (policy making as "battle of ideas"). The former approach to policy making may be dominated by conflict in the networks and "garbage cans" layer of policy processes, while the latter may be more dominated by cooperation.

The first would often be referred to as a technocratic approach, which interprets policy making only as rational linear or circular planning, failing to acknowledge that complex policy making implies many actors in networks and that policies are formed in a flow of actions, which cannot be anticipated in preplanned sequences. A technocratic approach focusing on the production of a policy *paper* may thus be a misguided effort if it is disconnected with the realities of real planning and practice in a sector or subject matter area. As indicated by Gould (2005), an overly technocratic approach to policy making may lead to two "disjunctures": between policy formulation and policy implementation, and between policy and politics. In addition to relatively useless "paper tigers," it may also lead to policy proposals that are not politically accepted. Many scholars underline the importance of policy formation that is sensitive to social realities and complexities; they argue for an understanding of policy formation as occurring in networks of interdependent actors (who all exercise influence at various degrees) and as a continuous process without beginning or end (e.g., Feldman and Khademian 2008; Kickert, Klijn, and Koppenjan 1997).

Policy processes, power, and knowledge: Descriptions of policy making as networking typically also address the role and influence of power and knowledge on the policy making process. Here, power and knowledge are purported to be held by many (rather than few) actors, although the influence may vary considerably across the actors. Individual actors are tied in a larger web of actors, which relates to a complex society. This implies that individuals (e.g., leaders representing an elite) who are trying to influence the agenda are constrained by other powers held in the wider system of (local, national, and international) actors and institutions. Nobody is really fully in charge of the system, i.e., of sectoral development. This description represents a stark contrast to other descriptions of policy making as a rational issue determined by a select group of influential actors (typically "decision makers and experts") interacting in a well-structured society of tangible institutions. Hence, in most countries, power is shared in networks of actors (e.g., Lindquist 2001; Kickert, Klijn, and Koppenjan 1997), which may cut across the formal structure of ministries, agencies, and other government organizations. One way of describing how policies emerge, therefore, is as a web of small decisions emanating from the actors, which add up to larger decisions on policy formulation. Therefore, steps to resolve policy issues (formulated in political goals) are often incremental (Lindblom 1959).

Whether influence can be exercised depends on the perceived benefits among the key influential actors in the political process; it helps if interests are organized and alliances (advocacy coalitions) are established based on these interests (Sabatier and Jenkins-Smith 1993). In developing countries, such advocacy coalitions typically consist of a mix of international and national organizations. The policy process becomes a "battle of discourses" in which arguments are sought to support positions already taken.

The incremental steps of policy formation are also parts of a social learning process, which may lead to a state of balance between (organized) interests ("countervailing powers"). Through social learning, subjects become aware that balance is needed to prevent one interest dominating the other, preventing change. These public organizations and associated institutions (for example, the sharing of power in a democratic system among judicial, legislative, and executive bodies, but also between planning authorities and implementing authorities), cannot be changed overnight, but incremental actions may add up to significant and sometimes sudden changes.

Implementation of policies: Arguably, policies are often poorly implemented (Pressman and Wildavsky 1973); official government policies create higher political expectations than can be met in practice. A large set of reasons may explain this. Besides lacking commitment and resources, actors responsible for development and implementation of public policies often lack sufficient knowledge of the local conditions in which the policy is to be implemented. The existing incentive structure may also be biased toward rewarding opportunistic (overly ambitious) policies rather than realistic policies. Realistic policies may look less ambitious and include fewer promises, and in democratic systems, such policies may not be rewarded in reelections. Causes behind failed implementation are not only found in the political system. They are also found in the inertia in actors' beliefs and preferences, in society's institutions, and in the realities on the ground, e.g., the functioning and structure of the local markets (e.g., Lipsky 1980). A significant challenge is therefore to find levers that actually can influence these beliefs and preferences, strengthen institutions, and meet the demands and realities on the ground.

Enabling leadership: Theories about complexity and leadership indicate that new forms of enabling leadership may emerge under complex conditions. Politicians who position themselves "above the battle of discourses," and who can reconcile social dilemmas (as the battle between discourses expresses), display enabling leadership (Uhl-Bien, Marion, and McKelvey 2007). Enabling leaders stimulate interaction and dialogue among many groups in order to identify a larger variety of possibilities. They are, in fact, increasing the number and variety of actors and ideas in the policy process, which is a requisite for adaptability to changing conditions (Ashby 1956; Uhl-Bien, Marion, and McKelvey 2007). Practical methods have been developed to achieve variety in policy processes, of which joint fact finding and process management are a few (e.g., De Bruin, Ten Heuvehof, and In 't Veld 1998; Susskind, Jain, and Martyniuk 2001).

3.2 SEA and Policy Processes

In general, the World Bank I-SEA approach (World Bank 2005; Ahmed and Sánchez-Triana 2008), and Feldman and Khademian (2008) in particular, is in line with modern public management theories about policy processes as described above. Central observations are that policy making is a continuous process and that individual policies mainly represent snapshots of ongoing policy processes. Influencing concrete policy interventions is a means to influence the policy process at large. Just as policy processes are continuous, so should be the process of integrating environmental considerations. A few key issues that need to be paid special attention in trying to influence policy formation through an I-SEA are outlined in the following paragraphs:

Context sensitivity: Research suggests that a critical success factor for SEA is the ability to adjust its scope and methodology to contextual factors (e.g., Hilding-Rydevik and Bjarnadóttir 2007). Hence, I-SEA practitioners need to understand which knowledge and actions are timely and useful in each specific policy formulation context. Developing such context sensitivity is primarily a learning process occurring at the level of individuals, but valuable experiences and tools for context mapping should also be essential elements to document in the evaluation of the I-SEA pilot program.

Discrete policy processes may provide windows of opportunity for institutional change: Ahmed and Sánchez-Triana (2008) and Feldman and Khademian (2008) put the idea of "windows of opportunity" at the heart of influencing policies. However, windows of opportunity are often not easy to discover when open and may close before opportunities are seized. Discrete policy processes should be seen as an opportunity for interaction which may or may not lead to important policy and institutional changes. Many times, discrete policy processes are subject to substantial lock-in and domination by vested interests, and provide only limited opportunities for larger change processes toward sustainable development. A key challenge for I-SEA is to utilize the opportunity provided by the policy process to move beyond assessing potential impacts of policies and assess the broader institutional constraints to environmentally sustainable development. In order to know which institutions to focus on, the I-SEA team may first identify the policies which seem unsustainable and then assess which institutions "control" these policies.

Since institutions tend to change slowly, a key challenge for an I-SEA team is to come up with proposals that may facilitate a long-term change process. Sometimes this will entail a particular focus on strengthening networks or long-term constituencies which are needed to demand institutional change. Research on public management indicates that through building powerful environmental organizations (i.e., public environmental agencies, civil society organizations) environmental issues may penetrate the agenda of sectoral actors and authorities. These environmental organizations can form a kind of countervailing power to other sector interests; they can force other sector agencies to listen more carefully to affected stakeholders and approve/disapprove public policies, which will stimulate adjustments along the policy formation continuum. For example, introducing legal requirements for environmental assessment in a country might prompt environmental agencies to serve as a countervailing power in policy processes.

A challenge for I-SEA is that it is difficult a priori to identify or explain the link between small steps and envisaged large institutional change that can lead to environmentally sustainable development. In evaluating the effectiveness of I-SEA, it is hence particularly important to assess the relationship between the *immediate* influence of an action (triggered by a specific opportunity occurring at a point in time) and the *future* influence of that action on institutions and on sustainable development. The supposition of I-SEA is that (smaller) opportunities in early stages of proposed policy change enable dialogue about the role of institutions and the need for changing them.

Interaction and social learning: Clearly, all policies have unexpected side effects, which may be adverse. Good policies are therefore developed in interaction with those who may be affected, given that adverse side effects cannot be completely prevented or compensated. I-SEA may ideally encourage policy makers to reach out to a broader range of stakeholders and prolong the interaction in the future, with the aim of minimizing adverse effects of new policies. In this process, incremental concessions or changes can be made by policy makers and different stakeholders, who themselves may seem symbolic in terms of economic significance, but who may be effective levers in the policy process. Interaction and a sense of interdependency between stakeholders is a key prerequisite for social learning to occur. A key issue to address for an I-SEA team is hence how policy processes can become more reflexive and stimulate interdependency between stakeholders.

Variety in policy processes: Since societal problems are complex, and therefore create ambiguity, it is assumed that they can only be solved by a policy process that meets the complexity (variety) of the problem (Ashby 1956; Uhl-Bien, Marion, and McKelvey 2007). This means that many possible solutions should be brought to the fore in policy processes for serious consideration. In reality, there is rarely only one unique first-best solution. Hence, it is unwise a priori to decide on or assess a single solution. Those influencing the organization of the policy process (e.g., through institutions) should allow for more variety, so more groups are challenged and invited to participate and develop solutions. They should advise decision makers to be inspired by many groups, and to organize interaction and dialogue with many groups to identify a variety of possibilities (De Bruin, Ten Heuvehof, and In 't Veld 1998; Susskind, Jain, and Martyniuk 2001).

We learn from this that whatever I-SEA does, to be effective it should bring more variety in policy processes. Obviously, there is a trade-off, since variety costs. Implications for I-SEA are that it should facilitate action and policy change in at least two respects:

1. *Create variety:* Imagine how a policy process could develop more variety, for example by creating transparency and participation and enhancing knowledge;
2. *Stimulate policy entrepreneurship:* Look for opportunities in the policy process to intervene effectively in order to achieve the changes imagined at the first level. In other words, I-SEA practitioners should ideally act as policy entrepreneur(s) (Kingdon 1995, by, e.g., attempting to understand the policy process and the actor networks they are trying to influence, and offer their knowledge.

4. IDENTIFYING ENVIRONMENTAL PRIORITIES

This section presents perspectives on environmental priority setting, and emphasizes the need to understand that environmental priorities are a subset of a larger set of other (political, social, economic, etc.) priorities in society, and must be identified in relation to them. A key message is that priority setting should not be the exclusive domain of experts, nor of public opinion, but rather of both. Economic and scientific tools that can be used to prioritize among environmental issues and environmental interventions are briefly outlined before priority setting is discussed in relation to SEA.

4.1 Perspectives on Environmental Priority Setting

Identifying environmental priorities requires an understanding of priority setting in general because environmental priorities are a subset of a larger set of other (political, social, economic, etc.) priorities in society. Hence, identifying environmental priorities must be done in relation to other societal issues and is thus a highly political process that cannot be reduced to a purely technical matter, or be isolated in an independent process. Politicizing environmental assessment and environmental priority setting[6] may thus be an effective way of influencing policy formation and formulation from an environmental perspective. Moreover, serious efforts to identify environmental priorities create opportunities to escape from environmentally unsustainable path dependencies.

Research on environmental priority setting can be structured into two broad areas: prioritization of environmental *issues* and prioritization of environmental *interventions*. The analytical approaches and processes for these two areas of research vary greatly. Specific related issues addressed in the research include the following: What tools are/can be used to prioritize among environmental issues, and environmental interventions, respectively? What are the political economy aspects related to these issues? Who sets priorities for environmental management? Who sets the environmental agenda?

Due to limited financial resources, competing general political priorities (health, education, environment, employment, etc.), and competing specific *environmental* interests and preferences, priorities have to be set in environmental management and in identification of environmental interventions.

Who sets priorities for environmental issues? In the identification of who is setting environmental priorities, it is critical to assess who is providing the environmental information. Research on this issue has inter alia focused on testing the agenda-setting hypothesis, which claims that governments' provision of environmental information is generally a very strong and influential means to set the environmental priorities, specifically in relation to other political actors and public opinion (Stephan 2002). Empirical studies by Lynn and Kartez (1994) and Hamilton (1995), who test the hypothesis in cases where government discloses pollution information, indeed find that information disclosure correlates with media coverage, determines the importance placed upon the issue by citizens and shareholders, and facilitates collective action. They also find that environmental nongovernmental organizations (NGOs) act as mediators and conduits of the information and assist in increasing public interest. Further knowledge obtained from this strand of research indicates that transaction costs may hamper public involvement in environmental priorities proposed by the government. However, explicit efforts to reduce transaction costs counteract this negative relationship and increase citizens' collective or private actions as well as buy-in on the government's proposed priorities (Stephan 2002).

Although governments rightly have a crucial role to play in environmental priority setting, there is always the risk that they misuse their powers and mandates. Bias toward scientific analysis and government-led, expert-based planning and environmental priority setting increases the risk of "benevolent despotism" as opposed to environmental planning based on public involvement, ownership, and priority setting. Arguably, too much focus on quantitative priority-setting tools and policy making creates a "closed loop" between scientific experts and policy makers, which increases the risk of leaving the public outside priority setting, planning, and decision making. Hence, striking the right balance between public involvement and scientific underpinnings is crucial to adequate and sustainable environmental policy making and policy implementation.

A point of departure for the analysis provided in this report is the stated objective to identify prioritization of environmental issues in the policy agenda *according to their effects on economic development* and *poverty alleviation* (World Bank 2005; Ahmed and Sánchez-Triana 2008). Although important, economic development and poverty alleviation are not always used as criteria or references for environmental prioritization. In reality, other issues and interests may dominate. Nevertheless, economic development and poverty alleviation are key development objectives of development cooperation agencies, including the World Bank, and of governments in developing and developed countries. Hence, a rationale for identifying environmental priorities in terms of their effects on economic development and poverty alleviation is the assumption (World Bank 2005) that these issues are *politicized,* i.e., that they are placed firmly in the policy agenda and catch the attention of key politicians. In the section on policy processes, we have seen that priority setting feeds into the policy process, where the agenda of influential actors may change on the basis of substantive arguments, but where often, substantive argument (i.e., the result of analysis which may be supported by minorities) does not influence the agenda of influential actors.

Further, prioritization among biophysical environmental issues (air pollution, water contamination, deforestation, etc.) is closely linked with the existing (and often competing) environmental *interests.* These interests are typically communicated by various interest groups, which can be more or less influential ("stronger/weaker") in the final priority setting made in the policy process.

Increasing awareness of the power of information has stimulated increased use of it among actors outside the ruling government as a means to influence the environmental agenda and priorities. This applies to government opponents in the political sphere, business companies, environmental NGOs, media, labor unions, etc. In this context, it is also evident that the extent and quality of the scientific evidence behind the disseminated environmental information vary a great deal across actors.

Although not always perfectly clear or delineated, a dividing line can be drawn between priority setting based on expert knowledge, on the one hand, and the preferences expressed by public opinion, on the other. Expert knowledge presupposes involvement of experts, who are expected to prioritize (or alternatively, suggest prioritization of) environmental issues under scrutiny in an objective (neutral and impartial) manner, by use of technical assessment tools (see examples below). Alternatively, preferences among public opinion are obtained by consulting various stakeholders; as opposed to expert judgment, environmental priorities of the public are defined as the sum of individual subjective (intuitive) preferences.

Depending on the level of democratic governance characterizing the prioritization process, expert knowledge and public opinion may be integrated to a greater or lesser extent. This is partly driven by the fact that knowledge and expert assessments seldom provide only one solution or represent neutrality or impartiality (Owens, Rayner, and Bina 2004). As pointed out by Wilkins (2003), increasing acknowledgment of practical knowledge and wisdom among the public has increased the need for, and attention to, negotiation between experts and public stakeholders in priority setting. This is reinforced by the fact that application and influence of technical methods depend on the institutional and cultural context. Many specific technical approaches exist, but due to contextual differences there is no generalized way of determining a priori the best method or approach. Knowledge and priorities need to be negotiated and contextualized. Hence, priority setting is conducted in arenas involving different stakeholders (including experts and project/reform proponents), who possess different analytical and knowledge capacities, and different negotiating powers (Rijsberman and Van de Ven 2000).

Who sets priorities for environmental management? Much like the priority setting of environmental issues, priority setting for environmental interventions is subject to stakeholder preferences, power relations, belief in technical rationality, and the relative influence of proclaimed technical experts. However, there is not necessarily a direct correspondence between environmental issues and environmental interventions. Priority environmental issues (defined in terms of the largest environmental threats or impacts) do not always translate into priority environmental interventions for various reasons. Some of the key environmental problems may be too difficult or too costly to address at present. Interventions for mitigation may have to wait until costs are reduced, or until political, social, scientific, or other issues and responsibilities are sorted out. Consequently, environmental priorities might focus on picking "low-hanging fruit" to achieve cost-effective and politically possible interventions in the short run.

Admittedly, there is a vast literature on tools for environmental analysis. While it is outside the scope of this report to present it, we present below some tools to prioritize among environmental *issues*, and tools to prioritize among environmental *interventions*.

Tools to prioritize among environmental issues: The tools to identify, analyze, and prioritize among environmental issues can broadly be divided into biophysical assessments and economic assessments. Biophysical assessment tools include, but are not limited to, comparative risk analysis, geo-based mapping, modeling and forecasting analysis, quality of life assessments, carrying capacity analysis, ecologically based multicriteria analysis, and vulnerability analysis. Economic assessment tools to prioritize among environmental issues include economic damage assessment, opportunity-cost analysis, loss of productivity assessment, and preventive expenditure analysis.

Tools to prioritize among environmental interventions: Tools to prioritize among environmental interventions include expert judgment, public opinion surveys; public participation–based rankings and ratings ("popular voting"), and comparisons or combinations of biophysical and monetary assessments, which attempt to reconcile pros and cons of a particular proposed reform or policy (process). Specific issues and key concepts to consider in priority setting pertaining to environmental interventions include (i) time horizon/intertemporal aspects; (ii) risks and uncertainties; (iii) distributional aspects—across geographical regions, different income groups; impacts on the poor or disadvantaged (vulnerable groups such as handicapped, women, children, ethnic/cultural/religious minorities, etc.); and (iv) ecological, social, and economic sustainability; efficiency and effectiveness; and transparency.

Principal tools for economic assessments, which are used to set priorities for environmental interventions, are cost-benefit analysis, cost-utility analysis, and cost-effectiveness analysis. Provided that it is appropriately undertaken, *cost-benefit analysis* (CBA) provides information on the allocative efficiency of an investment, and takes into account all costs and benefits relevant to the investment, distribution effects as well as (costs and benefits of) future impacts. In essence, CBA investigates society's gains from a project, program, or policy reform in relation to its costs. The advantage of conducting CBA for priority setting is that it provides the decision maker with alternatives which use the same (monetary) unit for comparison and transparency. Although criticized (see, e.g., Hausman and Diamond 1994; Hughey, Cullen, and Moran 2003), modern techniques for nonmarket valuation (e.g., contingent valuation) offer opportunities to identify environmental costs and benefits.

Cost-effectiveness analysis (CEA) is typically used to identify the lowest-cost alternative to meet a certain (environmental) objective. In the context of priority setting, CEA is in some respects more attractive than CBA, since it avoids some of the controversies associated with CBA in the measurement of environmental benefits in monetary units. On the other hand, CEA still requires data for each alternative under investigation, including costs of each alternative and biophysical or some other nonmonetary indicators representing the objective. The fact that CEA does not harmonize program/reform benefits into comparable units (unlike CBA) reduces the comparability across alternatives, compared to CBA.

Cost-utility analysis (CUA) is used to identify and compare project/reform alternatives when there is agreement on attaining a specific utility objective (e.g., an environmental health quality standard) and when there are several options and costs associated with achieving it. A slightly different way to understand and use CUA in the identification of priorities is to maximize an agreed environmental outcome within a given budget envelope. This has been applied in the area of biodiversity conservation (Weitzman 1998; Van der Heide, Van den Bergh, and Van Ierland 2005).

4.2 SEA and Environmental Priority Setting

Priority setting can be influenced through the application of analytical tools, which provide insights as to what the impacts of sectoral development are, and how these can be compared with alternative development. Priority setting can and should arguably also be influenced by stakeholder dialogue in an open political process. For this to happen, the proposed analytical and process tools for environmental priority setting in World Bank (2005) may be useful means in SEA to "politicize" key environmental issues in the broader policy agenda. The suggested focus on risks, costs, and public participation creates links to (impacts on) economic development and poverty alleviation. Specifically, by undertaking comparative risk assessments and cost-of-environmental-damage studies, and using various (complementary) participatory techniques, there is certainly the possibility that key environmental issues can be identified and aligned with other key development themes in the policy process, largely due to political sensitivity to risks, economic costs, and—in most cases—popular consent.

Consider a broader set of environmental analyses for priority setting: Provided that an SEA involves the right type of competence and capacity for the kinds of assessment tools alluded to above and in World Bank (2005), such analyses facilitate priority setting and may create opportunities for political uptake. However, it should be kept in mind that these proposed tools only form a subset of a larger set of analytical and priority-setting tools used in SEA (OECD 2006). As indicated above, other priority-setting tools, which potentially can be used in the analytical step of an I-SEA process tied to a specific policy process, also include, e.g., biophysical assessments (such as quality of life assessments, carrying capacity analysis, ecologically based multicriteria analysis, and vulnerability analysis), or other economic assessments (like opportunity-cost analysis, loss of productivity assessment, preventive expenditure analysis, which may be components of cost-benefit analysis, cost-utility analysis or cost-effectiveness analysis). There is thus a large set of analytical tools to choose between, and a priori no first-best assessment tool for priority setting; the choice has to be made depending on the terms of reference and broader conditions framing the I-SEA process—e.g., political acceptance and buy-in, availability of data and other information for quantitative (biophysical and economic) assessment, links with poverty and other key development themes, availability of expertise to undertake the assessment, etc.—and coupled with stakeholder representation techniques (see further in section 5).

Regarding economic assessments as part of an I-SEA process, it may be that other economic analytical tools are more effective in politicizing the environmental issues than the proposed cost-of-environmental-damage studies. Examples of such analyses include benefits of environmental management studies for prioritizing various environmental *interventions*, or public revenue assessments for using/depleting various natural resources, or studies of cost-effectiveness of various environmental economic policy instruments such as environmental taxes, fees, levies, or subsidies. Such (studies of) policy instruments may be compared with other policy instruments (e.g., command and control like environmental regulation, norms and standards, or environmental information disclosure and environmental education) as part of the I-SEA process.

Local capacity development for environmental priority setting: A common feature for applying proposed tools for environmental priority setting is the need for strong local capacity. Hence, applying any of the quantitative tools above requires significant elements of capacity and continuous learning in local institutions, which are subject to policy reforms and I-SEA. Hence, strengthening the use of tools for environmental priority setting in I-SEA also requires *strengthening local institutions' capacity to carry out such analyses* and to understand the results and implications for policy design/reform, and increasing ownership among local actors of the analyses underpinning policy processes.

Today, many of the impact-centered SEAs conducted in low-income countries are operationalized by foreign experts and resource persons with limited transfer of knowledge to local expertise. This constrains the possibilities for local analysis and local priority setting. Although the proposed I-SEA methodology recommends use of both quantitative and participatory methods (to facilitate a combination of expert judgment and broad-based popular involvement and prioritization in the policy process), there is also a need to stress structured, institutional learning and capacity building for locally owned and locally implemented analysis for priority setting. This provides the rationale for posing the questions: Who conducts the I-SEA? Based on whose analysis are the priorities set? Too often the technical analysis is carried out by expatriate experts, who typically fail to facilitate local learning in their prioritization analyses. Increasing the involvement of local resource persons in the prioritization analyses not only contributes to enhanced local ownership and buy-in, but also functions as a cost-effective means to strengthen local analytical capacity and institutions (e.g., government agencies).

Selectivity, timing, and sequencing of I-SEA is critical: In many instances, local capacity and government resources are limited for making environmental policy analysis. Hence, as indicated in World Bank (2005) and in Ahmed and Sánchez-Triana (2008), there is a need to be selective in the choice of I-SEAs in relation to proposed and envisioned discrete policy changes. Although policy formation is a continuous process, there are windows of opportunity for discrete interventions, and in order to have identified and (publicly) endorsed the official environmental priorities, there is a need to select key policy processes strategically and very selectively. From an environmental point of view, some policy processes or reforms are more important than others. Although some aspects or elements of I-SEA are continuous, the *timing* and *sequencing* of discrete I-SEA interventions are critical to achieve impact in the policy formation process. Linked to this is the fact that priorities arrived at in a policy-based I-SEA are certainly not eternally valid, and may have to be revisited and redefined. Hence, as indicated in World Bank (2005), priority-setting processes should take place periodically in light of policy revisions, new information, new research knowledge, changing preferences, and changing institutions. Accordingly, tools and criteria for priority setting should be revisited and possibly also redefined.

5. STRENGTHENING STAKEHOLDER REPRESENTATION

As indicated in the section on policy processes, the involvement of a variety of stakeholders in decision making increases the likelihood that solutions to complex problems like sustainable development will emerge. This section begins by briefly discussing different types of stakeholder representation before identifying common obstacles to "sound" participation and how these can be overcome. The section ends by identifying key challenges for I-SEA in relation to stakeholder representation.

5.1 Perspectives on Stakeholder Representation

Participation or representation? Representation of stakeholders in policy processes may be defined as the way in which affected groups can have an influence on public policy. There are gradations of difference between participation by representation and direct participation: representation can also be indirect participation by means of actors (organizations or people) who represent a stakeholder group. For example, a nongovernmental organization or a ministry of indigenous people may represent indigenous people.

   Different types of stakeholder representation: Five intensities of involvement by stakeholder groups, which have an increasing degree of influence on the outcomes of a public policy process, can be distinguished (Edwards 2007):[7]

- *Information exchange*: Citizens are informed and may ask questions during hearings; there is no commitment to take them into account.
- *Consultation*: Citizens are invited to comment on government proposals; this may occur through surveys or in hearings; government commits itself to take comments seriously but they cannot be held accountable for them.
- *Advising*: Citizens may come up with their own problems and suggest solutions; government takes these seriously and promises accountability on how the suggestions have been used.
- *Co-production*: Stakeholders representing different interests co-design policies with public officers and politicians; in principle, these solutions are taken over but well-accounted-for amendments are possible.
- *Co-decision making*: Stakeholders jointly design solutions and these are adopted.

Direct influence can only occur from the third intensity onward, because only in those cases are policy makers responsive to results of stakeholder involvement. Information exchange and consultation may have a more indirect effect; they may be the first step in a learning process that may have visible results only in subsequent policies. Stakeholders may also participate uninvited in the policy process, for example by demonstrating or lobbying, or by implementing or ignoring public policies if they can.

Obstacles to stakeholder representation: The extensive literature on participation in policy processes has revealed that positive effects of participatory approaches to public policy making cannot be taken for granted. A ladder of participation has been suggested, ranging from "manipulation" and "therapy" (in fact, nonparticipation), to "partnership," "delegated power," and "citizen control." In between there are different degrees of stakeholder involvement: "informing," "consultation," and "placation," in which participation is an "empty" exercise, not meant to have any real consequences (Arnstein 1969).

Common obstacles to sound stakeholder representation include the following:

Weak interests are difficult to identify: It is not always clear ex ante who the "weak interests" are and whose voice needs to be enhanced. In relation to, for example, SEA, there is a considerable amount of uncertainty about environmental effects of policies, so it is not always known which groups will be affected and which groups should be involved.

Their voice is often weak: Local communities, municipalities, or national arenas are typically not level playing fields. Organizing participation in unequal initial settings may give the most powerful most voice. According to Edwards (2007), the following measures help promote public participation and stakeholder representation: (i) give participants access to all available information, (ii) allow participants to question witnesses and to consult experts, (iii) use an independent moderator, and (iv) secure checks and balances in governance (as elaborated in the section on institutions).

It is difficult to involve larger groups that are not organized: Weak groups, let alone future generations, are often excluded from the current policy debate. It is widely known that this gets worse as public policies become more strategic and abstract, because it is difficult for people at large to imagine the links between abstract policy proposals, the individual situation, and individual and local/global impacts. A next best option can be to consult national advocates such as civil society organizations, but these organizations may have their own agendas and not adequately represent (individual) stakeholders' interests or communicate with the group they are supposed to represent.

Policy makers' intentions may not be sincere: Policy makers may use "participatory speak" without attaching any real content to it. Legislation or other mechanisms may require them to invite stakeholders for participation, but in reality there is no willingness to use their input, at least visibly in the short term.

Vested interests do not participate in the process: If powerful groups with great stakes in a certain policy process do not participate in the policy formulation phase, there is a risk that implementation will be obstructed by these groups, since they in fact control it when it comes to implementation.

If these types of obstacles to sound stakeholder representation are not addressed, then this "empty participation" may lead to participation fatigue and increasing distrust between government and civil society, or between government and society at large (Molenaers and Renard 2006).

Addressing obstacles to stakeholder representation: Stakeholder representation is severely restricted in policy making in many countries (e.g., Transparency International 2008). A completely open and transparent society is probably unrealistic, and since it is always painful for those who are forced to open up, the development toward more transparency and participation will most likely be a gradual shift toward a more democratic culture and procedures. Ways to address common obstacles and increase opportunities for stakeholder representation include:

Institutionalize formal laws that require participation or representation: Laws requiring governments to engage with stakeholders when developing certain policies can be an important basic institution for sound stakeholder representation. The basic rationale is that the existence of such laws provides a lever for national advocates to demand more openness. For example, laws on environmental impact assessments (EIA) normally require some form of stakeholder representation. However, while EIA laws have been implemented in countries all over the world, its contribution to enhanced stakeholder representation and influence on actual decision making vary a lot. Wood (2002) asserts that EIA and SEA may be effective to mitigate some smaller effects, but there is little evidence that it actually leads to a fundamental change of strategies and policies required for attaining sustainable development. Although introduction of EIA laws may promote increased participation and stakeholder representation, it is not a warrant of success. Unless the legislation is backed up by adequate institutions for its implementation, it risks being encapsulated and made harmless by opponents (Dijkstra 2005).

Propositions for public participation formulated in manuals and guidance developed by the World Bank and other institutions may be significant contributions to improved stakeholder representation. However, governments adhering to international treaties[8] can also be a step toward institutionalizing environment-related stakeholder representation.

Strengthen accountability: Bekkers et al. (2007) argue that participation processes should be linked to formal democratic organs or decision-making institutions such as elected councils or parliaments. These formal representative organs can hold governments to account and may make governments responsive to stakeholders' interests. Such a strengthening of institutions that make states more accountable to citizens' demands may create incentives for both policy makers and the public to increase participation. Stakeholders may be more inclined to participate since they know the policy makers have an incentive to take them seriously. Conversely, policy makers may be more inclined to listen to stakeholders, since they know stakeholders with opposing views have been granted greater freedom to issue complaints at later (and more costly) stages of the policy-making process (see also section 7, "Strengthening Social Accountability").

Involve weak and other stakeholders: Beierle and Konisky (2001) conjecture that one of the reasons of implementation failure was that neither all socioeconomic groups nor all relevant interests have been represented in the participation process; some excluded groups were apparently able to prevent the implementation of the agreed-on solutions. Possible remedies include enhancing the voice of the weak interests in participatory processes and (promoting) involvement of all interdependent socioeconomic groups and all possible interests.

Strengthen networks that can demand improved stakeholder representation: The emergence and growth of influential organizations which claim a stake in policy processes can be an important move toward improved representation. Supporting such a development can be seen as a form of network management (e.g., Kickert, Klijn, and Koppenjan 1997). In the longer, run these organizations can be important for the creation of institutions, which ensure future continued representation of weak interests or enforcement of transparency laws.

Focus on small improvements when the opportunities for broad stakeholder representation are limited: In some cases—where the possibilities for broad stakeholder representation are limited—it may be possible to take small but important steps toward broadening perspectives in a policy process. It might, for example, be possible for the first time to moderate a dialogue between two ministries which are not accustomed to listening to each other, or to discuss options that seemed impossible to address before. It might also be possible to get politicians, who represent sectoral interests, to raise questions in public about sustainable development, or to raise the need of considering certain institutional changes, like subscribing to international treaties. These small steps may be important, especially if they facilitate more long-term changes.

5.2 SEA and Stakeholder Representation

Ahmed and Sánchez-Triana (2008) suggest that I-SEA–based participatory approaches should identify weak and vulnerable groups and amplify their voice in policy formation. In this way, the likelihood increases that policy planning and implementation are responsive to views and preferences of multiple stakeholders, including the weak and vulnerable in society. The creation and maintenance of a community of participation is seen as central to ensuring that a variety of perspectives are represented in policy formation (World Bank 2005). While it is clearly difficult to prescribe in general how stakeholders ought to be identified and represented in highly context-dependent SEAs, the following key issues merit specific attention in I-SEA:

More people or more perspectives? Public participation is a key ingredient in most SEAs. It is important to note that the World Bank approach to stakeholder representation does not necessarily suggest a larger number of *people* participating in the policy process, but rather ensuring representation of a larger number of perspectives, especially those of the weak and vulnerable.

How are the perspectives of the weak and vulnerable identified? As stated above, it is not always clear ex ante who the "weak and vulnerable" are. How can an I-SEA team go about to ensure that the "right" perspectives are represented in the process? Specific attention may be paid to ensuring that perspectives represented are not biased with respect to gender, age, ethnicity, or religious beliefs.

How can communities of participation be created and maintained? World Bank (2005) suggests that the creation of a community of participation is central to facilitating inclusive management in an iterative policy process. Communities of participation are not fixed entities, but "any particular policy problem/choice opportunity is an occasion to create or modify the community of participation" (World Bank 2005, 36). Specific attention needs to be paid to how such communities of participation can be created and maintained during and after an I-SEA of a discrete policy formulation process.

6. ANALYZING INSTITUTIONAL CAPACITIES AND CONSTRAINTS

Analyzing and strengthening institutions and governance dimensions are put forward as key features of institution-centered SEA by the World Bank (2005). This shift in thinking about environmental assessment can be seen as a reflection of the remarkable growth in attention to the role of institutions for economic and social development within the social sciences during the last decades. This section discusses how the concept of institutions can be disentangled, understood, and analyzed in the context of SEA.

6.1 Perspectives on Institutions

What are institutions? The study of institutions has a long tradition, but a new institutionalism emerged in the late 1980s as a reaction to the then-dominating actor-centered analyses in the social sciences (Nilsson 2005; Vatn 2005). The literature on institutions is very rich and complex and several different definitions of institutions exist. One of the most famous is put forward by Nobel laureate Douglas North (1994, 360): "Institutions are the humanly designed constraints that structure human interaction. They are made up of formal constraints (e.g., rules, laws, constitutions), informal constraints (e.g., norms of behavior, conventions, self-imposed codes of conduct), and their enforcement characteristics. Together they define the incentive structure of societies and specifically economies."[9]

The concept of institutions is thus much broader than that of organizations. While institutions make up the rules, organizations[10] are the players. The distinction between institutions and organizations is important since there is a tendency to equate the two concepts in discussions on institutional capacity building for improved environmental management (OECD 1999). A too-limited focus on environment sector organizations (such as environment ministries and agencies) risks diverting the attention from other institutions which may be equally or more important for environmentally sustainable development.

There are various attempts to disentangle the broad view of institutions as formal and informal constraints or rules into more tangible analytical units. In its *World Development Report*, the World Bank (2003) depicts institutions as a continuum where, on the informal end, they go from trust and other forms of social capital to networks for coordination. On the formal end, institutions codify rules and laws as well as formal organizations such as courts and government agencies (figure 3). The World Bank (2003, 37) suggests that "institutions must perform three key functions in order to contribute to a sustainable development: (i) *pick up signals* about needs and problems . . . (which) involves generating information,

FIGURE 3
Institutions as Formal and Informal Rules

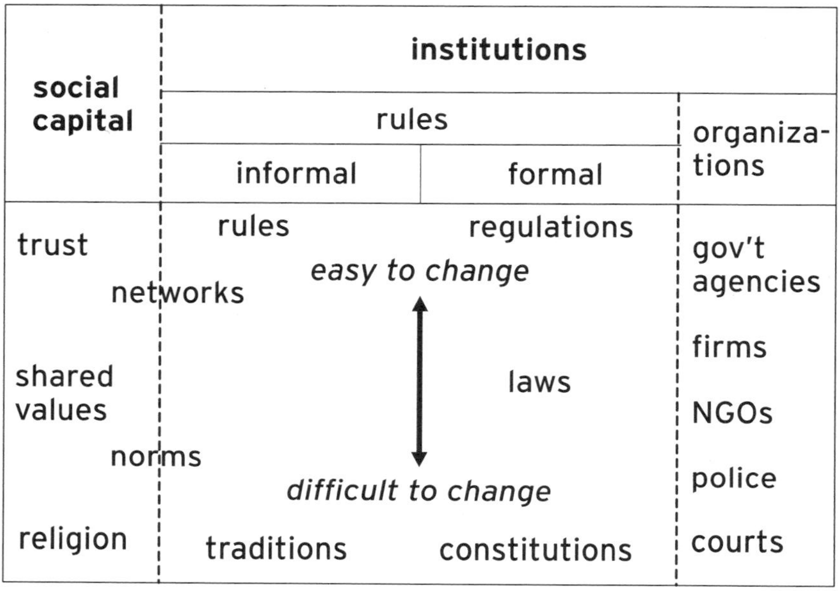

social capital	institutions		organiza-tions
	rules		
	informal	formal	
trust	rules networks	regulations easy to change	gov't agencies
shared values norms	laws		firms NGOs police
religion	traditions difficult to change	constitutions	courts

Source: World Bank 2003.

giving citizens a voice, responding to feedback, and fostering learning; (ii) *balance interests* by negotiating change and forging agreements, and by avoiding stalemates and conflicts; (iii) *execute and implement solutions* by credibly following through on agreements."

Williamson (2000) identifies different levels of institutional analysis (figure 4).[11] In this framework, the institutions at higher levels constrain choices at lower levels, but changes at lower levels can also occur through different feedback mechanisms, generating changes at the higher levels.

The first level identified by Williamson is *social embeddedness*, which comprises informal institutions such as norms, religion, and culture. Institutions at this level have evolutionary origins and normally change very slowly (100–1,000 years, according to Williamson).[12]

The second level is the *institutional environment* or the formal rules of the game, including constitutions and the executive, legislative, judicial, and bureaucratic functions of government. The definition and enforcement of property rights and contract laws are important elements at this level. Changes in the institutional environment normally happen slowly (10–100 years), but sudden crises can occasionally produce a sharp break from established procedures. The third level is the *institutions of governance*, where much of the day-to-day policy making takes place. Institutions at this level include the different parts of the government bureaucracy and laws and regulations. Changes in institutions at this level normally happen more rapidly (1–10 years). The fourth level is *resource allocation and employment*, where incentives resulting from the institutions on the other levels affect the choices of the different actors in society. Change at this level is continuous.

Which institutions are important for sustainable development? There is a growing consensus that good institutions matter greatly for economic and democratic development as well as social and environmental sustainability. Institutions are for example increasingly seen as one of the key fundamental causes of long-run growth and cross-country differences in economic performance (Acemoglu, Johnson, and Robinson 2004). Similarly, institutions are viewed as essential to the solution to many environmental problems, which require "motivating individuals to take a long-term perspective and the interest of a wide diversity of unknown individuals into account when making choices" (Ostrom, Schroeder, and Wynne 1993, 214). There are however a number of different perspectives on what institutions need to be put in place to generate these favorable outcomes, for example:

FIGURE 4
Levels in Institutional Analysis

level	frequency of change
customs, traditions, norms, religion	100–1,000 yrs.
formal rules of the game (judiciary, bureaucracy, etc.)	10–100 yrs.
governance: play of the game (contracts, aligning structures)	1–10 yrs.
resource allocation and employment (budget, policy)	continuous

Source: Adapted from Williamson 2000.

Institutions for economic development: Rodrik (2000) identifies five types of nonmarket institutions necessary for supporting a flourishing market economy: property rights, regulatory institutions, institutions for macroeconomic stabilization, institutions for social insurance, and institutions of conflict management. *Institutions for good governance:* The governance indicators produced by Kaufman, Kraay, and Mastruzzi (2008),[13] widely used for cross-country comparisons, include six different dimensions: voice and accountability, political stability and absence of violence, government effectiveness, regulatory quality, rule of law, and control of corruption. These indicators can be seen as pointing to the kind of institutions considered to be essential for good governance.

Institutions for environmental sustainability: OECD (2009) identifies specific environmental institutions, such as constitutional provisions for a right to a clean environment, environmental protection laws, and public environmental agencies, as key prerequisites for environmentally sustainable development. Building on the broader framework from the *World Development Report 2003* (World Bank 2003), Pillai and Lunde (2006) develop a checklist for assessing the institutional capacity for environmental management in different countries (appendix).

For several reasons, however, it is problematic to identify a generic set of good institutions that contribute to sustainable development. Since informal norms matter greatly for the outcomes of formal rules, the institutional solutions to specific problems will be highly context dependent. Conversely, the same institutional function (e.g., picking up signals) can take many different institutional forms. A meaningful answer to which institutions are important for sustainable development must thus first involve an identification of the specific obstacles to sustainable development in a particular context. An institutional analysis should begin by identifying "institutions for what."

How can institutions be transformed? If institutions are so crucial for development, why do countries not improve them? This simple question has puzzled researchers. North (1994) notes that institutions are not necessarily or even usually designed to be socially efficient. Formal rules are rather created to serve the interests of those with the bargaining power to create new rules. Acemoglu, Johnson, and Robinson (2004) portray institutions as having long historical roots (or "colonial origins") and being persistent over time since powerful groups block reforms and possess de jure and/or de facto political power. The search for a general theory of how to improve institutions is seen by some as the Holy Grail of social sciences (Acemoglu, Johnson, and Robinson 2004).

The slow-changing nature of norms, as well as their importance in the enforcement of formal rules, is one important factor explaining the difficulties involved in changing institutions. While formal rules may be changed overnight, informal norms usually change only gradually. Since norms provide "legitimacy" to a set of rules, societies that adopt the formal rules of another society will have very different performance characteristics because of different informal norms and enforcement (North 1994). The difficulties in transferring the formal political and economic institutions from Western market economies to Eastern European economies in the 1990s is a commonly cited example where the same formal institutions resulted in very different outcomes (North 1994; Rodrik 2000).

Rodrik (2000, 11–14) distinguishes between a "blueprint approach" and a "local knowledge (or experimentalist) approach" for institutional change. In the blueprint approach, best practice solutions from elsewhere are identified, imported, and implemented. However, given the many different perspectives of what best practice institutions are, the current attention to "getting the institutions right" may lead to a long wish list of policy reforms that is impossible to fulfill for poor countries (Grindle 2004; Rodrik 2006).[14] The local knowledge approach to institutional change on the other hand stresses that institutions need to be developed locally, relying on hands-on experience, local knowledge, and experimentation. This view can, however, serve privileged interests who want to conserve a certain set of institutions despite the fact that there are clearly better institutions elsewhere. It can also be quite costly to develop all the institutions locally when imported blueprints may serve just as well in some cases. Rodrik suggests that the blueprint approach may be appropriate for more narrow and technical issues, while large-scale institutional development by and large requires a process of discovery of local needs and capabilities. Participatory political institutions can be seen as a "meta-institution" that can ensure that institutional development is grounded in local knowledge (Rodrik 2000). They also can be seen as levers that stimulate a social learning process, over time creating more legitimacy (democratic support) for making new steps in institutional development (Nooteboom 2007).

6.2 SEA and Institutions

Despite the central role of institutions in I-SEA, the concept is not explicitly defined or discussed in the World Bank publications on policy-level SEA (World Bank 2005; Ahmed and Sánchez-Triana 2008). However, several aspects that should form part of an institutional analysis as part of an I-SEA are identified: (i) historical analysis to understand how current policies become locked in; (ii) political economy analysis, including goals, values, behaviors, and incentives of stakeholders involved in policy formulation and implementation; (iii) analysis of intersectoral (horizontal) and vertical coordination mechanisms within government to better understand implementation hurdles; (iv) analysis of mechanisms to promote social accountability and learning; and (v) identification of efficient and politically feasible interventions to overcome priority issues (Ahmed and Sánchez-Triana 2008).

This implicit definition captures the Bank's idea that an SEA needs to go beyond assessing the potential social and environmental impacts of policies and address the forces that drive policies (and their implementation). It also suggests that institutional analysis as part of an SEA should take a broad focus and not be limited to specific institutional arrangements for environmental management.

However, there seems to be a need for further and more specific guidance and learning on how to perform good institutional assessments as part of SEAs. Important lessons can be learned from the growing focus on governance and institutional factors in SEA literature. For example, Turnpenny et al. (2008) undertook a layered form of institutional analysis, based on a framework similar to Williamson's (2000) above, to analyze capacities and constraints for integrated policy assessment in four different European countries. On the *micro level,* the analysis concerned the individuals involved in doing assessments in the bureaucracy and the availability of resources (time, money, staff) and human resources (skills, educational background, etc.) for doing the assessments. On the *meso level,* organizational issues such as management structures, coordination procedures, and incentive systems were analyzed. Finally, on the *macro level,* the analysis focused on wider issues such as the administrative and legal context as well as the role of stakeholders in the decision-making process. This type of layered framework could be a way of structuring institutional analyses conducted as part of SEAs as well.

Lessons can also be drawn from the rapidly growing body of broader literature on environmentally related institutional assessments. A recent review of institutional assessments conducted as part of World Bank Country Environmental Analysis indicates that institutional assessments need to (i) move beyond an analysis of organizational mandates, functions, and gaps in formal rules, to include informal rules, political economy issues, and power relationships; (ii) put a stronger focus on the demand side of environmental governance and the role of private sector and civil society institutions; (iii) include subnational levels and resource flows between national and subnational levels; and (iv) focus on specific themes and sectors (Pillai 2008).

The importance of including an analysis of budget processes in institutional assessments is highlighted by Lawson and Bird (2008). Drawing on a four-country comparative study,[15] they conclude that while the environmental policy and legislative frameworks were generally well articulated and clear, the most important obstacle to implementation lies in deficient financing of public environmental actions. The study identifies the existence of three essentially parallel budget processes determining the level and direction of environmental financing: (i) a national budget process limited essentially to the recurrent budget, (ii) a process for the allocation of external project finance, and (iii) a process of negotiating rights to collect revenues and fees and retain control over their use. This fragmented budgetary system resulted in generally very low budgets for recurrent expenditures to cover core functions such as monitoring, control, and supervision, and relatively large portfolios of externally financed projects.[16] This was found to have led to a diversion from addressing national environmental priorities. Another consequence of this fragmented budgetary system is that a large part of the resources available for environmental action are beyond the control of the ministry of finance and ultimately also the parliament, undermining accountability and public management capacities.

While it may be appropriate to assess the institutional capacities and constraints for environmental management on a national level, for many SEAs of sector reforms a more focused assessment of institutions of particular relevance for the sector is more appropriate. For example, in relation to forestry or mining reforms, a thorough assessment of the institutions for land tenure may be more important than assessing the formal mandates of different environmental functions on a national level. The scope and priorities for institutional assessments to be conducted as part of an SEA will thus always be important to discuss. A good understanding of the context of the particular reform process will be key for making good judgments on what institutions with environmental relevance to prioritize.

7. STRENGTHENING SOCIAL ACCOUNTABILITY

Promoting social accountability as part of an I-SEA is identified by the World Bank (2005) as a key mechanism to ensure that I-SEA can have an influence beyond a discrete policy intervention and contribute to more long-term improvements of environmental governance. Accountability is, however, a broad concept with different interpretations and has been described as "probably one of the most basic yet most intractable of political concepts" (Hill 2005, 259). This section begins by relating social accountability to other types of accountability and then discusses accountability in relation to SEA.

7.1 Perspectives on Accountability

Accountability basically concerns preventing and redressing the abuse of political power through three general dimensions: (i) by subjecting power to the threat of sanctions (enforceability), (ii) by obliging it to be exercised in a transparent way, and (iii) by forcing it to justify its acts (Schedler 1999). Accountability refers to a relationship between two parties,[17] and a first step to understanding this relationship is to identify (i) who is the agent being held accountable, (ii) who is the agent demanding accountability, (iii) for what type of activities or duties are organizations or people being held accountable, (iv) in what forum are they being held to account, and (v) how is accountability being delivered.

Political accountability refers to the role of political institutions in holding government, civil servants, and politicians accountable to the public. A distinction is often made between vertical and horizontal accountability. The existence of free and regular *elections* is often viewed as the most basic mechanism for assuring vertical accountability in a democratic system. In theory, elections allow citizens to punish politicians, and the credible threat of losing office in the next period compels policy makers to respond to voters' interests (Adsèra, Boix, and Payne 2003). Information asymmetry (i.e., differences in access and capacity to interpret information) between the public and politicians, however, severely limits the possibilities for citizens to hold politicians accountable through elections.[18]

Another type of vertical accountability, which is a top-down relationship, exists when elected representatives are to appoint and hold the public servants in the bureaucracy accountable for the implementation of different policies. A similar problem of information asymmetry is also present here, since it is difficult for the politicians to know exactly how the civil servants go about implementing policies (see section on policy processes above). This is in one way a classic public administration problem, where there is a tension between rule-based control of the administration and the discretion of public servants necessary to do a good job. Civil service reform, improvement of internal auditing, evaluation, and surveillance are normally central elements of *proaccountability public administration reform*. This is sometimes referred to as administrative accountability and professional accountability. In weaker political economies, these are often highly contentious issues, since, as noted by Batley (2004, 35) "the bureaucratic arena is itself highly politicized and inter-connected with societal interests; it is where power, employment and patronage are concentrated, so the stakes are high."

Horizontal accountability refers to a relationship between more or less independent state agencies that monitor and discipline each other, and presupposes an internal functional differentiation of the state (Schedler 1999). The sharing of powers between the executive, legislative, and judiciary, together with checks and balances between different branches of government, constitutes the most typical mechanism for horizontal political accountability. In practice, this balancing of powers is weak in many countries. Veit et al. (2008) pay specific attention to the need to strengthen the role of the legislature in many African countries in order to address the often-neglected environmental priorities of rural populations. The lack of autonomy and authority of many African parliaments in relation to the executive severely undermines accountability.

Other examples of horizontal accountability mechanisms are the creation of *independent proaccountability agencies,* such as corruption control bodies, ombudsmen, and auditing agencies, which have been set up in many countries during recent years. These agencies are normally responsible for holding the government accountable in specific issue areas (Ackerman 2004, 2005).

Social accountability: Despite the implementation of many different measures to improve top-down accountability, corruption and other types of bad governance are persistent problems, not least in many developing countries.[19] Many analysts suggest that approaches to improve top-down accountability need to be complemented by bottom-up approaches to accountability that emphasize the demand side of good governance (Ackerman 2005). Social accountability is a broad term for this type of demand-side approach to accountability. While Blair (2008, 128) refers to social accountability as "the accountability of the state to the society as a whole (as opposed to some individual sector of society)," Malena, Forster, and Singh (2004, 3) define it as "an approach towards building accountability that relies on civic engagement, i.e. in which it is ordinary citizens and/ or civil society organizations who participate directly or indirectly in exacting accountability." Social accountability mechanisms refer to the broad range of initiatives that citizens can use to hold the state accountable, including citizen monitoring of public services, participatory expenditure tracking, social auditing, and civil society monitoring of the impacts of public policies.[20]

Public participation and voice: Some social accountability initiatives focus on enhancing public participation and giving *voice* to people to express views and interests and demand action of those in power. The focus is not on the creation of voice for its own sake but on enhancing the capacity to access information, scrutinize, and demand answers in order to influence governance processes (O'Neil, Foresti, and Hudson 2007). Voice can be exercised directly by poor people through, for example, elections, but many times it is channeled through indirect mechanisms such as civil society organizations or media.

This is clearly related to the opportunities and constraints discussed in the section above about participation. A general observation is that social accountability initiatives tend to be most effective if they are combined with accountability mechanisms "internal" to the state, i.e., are institutionalized and systematically implemented by a civil society, state, or "hybrid" institution (Malena, Foster, and Singh 2004). This institutionalization is important to overcome the "event culture" that tends to prevail when concepts of societal participation and civic engagement are brought to the table (Eberlei 2001, cited in Ackerman 2005). It should also be noted that there is disagreement on how much and what kind of participation is good for a democracy. For example, Kaufman (2003, cited in Ackerman 2004, 458) argues that "some forms of inclusion such as partnerships with NGOs may enhance capacity, others such as popular assemblies may be a step backward in terms of the efficiency, effectiveness and even the accountability of state organizations." Ackerman (2004) on the other hand argues for the merits of full inclusion of the citizenry as a whole in the core activities of government.

Rights to access to information and justice: In order for people to be able to exercise their voice and demand accountability from public authorities, legal rights pertaining to access to information, participation, and justice are essential. For environmental matters, these access rights are stated as commitments in Principle 10 in the Rio Declaration, as well as in the Aarhus Convention, which turns these commitments into legal obligations. Access to information can include the right to examine public records and to obtain data from environmental monitoring or reports from environmental agencies. At a more general level, access rights are rooted in civil and political human rights and part of international law on these issues. Using a human rights–based approach, accountability can be expressed as relations between the public, which has rights of access to information and justice, and the state, which is the bearer of the duty to fulfill these rights.

Freedom of press: The degree of citizen information has been shown to be a significant factor in explaining the level of corrupt practices in different countries (Adsèra, Boix, and Payne 2003).

7.2 SEA and Accountability

Reinforcing social accountability as part of an SEA is put forward by the World Bank (2005) as a key mechanism for improved environmental governance. Ahmed and Sanchéz-Triana (2008) note that in addition to the disclosure of information and public participation which are encouraged in traditional SEA methodologies, institution-centered SEA should in particular focus on strengthening the underlying legislation and implementation practices on information disclosure, public participation, and access to justice on environmental matters. This is consistent with Principle 10 of the Rio Declaration and the 1998 Aarhus Convention.[21] Moreover, small steps in increasing accountability by putting in place institutions that create more transparency can be seen as levers for social learning that eventually create legitimacy for next steps in developing accountability.

The focus on *access rights* is likely to be an important evolution in SEA approaches, since these rights can become an important lever for public demands. The rapidly growing Access Initiative is one example of how a network of civil society organizations can utilize access rights for political mobilization.[22]

While many governments have made progress in establishing legal frameworks for access rights, the implementation of these frameworks is often weak (Foti et al. 2008). This highlights the need for I-SEA to focus on the *mechanisms for enforcing access rights*. As stated in the beginning of this section, subjecting power to the threat of sanctions through effective enforcement mechanisms is a crucial element of accountability. At least parts of these enforcement mechanisms are likely to be found within the government system. It can be questioned whether increased transparency and participation will lead to improved governance without a system of checks and balances and strengthening of competing agencies (or countervailing powers), which can challenge the interests dominating, for example, a sector (Fung 2002; Galbraith 1952). It should thus also be considered if I-SEA can analyze and strengthen "government internal" horizontal accountability systems. An analysis of horizontal (cross-sector) and vertical mechanisms for coordination and sanctions as well as incentive systems within the public administration may very well be performed as part of an SEA.

While the focus on access rights is clearly relevant, one could discuss whether an I-SEA could also strengthen *other types of social accountability mechanisms.* For instance, it may be possible to institutionalize different types of participatory elements in the implementation of sector policies or management of natural resources. Although the form these institutions take will be highly context dependent, there seem to be a great need for further studies on how these types of arrangements can be influenced as part of an SEA.

The importance of *strengthening long-term constituencies* that can demand accountability and improved environmental governance is analyzed by Blair (2008) and recognized as important for I-SEA by Ahmed and Sánchez-Triana (2008). Environmental civil society organizations, the media, and the legislature are examples of actors that may form important parts of constituencies for environmental change.

Finally, how to prioritize between and sequence different types of initiatives to improve accountability and environmental governance merits further attention. Is it preferable to begin by strengthening environmental constituencies and a system of competing interests and checks and balances, which then can demand transparency and improved environmental governance? Or should the primary focus be on improving transparency, which then allows environmental constituencies to get engaged?

8. ENSURING SOCIAL LEARNING

Strategic environmental assessments commonly involve both analytical and participatory approaches (OECD DAC 2006). In institution-centered SEA, the role of learning is emphasized, and this is an important feature distinguishing I-SEA from impact-centered SEA approaches (Ahmed and Sánchez-Triana 2008). However, understanding what type of learning takes place in a policy process is a complex endeavor. First of all, social learning is conceptually difficult, since it is a very broad term that brings together several of the other key aspects of institution-centered SEA discussed in this literature review. Second, it is empirically difficult to evaluate if social learning has taken place and what effect it has had on specific policy outcomes (Bennett and Howlett 1992). This section discusses how learning can be conceptualized in the context of SEA and how it may be evaluated.

8.1 Perspectives on Social Learning

A learning approach to understanding policy changes generally claims that states (and public bureaucracies) can learn from experiences and modify present action on the basis of the results of previous action. A learning approach should be viewed as a complementary rather than an alternative hypothesis to theories emphasizing the importance of power and conflict for policy change (Bennet and Howlett 1992). While policy processes always take place in a context of power struggles and political conflicts, learning can be an important factor for change as well.

Different types of learning: In the literature, different types of learning that may take place in policy processes are identified (Ebrahim 2008):[23]

Technical learning involves a search for new policy instruments in the context of fixed policy objectives, and change occurs without fundamental discussion of objectives or basic strategies.

Conceptual learning involves a more fundamental redefinition of policy goals, problem definitions, and strategies. In, for example, the energy sector, conceptual learning can imply a redefinition of the policy goals from energy production to energy security, and this new policy goal is shared by key actors that may have opposing political interests (Nilsson 2005). Such a redefinition of policy goals is often crucial for environmental improvements, since implementation of environmental policies often requires the collaboration between different sectors (Fiorino 2001).

The distinction between technical and conceptual learning has connotations to the distinction between single-loop learning and double-loop learning in organizational theory (Argyris and Schön 1996). Single-loop learning is "concerned primarily with effectiveness: how best to achieve existing goals and objectives," while double-loop learning involves "inquiry through which organizational values and norms themselves are modified" (Argyris and Schön 1996, 22; cited in Ebrahim 2008, 160).

Social learning builds on both technical and conceptual learning but focuses on interactions and communications among actors (Fiorino 2001). With its emphasis on relations among actors and the quality of the dialogue, social learning is clearly linked to stakeholder participation in policy processes as well as accountability. The extent to which stakeholder participation and other types of social interactions result in learning is influenced by formal and informal institutional rules related to the policy process. Institutional rules shape power relations and determine how and where decisions are being made, who is in charge, and who gets to participate. Thus, changing institutional rules can affect the possibilities for learning to occur (Nilsson 2006).

In addition, the concept of *political learning* is used by some analysts to describe situations where new concepts are introduced and strategies improved, but with the purpose of strengthening fixed policy positions and objectives. The use of the political learning concept "allows for an often-neglected distinction to be made between strategic behavior and genuine shifts in beliefs" (Nilsson 2005, 209).

The role of research and evidence for learning and policy making: Research may greatly influence policy (recent examples include the biophysical and economic research on climate change; see, e.g., IPCC 2007; Stern et al. 2006). However, as pointed out by, e.g., Carden (2004), Owens (2005), and Neilson (2001), more information generated through research, policy assessments, or evaluations does not automatically translate into improved decisions or learning. Factors such as incentives, timing, costs, capacity (to absorb or understand research knowledge), and public opinion can constrain transfer of knowledge to policy making.

Tracing the influence of research knowledge on policy processes is associated with difficulties, partly due to the multitude of indirect links between research and policy processes, and to time lags. It may be that policy processes internalize research knowledge years or decades after the original research was undertaken (Neilson 2001). The research-policy links are also obscured by the fact that most research is incremental and cumulative, and requires translation, interpretation, and adaptation in the policy process. Disentangling research knowledge from other knowledge, information, and opinion in the policy process is therefore an additional difficulty. Some go as far as claiming that there is a cultural gap between the academic and the political spheres ("communities"), which substantially inhibits policy uptake of research (Caplan 1979). This view is somewhat moderated by Weiss (1977), who claims that we should not generally expect research to have a direct and immediate (linear) impact on policy. Rather, policy uptake of research knowledge is slow and incremental, and determined by organizations' (the political sphere's) openness toward new scientific knowledge. Research has an enlightenment function which slowly creeps into the policy sphere and gradually changes the mind set of politicians/policy makers. Research can suddenly change political priorities if other actions and events have worked in favor of taking the research knowledge on board.

Time is thus an important factor to consider when discussing the role of research and assessments in learning and policy making. Although new evidence in many cases may have little impact on policy making in the short run, the impact in the long run may be greater.

Learning in different types of policy processes: Among the factors that determine how wide a role evidence and learning play in a policy process, Lindquist (2001) underlines the importance of the decision mode of the organizations or networks involved in the policy process. He distinguishes between routine, incremental, and fundamental decision modes. *Routine decision regimes* focus mainly on matching and adapting existing programs to emerging conditions, and are generally not receptive to research or analytical work suggesting major changes. *Incremental* decision-making processes deal with selective issues as they emerge and can be receptive to policy analysis that identifies alternatives that address selective issues that do not involve wholesale rethinking of existing policies. *Fundamental* decisions are relatively infrequent opportunities to rethink approaches to policy problems, for example, as a result of crisis or new governments. In anticipation of fundamental policy decisions, or following sharp regime shifts, openness to and demand for research and new information can be expected. These fundamental decision regimes provide windows of opportunities for social learning as well as change in a broader perspective.

The scope of learning in relation to knowledge base and degree of social conflict: Several analysts use a simple typology (displayed in table 1) to discuss how learning (Nilsson and Persson 2003), the role of policy assessments (Kornov and Thissen 2000), and implementation of policies (Matland 1995) depend on the availability of substantive knowledge and the degree of social conflict in a decision-making process.

In situations where a high degree of social consensus is combined with a good knowledge base, rational problem solving based on facts and technical (rather than conceptual) learning is more likely to occur. When a high degree of social consensus is combined with a weak knowledge base, additional research can play an important role. Experimentation and learning during the implementation of decisions become important due to ambiguity involved at the decision

TABLE 1
Typology of Problem Situations with Indicated Support Approach

	Low conflict of values/interests	Strong conflict of values/interests
Good knowledge base	Rational problem-solving approach	Mediation
Low uncertainty/ambiguity	Technical learning	Negotiation support
Weak knowledge base	Risk approach, experimentation	Catalytic and entrepreneurial approaches
High uncertainty/ambiguity	Additional research	

Source: Adapted from Kornov and Thissen 2000.

stage. Ambiguity "provides an opportunity to learn new methods, technologies, and goals" (Matland 1995). In situations where there are strong social conflicts, the prospects for learning are bleaker, especially if this is combined with a weak knowledge base. Political learning rather than genuine shifts in beliefs are more likely, since actors tend to have clearly defined and incompatible goals and are less willing to interact. More analytical inputs are unlikely to result in improved decisions, since actors act strategically, and power rather than learning governs the outcome of decision making in these situations (Matland 1995). Approaches focusing on stimulating interaction, dialogue, and negotiation between different interests may be more fruitful, feeding more new information to the stakeholders (Nilsson and Persson 2003; Kornov and Thissen 2000).

This basic and rather crude typology may involve a risk of oversimplification, but the point is to illustrate that the level of knowledge and degree of social conflict matter greatly, not only for the opportunities for learning to occur but also for how to design an appropriate SEA approach (Kornov and Thissen 2000).

Institutions for learning: Different institutions may be more or less condu-cive to social learning processes. Formal and informal rules for how and where decisions are made and who gets to participate are important determinants for learning outcomes. For example, many central governments can be characterized as based on a bargaining model, where each ministry is looking out for its core interests in an interdepartmental negotiation process. Instead of being conducive to learning, this institutional setup often leads to positional wars and strategic use of knowledge. Parliamentary committees, or cross-sector working groups created around certain themes, are examples of institutions that have been more conducive to learning (Nilsson 2005; Pillai 2008).

Organizational research has shown that the ability of organizations to learn and incorporate new understandings is often limited. Organizations tend to accept knowledge that confirms their world views and resist knowledge that challenges them (Nilsson 2006). March (1991, 71) claims that organizations face a trade-off between "the exploration of new possibilities and the exploita-tion of old certainties." The essence of explorations is experimentation with new alternatives, and the resulting returns from this learning endeavor are often long term. Since the essence of exploitation is the refinement and extension of existing competences, technologies, and ideas whose payoffs are more immediate, there are strong incentives for organizations to favor exploitation over explora-tion (March 1991). Given these incentives that restrain learning, it is often held that a force from outside is necessary in order to induce learning (Sabatier and Weible 2007; Nilsson 2006). Such a force from outside is often viewed in terms of external shocks leading to changes in power relations among influential actors or networks (Sabatier and Weible 2007).

Network theory states that learning occurs when actors with different interests and beliefs interact in the policy arena. The literature does not, however, give any clear guidance on how to design institutions that create the type of interactions that result in social learning. For example, Nooteboom (2007) claims that EIA, as an example of a formal institution, has contributed to a learning process with far-reaching effects in the Netherlands. The effects on learning of institutionalizing mandatory participation systems, requiring governments to involve civil society in the development of poverty reduction strategy papers, are mixed. In some countries like Honduras, mandatory participation has given NGOs a more important role and contributed to political openness (Seppanen 2005). But in many other countries, it did not seem to deliver a lot of visible result (IEO 2004; OED 2004). For example, in Bolivia it resulted in a larger gap between expectations and results, frustrating the poor population (Dijkstra 2005).

8.2 SEA and Social Learning

Social learning is important in the World Bank I-SEA approach, since it is seen as a key mechanism to ensure that I-SEA can have an influence beyond the discrete policy intervention. The World Bank (2005, 56) suggests that "improving policy learning—technical, conceptual and social—relies on enhancing communication and dialogue among actors and constant evaluation." While "systems for monitoring and evaluation that are publicly available are crucial not only for technical learning but also for democratic legitimacy and public confidence," promoting social learning in environmental policy is more about "creating a culture of stakeholder involvement and scrutiny among policy makers and implementers." Ahmed and Sánchez-Triana (2008) suggest that in order to promote social learning, an I-SEA should focus on aspects such as these:

- "politicizing" environmental issues, by linking them to broader development issues and integrating agendas of environmental ministries with those of more influential ministries
- strengthening policy advocacy networks and creating public forums for policy debate to ensure that diverse perspectives are repeatedly placed on policy makers' agendas
- putting effective transparency mechanisms in place and supporting media scrutiny of policy and implementation to strengthen accountability

The suggested aspects an I-SEA should focus on in order to promote social learning illustrate that social learning is viewed as an outcome resulting from the implementation of many different activities. The World Bank approach to social learning seems to be well grounded in modern theories of adaptive management, collaborative planning, and interactive policy making; see for example Feldman and Khademian (2008); Healey (1997); and Innes and Booher (1999). There is no single best way to stimulate social learning, which is extremely sensitive to context. It may be more an art than a science, and I-SEA should primarily consider what is feasible given the specific context.

An interesting development of the framework would be an explicit discussion of how I-SEA best can contribute to social learning in different types of decision-making contexts (in line with the discussion above; see Kornov and Thissen [2000]; Lindquist [2001]). It would be interesting if the evaluation of the I-SEA pilots could explore whether there may be a trade-off between making an SEA process as open as possible on the one hand and maximizing learning on the other. Do stakeholders need an environment that is not completely open to media and public scrutiny to be willing to challenge old positions?

The broad nature of the social learning concept may be the main weakness of this part of the I-SEA approach. The broad concepts related to learning and the slow nature of learning processes are likely to make it difficult to empirically evaluate if learning has taken place and to attribute possible changes to I-SEA. Aware of this, the World Bank (2005) suggests that the effects of learning should be studied over long time frames and that one should have conservative expectations about the potential for actual learning. But even so, as Bennet and Howlett (1992, 290) note, "it may be impossible to observe the learning activity in isolation from the change requiring explanation," and "we may only know that learning is taking place because policy change is taking place." In relation to SEA, it seems important to distinguish the learning activities more clearly from the objective of integrating key environmental concerns into policy formation. As a starting point it would be desirable to further disentangle the concepts related to policy learning and I-SEA and to clarify the following (Bennet and Howlett 1992; Nilsson 2006):

- *Who learns?* Is it primarily government officials and policy makers or a broader set of societal actors?
- *What is learned?* Is it mainly technical learning or are more fundamental problems and strategies reconceptualized?
- *What are the key elements of learning?* Is it mainly new knowledge acquisition, lessons drawing, or institutionalization?
- *What are the results of learning?* What effect does learning have on policy outcomes?

Finally, social learning is something that the social actors should do themselves, if they want. Interventions cannot force any actor to learn. As the saying goes, "One can bring a camel to a well, but one cannot force him to drink." Instruments that create accountability may increase a sense of interdependency, but the actors may still refrain from agreeing on joint interests. Therefore, progress on social learning should in the first place be observable as changes in the attitude of individuals toward others who ask attention for the environment.

C. Evaluating I-SEA

9. FRAMEWORK FOR EVALUATING I-SEA PILOTS

This section provides guidance for the evaluation of the different SEAs in the World Bank pilot program. For each pilot to be evaluated, there will be separate terms of reference developed containing more detailed information and guidance.

The evaluation framework[24] aims at (i) forming a shared understanding of the objectives, concepts, and methodologies used in institution-centered SEA; (ii) establishing joint objectives and a common scope for the pilot evaluations; and (iii) facilitating the cross-analysis of the results of the different pilot evaluations. Although these are some general objectives to attain, the evaluators should be flexible in applying this framework, adjusting the evaluations to the unique contextual factors that set the stage for each pilot that will be evaluated.

9.1 Evaluation Objectives

The general objective of evaluating the SEA pilots is *to learn how effective the I-SEA approach is in integrating environmental and social considerations in policies, plans, and programs, and understand the contextual factors that explain its influence or lack thereof.*

The specific objectives of the pilot evaluations are the following:

1. to evaluate the pilot's actual and potential influence on a concrete policy, plan, or program and on the underlying institutional framework in which this policy, plan, or program has been formulated and implemented
2. to evaluate how and to what extent contextual influencing factors and processes explain the influence or lack of influence of the pilot
3. to evaluate how the pilot used the I-SEA methodological framework while adapting to contextual influencing factors and processes
4. to evaluate to what extent the pilot has achieved the process outcomes of I-SEA

9.2 Evaluation Considerations

The evaluation of the SEA pilots involves several challenges. The evaluators should especially consider the following issues.[25]

Evaluating outcomes rather than impact: Since the evaluations will take place shortly after the completion of the different SEA pilots, the longer-term impacts[26] on the underlying institutional framework and political economy context will not be evaluated. A more tangible scope for the evaluation than to evaluate impacts is therefore to assess the outcomes of the SEA pilots. Outcomes can be defined as changes in the behavior, relationships, activities, or actions of people, groups, organizations, and institutions with which the SEA pilot has engaged (Earl, Carden, and Smutylo 2001).[27] The evaluation should thus focus on detecting the many different types of expected and unexpected outcomes (or changes) that may have evolved in the limited time frame since the initiation of the SEA pilot. The I-SEA model as outlined in this report suggests that important expected outcomes would be raised attention to environmental priorities, strengthened environmental constituencies, enhanced social accountability, and greater capacity for social learning. For some pilots, it may also be possible to find that key environmental issues have been incorporated in policy formulation and implementation. More examples of what expected outcomes can be, and suggestions for how these can be detected, are found in the evaluation questions below.

The key challenge of not having access to a baseline or counterfactual when mapping these kinds of outcomes would be at least partially addressed by building a sound narrative on how the SEA pilot intended to incorporate environmental and social considerations in specific interventions, what actually happened, and why this may have happened (see "Evaluation Report" in subsection 9.3). The evaluator may as well consider other experience in the sector for influencing decision making and institutional strengthening in an attempt to anticipate conclusions on "what may happen" in the future as a result of the SEA being evaluated. There is a wealth of experience on capacity building and influencing strategic decision making that can be brought to bear, at least to point out potential strengths or weaknesses of the pilot SEA being evaluated.

Analyzing the contribution of I-SEA to outcomes rather than establishing causality: A second challenge in evaluating the influence of the SEA pilots concerns the difficulty of determining if observed changes are caused by the SEA or by other factors. Changes are likely the result of many contributing factors, and an SEA can at best be one of these. Rather than attempting to establish a direct causality between the SEA and the observed outcomes, the evaluation should analyze if it is likely that the SEA pilot has made an important contribution to these outcomes. The evaluation may trace logical links between SEA activities and outcomes, but should be careful in not framing these in terms of causality.

Analyzing the interaction between contextual factors and I-SEA in explaining outcomes: A critical success factor for SEA effectiveness is the ability to adjust the scope and methodology of an SEA to contextual factors (e.g., Hilding-Rydevik and Bjarnadóttir 2007). The interaction between the pilot and its context therefore merits attention in evaluating the contribution of an SEA pilot to observable outcomes. The evaluator should distinguish between factors under control of the SEA team and external factors. Formal as well as informal institutions in the country,[28] windows of opportunity for policy reform, and political economy conditions affecting the implementation viability of reforms are examples of external factors that could define (favorably or unfavorably) I-SEA outcomes. It is difficult to identify ex ante which contextual factors are most important in explaining I-SEA outcomes. As a rule of thumb, the evaluator should intend, early in the evaluation process, to get a broad overview of the historical, political, economic, social, cultural, and institutional factors that may be crucial to the policy intervention at hand. The evaluator should then try to narrow the focus to those contextual factors that seem to be most important in explaining the influence or lack of influence of the SEA pilot.

In evaluating the interaction between the pilot and its context, the evaluator should also analyze the role of the factors potentially under control of the SEA team. Among those that merit consideration are the ability to access and involve key stakeholders and decision makers in the I-SEA process, communication of I-SEA findings and results, and the ability to take advantage of windows of opportunity for influencing decision making and effecting institutional change.

9.3 Evaluation Process

Evaluation team: The evaluation of pilots will be carried out by specialists independent of the World Bank.[29] Evaluators are encouraged to team up with local expertise or seek assistance from local specialists to undertake the evaluation of the SEA pilots.

Evaluation steps: The evaluation of each pilot will involve the following steps:

Preparatory work: Thorough preparations will be key for successful fieldwork. Preparatory activities suggested include (i) document review, (ii) development of a plan for the fieldwork including an interview guide, and (iii) draft context analysis.

Fieldwork: Each pilot evaluation will include at least one trip for carrying out fieldwork activities.

Report writing: A draft evaluation report may be written during the field trip. This may allow for a validation of some of the findings during the field trip. The final report should incorporate comments received on the draft report.

Documentation of findings: Each evaluation team should establish an electronic database including documents, interview protocols, and other sources of information on which the findings of the evaluation report are based. The database is one way of strengthening the reliability of the different evaluations.

Evaluation materials: The evaluation will build on the following materials:

Documents: The evaluators will have access to the documentation of the pilots, including concept notes, terms of reference, inception reports, mid-term reports, final reports, and lessons learned reports. In addition, the evaluators are expected to collect additional documentation necessary for fulfilling the objectives of the evaluation.

Interviews: Three sets of actors should be interviewed in order to base the evaluation on different points of view and multiple sources of evidence:

1. *The I-SEA team.* From the I-SEA team, the evaluators are expected to interview (i) the task manager of the project with which the pilot was associated, (ii) World Bank staff who actively participated in the implementation of the pilot, and (iii) the main consultant(s) in charge of the implementation of the SEA. The World Bank will provide the evaluators with names and contact addresses of these interviewees.

2. *Policy makers and implementers.* For the group of policy makers and implementers, the evaluators will interview government officials involved in the implementation of the policy and the use of the SEA recommendations at the strategic decision level like ministers, directors, principal secretaries, policy advisers, policy think tanks, etc.

3. *Key stakeholders.* The evaluators will prepare a list of potential interviewees based on the stakeholder analysis of the I-SEA. This list should include, but not be limited to, representatives of civil society stakeholders, grassroots organizations, lobbyists, local communities, relevant sector organizations (such as professional organizations), and the private sector significantly affected directly or indirectly by the intervention assessed through the I-SEA. By using and describing (in the evaluation report) broad-based soliciting, the list should strive to be representative of key stakeholders and appropriately consider multiple visions and perspectives. The interviewee list should be cleared by the World Bank prior to fieldwork.

Evaluation report: The evaluators will prepare the evaluation report as a narrative comprising four parts.

1. *The first part* (actual and potential influence of I-SEA) will discuss the discrete intervention (policy, plan, or program) and the extent to which the I-SEA pilot has contributed to integrating environmental and social considerations into this intervention through
    a. influencing decision makers and constituencies with a stake in the policy, plan, or program formation in the sector, country, or region;

b. influencing country work supported by the World Bank (i.e., preparation of loans), and, more broadly, World Bank staff working across the region or the world on similar sectoral interventions (i.e., mining reform, forest reform, urban planning, etc.)

This analysis should identify policy and institutional changes that may have already taken place and processes that may lead to future policy and institutional changes.

2. *The second part* (context and application of I-SEA) will contain a discussion of the context in which the SEA was undertaken, including historical, political, economic, social, cultural, and institutional factors that may explain the influence or lack of influence of the SEA pilot. The evaluator should then discuss how I-SEA methods and tools were applied in undertaking the pilot, given the constraints and opportunities of the context.

3. *The third part* (achievement of I-SEA process outcomes) will discuss the extent to which the I-SEA process was able to raise attention to environmental and social priorities associated with the discrete intervention, strengthen constituencies, and improve social accountability and social learning.

4. *In the fourth part* (I-SEA effectiveness and analysis of strengths and limitations), the evaluator should draw conclusions about and recommendations for effective I-SEA and discuss the strengths and limitations of the SEA pilot evaluated. The discussion should include an analysis of the interaction between the I-SEA process and its historical, political, economic, social, cultural, and institutional contexts.

In addition, the evaluation report should contain information about how the evaluation was conducted and how the findings are substantiated. This "approach" section of the evaluation report should make a clear distinction between findings that are derived directly from document reviews or interviews, and the expert opinions of the evaluation team. Detailed information on the sources of information for the evaluation should be provided in appendixes to the main evaluation report.

9.4 Evaluation Questions/Evaluation Criteria

This section outlines a set of evaluation questions which are intended to *guide* the evaluation teams in fulfilling the evaluation objectives. The questions are posed to the evaluators and should not be interpreted as interview questions that should be posed to different respondents. In order to assist the evaluators in answering the general evaluation questions, detailed evaluation questions are specified. The detailed evaluation questions can also be seen as interim markers of progress (Weiss 1998) in relation to the influence of the SEA pilot (evaluation question 1) and the achievement of envisaged process outcomes of the SEA pilot (evaluation question 3).

General Questions for the Evaluation of SEA Pilots

1. How and why has the SEA pilot influenced decision-making processes?
- In relation to policy, plan, or program formation in the sector, country, or region?
- In relation to country work supported by the World Bank?
- In relation to other actors and processes?
- What are the factors that may explain the pilot's influence or lack thereof?
- Which trends or processes may favor or hinder the influence of the SEA pilot in the future?

2. How was the pilot undertaken given the context?
- How were key contextual factors identified and taken into account?
- How were analytical and participatory tools and methods used?
- How were stakeholders' vulnerability aspects considered?
- Appropriateness, strengths, and weaknesses of tools and methods used?

3. To what extent did the pilot achieve key I-SEA process outcomes? How and why?
Intended outcomes:
- Raised attention to environmental and social priorities for policy reform, plans, and programs
- Strengthened constituencies
- Improved social accountability
- Enhanced social learning
Other outcomes of the SEA pilot?

4. What were the strengths and weaknesses of the SEA pilot for influencing decision-making processes?

Detailed Questions for the Evaluation of SEA Pilots

1. *How and why has the SEA pilot influenced decision-making processes?*
    a. *In relation to policy, plan, or program formation in the sector, country, or region?*
        *   Increased integration of environmental and social priority issues?
        *   Specific policy decisions including, if relevant, the preparation of laws, executive power, or judiciary decisions and regulations?
    b. *In relation to country work supported by the World Bank?*
        *   The preparation of a World Bank project or loan to support a client country's policy, plan, or program?
        *   The dialogue between the client country and the Bank?
        *   Other processes and actors within the World Bank such as staff working across the region or the world on similar sectoral interventions?
    c. *In relation to other actors and processes?*
        *   Other expected or unexpected changes in the behavior, relationships, or actions of people, groups, organizations, and institutions with which the SEA pilot has engaged?
    d. *What are the factors that may explain the pilot's influence or lack thereof?*
    e. *Which trends or processes may favor or hinder the influence of the SEA pilot in the future?*
        *   How has the SEA pilot attempted to ensure that its influence reaches beyond the discrete policy intervention?
2. *How was the SEA pilot undertaken given the context?*
    a. *How were key contextual factors identified and taken into account?*
        *   Historical, political, economic, social, cultural, and institutional factors (formal/informal) critical for the decision-making process?
        *   Political economy factors affecting the viability of the proposed intervention?
        *   Seizing windows of opportunity for influencing the decision-making process related to the discrete intervention or dealing with the effects of the closing of these windows of opportunity?

b. *How were analytical and participatory tools and methods used for the following:*
- Stakeholder dialogue?
- Identifying and selecting environmental and social priorities?
- Institutional and political economy analysis?
- The validation of pilot recommendations and dissemination?

c. *How were stakeholders' vulnerability aspects, such as gender discrimination, youth unemployment, weak land titling/property rights of farmers, etc., considered?*

d. *Appropriateness, strengths, and weaknesses of tools and methods used?*

3. *To what extent did the pilot achieve intended I-SEA process outcomes? How and why?*

a. *Raised attention to environmental (and social) priorities*
- Are priorities more clearly defined? How is this documented?
- Have environmental priorities been "politicized" and linked to growth, poverty reduction, or other key development issues?
- To what extent are priorities shared among key stakeholders?
- How has the pilot helped to raise attention to priorities?

b. *Strengthened constituencies*
- Which constituencies have been strengthened (CSOs, CBOs, private sector, networks within the bureaucracy, networks involving many different kinds of actors)?
- Have stakeholder engagement and networks been maintained after completion of the SEA report?

c. *Improved social accountability*
- New or improved legislation on access to information, public participation, or justice in environmental matters?
- Strengthened institutional mechanisms for the implementation/enforcement of legislation on access rights?
- Mechanisms for stakeholder participation or involvement in strategic decision making, particularly by weak and vulnerable stakeholders?
- Enhanced transparency and media scrutiny of policy decision making?
- Other accountability mechanisms that have been strengthened through the SEA pilot?

d. *Enhanced social learning*
- Who has learned? Is it primarily government officials and policy makers or a broader set of societal actors?
- In the Bank, is it just at the level of an individual task team leader, or more broadly among sectoral task team leaders, that learning has occurred?

- What has been learned? Is it mainly technical learning or have more fundamental problems and strategies been reconceptualized?
- Has the SEA pilot initiated or strengthened mechanisms for
  - intersector or multisector coordination?
  - dialogue on policy reform that includes environmental and social perspectives and involves multiple stakeholders?
  - compensating potential losers of policy changes?
  - monitoring and evaluation, creating feedback for policy and planning fine tuning?
  - linking policy making with research communities?
  e. *What other outcomes did the SEA pilot lead to?*
4. *What were the strengths and weaknesses of the SEA pilot for influencing decision-making processes?*

Appendix

Checklist for Analyzing Institutional Capacity for Environmental Management

Picking up signals	Balancing interests and reaching agreements	Executing and implementing decisions
Monitoring environmental quality for priority setting and informing public policies	Identification of key agencies and stakeholders and linking them with their mandates (including those relating to EA), interests, and incentives facing them (organizational mapping very useful here)	Gaps in formal rules (e.g., constitutional framework, legal and regulatory framework, EA legislation) shaping the incentives of key actors
Public disclosure of information; presence of an effective mechanism for responding to citizen concerns	Processes within key organizations (for example, leadership, organizational culture, quality and quantity of personel, conflicts of interest)	Divergence between formal and informal rules (e.g., respect for rule of law and property rights, presence of internal and external accountability mechanisms)
Assessment of demand for specific environmental priorities	Adequacy and transparency in allocation and execution of financial resources for managing environmental priorities	Independence of oversight institutions
	Formal and informal rules shaping coordination between sector ministries and key stakeholders; horizontal accountability mechanisms: capacity for EA in sector ministries	Role of the judiciary
	Environmental management at sub national levels and accountability mechanisms between different administrative levels; mandate and capacity for EA at sub national levels	

Source: Pillai and Lunde 2006.

Notes

1 Environmental Economics Unit, Department of Economics, University of Gothenburg (daniel.slunge@economics.gu.se).

2 Department of Public Administration, Erasmus University Rotterdam (nooteboom@fsw.eur.nl).

3 Environmental Economics Unit, Department of Economics, University of Gothenburg (anders.ekbom@economics.gu.se).

4 Department of Public Administration, Erasmus University Rotterdam (dijkstra@fsw.eur.nl).

5 Netherlands Commission for Environmental Assessment (Rverheem@eia.nl).

6 That is, putting environmental issues on the broader political agenda and linking them with key development issues, e.g., poverty reduction and economic development (World Bank 2005; Ahmed and Sánchez-Triana 2008).

7 The number of possibilities, forms, and techniques for stakeholder representation is large. For an overview, see for example Kende-Robb and Van Wicklin (2008) or Innes and Booher (1999).

8 See, e.g., the Espoo Convention on transboundary environmental assessment, the Aarhus Convention granting the public rights regarding access to information, public participation, and access to justice in governmental decision-making processes and the Kiev Protocol on SEA implementing the Espoo convention.

9 For alternative definitions, see for example the 2005 book by Arild Vatn, *Institutions and the Environment*. North's definition can be said to be a form of *rational institutionalism*, which emphasizes incentives and how rational individuals act within the constraints of rules. A *normative institutionalism* on the other hand stresses that values and norms and "a logic of appropriateness" are the central factors in explaining behavior and choice (March and Olsen 1989).

10 According to North (1990, 5), organizations can be thought of as "groups of individuals bound by some common purpose to achieve objectives."

11 The institutions and development framework (IAD) is an analogous layered framework for institutional analysis developed by Elinor Ostrom and colleagues (Ostrom 2005). The levels of analysis in the IAD framework are the constitutional arena, the collective choice arena, and the action arena. The IAD framework is much more elaborate than the one discussed by Williamson but it has not been possible to go into details here.

12 Chang (2007, chapter 9), however, describes how cultures can change more rapidly when incentives and/or transaction costs change.

13 Published by the World Bank Institute, http://www.govindicators.org.

14 Or as Rodrik (2006, 12) notes, "telling poor countries in Africa or Latin America that they have to set their sights on the best-practice institutions of the U.S. or Sweden is like telling them that the only way to develop is to become developed—hardly useful policy advice!"

15 Tanzania, Mozambique, Mali, and Ghana.

16 As an example: in 2005–06 the Ghanaian Environmental Protection Agency was managing 28 separate projects financed by 10 different funding agencies.

17 A is accountable to B when A is obliged to inform B about A's actions and decisions, to justify them, and to suffer punishment in the case of eventual misconduct.

18 This is often analyzed in terms of a principal agent framework, where the principal (the public) delegates an instrument to accomplish certain goals to the agent (the politicians or policy makers). In the next step, the principal is the politician and the agent the civil servant in the bureaucracy (Batley 2004; Adsèra, Boix, and Payne 2003).

19 It should be noted that corruption is often linked to natural resources management (Veit et al. 2008; Transparency International 2008).

20 For an overview see the World Bank Social Accountability Sourcebook.

21 Aarhus Convention on Access to Information, Public Participation in Decision-Making and Access to Justice on Environmental Matters.

22 See http://www.accessinitiative.org.

23 This conceptualization follows Glasbergen's (1996) work on environmental policy in the Netherlands and is used by several analysts, including Fiorino (2001), Ebrahim (2008), and (with some modifications) Nilsson (2006). Other concepts in the "learning literature" include government learning, lessons drawing, and political learning (Bennett and Howlett 1992).

24 The evaluation framework presented in this section builds partly on the section on evaluation in the OECD DAC (Development Assistance Committee) SEA guidance (OECD DAC 2006; see 123–28). It contains however less of "SEA quality control check-elements," which is one of the evaluation checklists presented by the OECD DAC as benchmarks for good practice. It can be found in a recent proposal of a "Generic SEA Quality Review Methodology" (Sadler and Dalal-Clayton 2009).

25 More elaborate information on these and other challenges in evaluating complex change processes can be found in e.g. Weiss (1998); George and Bennett (2005); and Yin (2003).

26 "Impacts" refers to "the positive and negative changes produced by a development intervention, directly or indirectly, intended or unintended. This involves the main impacts and effects resulting from the activity on the local social, economic, environmental and other development indicators" (OECD DAC 2008).

27 This definition of "outcomes" comes from the International Development and Research Centre's and others' work on outcome mapping as an evaluation methodology. The term "institutions" has been added for the purpose of this evaluation, but is not included in the definition of outcomes suggested by Earl, Carden, and Smutylo (2001). That study uses the term "boundary partners" for the individuals, groups, and organizations that a program interacts with directly.

28 See the discussion in section 6.1 on the importance of informal institutions for the actual performance of formal institutions.

29 EEU and NCEA will each evaluate two pilots, and the Swedish EIA Centre will evaluate one pilot. The remaining pilots will be commissioned by the World Bank to individual consultants with expertise in policy/institutional analysis, case study research strategy, and, preferably, experience in SEA.

References

Executive Summary

Ahmed, Kulsum, and Ernesto Sánchez-Triana, eds. 2008. *Strategic Environmental Assessment for Policies: An Instrument for Good Governance.* Washington, DC: World Bank.

North, D. C. 1994. "Economic Performance Through Time." *American Economic Review* 84: 359–68.

World Bank. 2005. "Integrating Environmental Considerations in Policy Formulation: Lessons from Policy-Based SEA Experience." Report 32783, World Bank, Washington, DC.

1. Introduction

Ahmed, Kulsum, and Ernesto Sánchez-Triana, eds. 2008. *Strategic Environmental Assessment for Policies: An Instrument for Good Governance.* Washington, DC: World Bank.

Fischer, Thomas B. 2007. *Theory and Practice of Strategic Environmental Assessment: Towards a More Systematic Approach.* London: Earthscan.

OECD DAC (Organisation for Economic Co-operation and Development, Development Assisstance Committee). 2006. *Applying Strategic Environmental Assessment: Good Practice Guidance for Development Cooperation.* Development Assistance Committee Guidelines and Reference Series. Paris: OECD Publishing.

Partidario, Maria R. 2000. "Elements of an SEA Framework: Improving the Added Value of SEA." *Environmental Impact Assessment Review* 20: 647–63.

World Bank. 2001. *Making Sustainable Commitments: An Environment Strategy for the World Bank.* Washington, DC: World Bank.

————. 2004. *Operational Policies. Development Policy Lending O.P. 8.60,* The World Bank Operational Manual. http://go.worldbank.org/ZODRFHOQI0.

————. 2005. "Integrating Environmental Considerations in Policy Formulation: Lessons from Policy-Based SEA Experience." Report 32783, World Bank, Washington, DC.

2. Institution-Centered SEA—A Conceptual Model

Blair, Harry. 2008. "Building and Reinforcing Social Accountability for Improved Environmental Governance." In *Strategic Environmental Assessment for Policies: An Instrument for Good Governance,* ed. Kulsum Ahmed and Ernesto Sanchéz-Triana, 127–57. Washington, DC: World Bank.

Cohen, Michael D., James G. March, and Johan P. Olsen. 1972. "A Garbage Can Model of Organizational Choice." *Administrative Science Quarterly* 17 (1): 1–25.

Kingdon, J. W. 1995. *Agendas, Alternatives, and Public Policies.* New York: Harper Collins.

World Bank. 2005. "Integrating Environmental Considerations in Policy Formulation: Lessons from Policy-Based SEA Experience." Report 32783, World Bank, Washington, DC.

————. 2008. *Evaluation of the World Bank's Pilot Program on Institution-Centered SEA: Concept Note.* Washington, DC: World Bank.

3. Understanding Policy Processes

Ahmed, Kulsum, and Ernesto Sánchez-Triana, eds. 2008. *Strategic Environmental Assessment for Policies: An Instrument for Good Governance.* Washington, DC: World Bank.

Ashby, W. R. 1956. *Introduction to Cybernetics.* London: Chapman and Hall.

Beck, U. 1992. *Risk Society: Towards A New Modernity.* London: Sage.

Cohen, Michael D., James G. March, Johan P. Olsen. 1972. "A Garbage Can Model of Organizational Choice." *Administrative Science Quarterly* 17 (1): 1–25.

De Bruin, J. A., E. F. Ten Heuvelhof, and R. J. In 't Veld. 1998. *Procesmanagement: over procesontwerp en besluitvorming* [Process management: About process design and decision-making]. Schoonhoven, Netherlands: Academic Service.

Feldman, Martha, and Anne Khademian. 2008. "The Continuous Process of Policy Formulation." In *Strategic Environmental Assessment for Policies: An Instrument for Good Governance,* ed. Ahmed Kulsum and Ernesto Sánchez-Triana, 37–59. Washington, DC: World Bank.

Gould, J., ed. 2005. *The New Conditionality: The Politics of Poverty Reduction Strategies.* London and New York: Zed Books.

Hilding-Rydevik, T., and H. Bjarnadóttir. 2007. "Context Awareness and Sensitivity in SEA Implementation." *Environmental Impact Assessment Review* 27: 666–84.

Hill, Michael. 2005. *The Public Policy Process,* 4th ed. Essex, UK: Pearson.

Kickert, W. J., E. H. Klijn, and J. F. Koppenjan. 1997. *Managing Complex Networks: Strategies for the Public Sector.* London: Sage Publications.

Kingdon, J. W. 1995. *Agendas, Alternatives, and Public Policies.* New York: Harper Collins.

Kornov, L., and W. A. H. Thissen. 2000. "Rationality in Decision- and Policy-Making: Implications for Strategic Environmental Assessment." *Impact Assessment and Project Appraisal* 18 (3): 191–200.

Lindblom, C. 1959. "The Science of Muddling Through." *Public Administration Review* 19: 79–88.

Lindquist, E. 2001. *Discerning Policy Influence: Framework for a Strategic Evaluation of IDRC-Supported Research.* Ottawa: International Development Research Centre Evaluation Unit.

Lipsky, M. 1980. *Street-Level Bureaucracy: Dilemmas of the Individual in Public Services.* New York: Russell Sage Foundation.

Nooteboom, S. 2006. *Adaptive Networks: The Governance for Sustainable Development.* Delft, Netherlands: Eburon.

Pressman, J. L., and A. Wildavsky. 1973. *Implementation: How Great Expectations in Washington are Dashed in Oakland.* Berkeley, CA: University of California Press.

Ritter, H. W. J., and M. M. Webber. 1973. "Dilemmas in a General Theory of Planning." *Policy Sciences* 4: 155–69.

Sabatier P. A., and H. C. Jenkins-Smith, eds. 1993. *Policy Change and Learning: An Advocacy Coalition Approach.* Boulder, CO: Westview.

Schön, D. A., and M. Rein. 1994. *Frame Reflection: Toward the Resolution of Intractable Policy Controversies.* New York: Basic Books.

Simon, H. A. 1957. *Administrative Behavior: A Study of Decision-Making Processes in Administrative Organizations.* New York: MacMillan.

———. 1991. "Bounded Rationality and Organizational Learning." *Organization Science* 2 (1): 125–34.

Susskind L. E., R. K. Jain, and A. O. Martyniuk. 2001. *Better Environmental Policy Studies. How to Design and Conduct More Effective Analyses.* Washington, DC: Island Press.

Uhl-Bien M., R. Marion, and B. McKelvey. 2007. "Complexity Leadership Theory: Shifting Leadership from the Industrial Age to the Knowledge Era." *Leadership Quarterly* 18 (2007): 298–318.

World Bank. 2005. "Integrating Environmental Considerations in Policy Formulation: Lessons from Policy-Based SEA Experience." Report 32783, World Bank, Washington, DC.

4. Identifying Environmental Priorities

Ahmed, Kulsum, and Ernesto Sánchez-Triana, eds. 2008. *Strategic Environmental Assessment for Policies: An Instrument for Good Governance.* Washington, DC: World Bank.

Hamilton, James. 1995. "Pollution as News: Media and Stock Market Reactions to the Toxics Release Inventory Data." *Journal of Environmental Economics and Management* 28: 98–113.

Hausman, Jerry A., and Peter A. Diamond. 1994. "Contingent Valuation: Is Some Number Better than No Number?" *Journal of Economic Perspectives* 8 (4): 45–64.

Hughey, Kenneth F. D., Ross Cullen, and Emma Moran. 2003. "Integrating Economics into Priority Setting and Evaluation in Conservation Management." *Conservation Biology* 17 (1): 93–103.

Lynn, Frances M., and Jack D. Kartez. 1994. "Environmental Democracy in Action: The Toxics Release Inventory." *Environmental Management* 18 (4): 511–21.

OECD DAC (Organisation for Economic Co-operation and Development, Development Assistance Commitee). 2006. *Applying Strategic Environmental Assessment: Good Practice Guidance for Development Cooperation.* Development Assistance Committee Guidelines and Reference Series. Paris: OECD Publishing.

Owens, Susan, Tim Rayner, and Olivia Bina. 2004. "New Agendas for Appraisal: Reflections on Theory, Practice, and Research." *Environment and Planning* 36: 1943–59.

Rijsberman, Michiel A., and Frans H. M. van de Ven. 2000. "Different Approaches to Assessment of Design and Management of Sustainable Urban Water Systems." *Environmental Impact Assessment Review* 20: 333–45.

Stephan, Mark. 2002. "Environmental Information Disclosure Programs: They Work, But Why?" *Social Science Quarterly* 83 (1): 190–205.

Van der Heide, C. Martijn, Jeroen C. J. M. van den Bergh, and Ekko C. van Ierland. 2005. "Extending Weitzman's Economic Ranking of Biodiversity Protection: Combining Ecological and Genetic Considerations." *Ecological Economics* 55: 218–23.

Weitzman, M. L. 1998. "The Noah's Ark Problem." *Econometrica* 66: 1279–98.

Wilkins, Hugh. 2003. "The Need for Subjectivity in EIA: Discourse as a Tool for Sustainable Development." *Environmental Impact Assessment Review* 23: 401–14.

World Bank. 2005. "Integrating Environmental Considerations in Policy Formulation: Lessons from Policy-Based SEA Experience." Report 32783, World Bank, Washington, DC.

5. Strengthening Stakeholder Representation

Ahmed, Kulsum, and Ernesto Sánchez-Triana, eds. 2008. *Strategic Environmental Assessment for Policies: An Instrument for Good Governance.* Washington, DC: World Bank.

Arnstein, Sherry R. 1969. "A Ladder of Citizen Participation." *Journal of the Institute of Planners* 35: 216–24.

Beierle, Thomas C., and David M. Konisky. 2001. "What Are We Gaining from Stakeholder Involvement? Observations from Environmental Planning in the Great Lakes." *Environment and Planning C: Government and Policy* 19: 515–27.

Bekkers, Victor, Geske Dijkstra, Arthur Edwards, and Menno Fenger, eds. 2007. *Governance and the Democratic Deficit: Assessing Democratic Legitimacy of Governance Practices.* Aldershot, UK: Ashgate.

Dijkstra, Geske. 2005. "The PRSP Approach and the Illusion of Improved Aid Effectiveness: Lessons from Bolivia, Honduras and Nicaragua." *Development Policy Review* 23 (4): 443–64.

Edwards, Arthur. 2007. "Embedding deliberative democracy: Local environmental forums in The Netherlands and the United States." In *Governance and the Democratic Deficit: Assessing the Democratic Legitimacy of Governance Practices,* ed. V. Bekkers, G. Dijkstra, A. Edwards, and M. Fenger. Aldershot/Burlington, UK: Ashgate.

Innes, J. E., and D. E. Booher. 1999. "Consensus Building and Complex Adaptive Systems: A Framework for Evaluating Collaborative Planning." *Journal of the American Planning Association* 65 (4): 412–23.

Kende-Robb, Caroline, and Warren A. van Wicklin III. 2008. "Giving the Most Vulnerable a Voice." In *Strategic Environmental Assessment for Policies: An Instrument for Good Governance,* ed. Kulsum Ahmed and Ernesto Sánchez-Triana, 95–126. Washington, DC: World Bank.

Kickert, W. J., E. H. Klijn, and J. F. Koppenjan. 1997. *Managing Complex Networks: Strategies for the Public Sector.* London: Sage Publications.

Molenaers, Nadia, and Robrecht Renard. 2006. "Participation in PRSP Processes: Conditions for Pro Poor Effectiveness." Discussion Paper 2006.03, Institute of Development Policy and Management, University of Antwerp.

Transparency International. 2008. *Global Corruption Report 2008: Corruption in the Water Sector.* Cambridge, UK: Cambridge University Press.

Wood, C. M. 2002. *Environmental Impact Assessment: A Comparative Review.* 2nd ed. Harlow, UK: Pearson/Prentice Hall.

World Bank. 2005. "Integrating Environmental Considerations in Policy Formulation: Lessons from Policy-Based SEA Experience." Report 32783, World Bank, Washington, DC.

6. Analyzing Institutional Capacities and Constraints

Acemoglu, D., S. Johnson, and J. Robinson. 2004. "Institutions as the Fundamental Cause of Long-Run Growth." National Bureau of Economic Research Working Paper 10481, National Bureau of Economic Research, Cambridge, MA.

Ahmed, Kulsum, and Ernesto Sánchez-Triana, eds. 2008. *Strategic Environmental Assessment for Policies: An Instrument for Good Governance.* Washington, DC: World Bank.

Chang, Ha-Joon. 2007. *Bad Samaritans: Rich Nations, Poor Policies and the Threat to the Developing World.* London: Random House Business Books.

Grindle, Merilee S. 2004. "Good Enough Governance: Poverty Reduction and Reform in Developing Countries." *Governance* 17 (14): 525–48.

Kaufmann, D., A. Kraay, and M. Mastruzzi. 2008. "Governance Matters VII: Aggregate and Individual Governance Indicators 1996–2007." Policy Research Working Paper 4654, World Bank, Washington, DC.

Lawson, Andrew, and Neil Bird. 2008. *Government Institutions, Public Expenditure and the Role Of Development Partners: Meeting The New Challenges Of The Environmental Sector.* London: Overseas Development Institute.

March, J. G., and J. P. Olson. 1989. *Rediscovering Institutions: The Organizational Basis of Politics.* New York: Free Press.

Nilsson, M. 2005. "Learning, Frames, and Environmental Policy Integration: The Case of Swedish Energy Policy." *Environment and Planning* 23: 207–26.

Nooteboom, S. 2007. "Impact Assessment Procedures and Complexity Theories." *EIA Review* 27: 645–65.

North, D. C. 1990. *Institutions, Institutional Change and Economic Performance.* Cambridge, UK: Cambridge University Press.

———. 1994. "Economic Performance Through Time." *American Economic Review* 84: 359–68.

OECD (Organisation for Economic Co-operation and Development). 1999. *Donor Support for Institutional Capacity Development in Environment: Lessons Learned.* Paris: Working Party on Aid Evaluation.

———. 2009. "Assessing Environmental Management Capacity: Towards a Common Reference Framework." Environment Working Paper No. 8, background report for the joint Task Team on Governance and Capacity Development for Natural Resource and Environmental Management, OECD Publishing, Paris.

Ostrom, E. 2005. *Understanding Institutional Diversity* Princeton, NJ: Princeton University Press.

Ostrom, E., L. Schroeder, and S. Wynne. 1993. *Institutional Incentives and Sustainable Development: Infrastructure Policies in Perspective.* San Francisco: Westview Press.

Pillai, Poonam. 2008. "Strengthening Policy Dialogue on Environment: Learning from Five Years of Country Environmental Analysis." Environment Department Paper 114, World Bank, Washington, DC.

Pillai, P., and L. Lunde. 2006. "CEA and Institutional Assessment: A Review of International and World Bank Tools." Environment Strategy Paper 11, World Bank, Washington DC.

Rodrik, Dani. 2000. "Institutions for High-Quality Growth: What They Are and How to Acquire Them." *Studies in Comparative International Development* 35 (3): 3–31.

———. 2006. "Goodbye Washington Consensus, Hello Washington Confusion? A Review of the World Bank's Economic Growth in the 1990s: Learning from a Decade of Reform." *Journal of Economic Literature* 44 (4): 973–87.

Turnpenny, John, Måns Nilsson, Duncan Russel, Andrew Jordan, Julia Hertin, and Björn Nykvist. 2008. "Why Is Integrating Policy Assessment So Hard? A Comparative Analysis of the Institutional Capacities and Constraints." *Journal of Environmental Planning and Management* 51 (6): 759–75.

Vatn, Arild. 2005. *Institutions and the Environment*, Cheltenham, UK: Edward Elgar.

Williamson, O. E. 2000. "The New Institutional Economics: Taking Stock, Looking Ahead." *Journal of Economic Literature* 38: 593–613.

World Bank. 2003. *World Development Report 2003, Sustainable Development in a Dynamic World: Transforming Institutions, Growth, and Quality of Life.* Washington, DC: World Bank.

————. 2005. "Integrating Environmental Considerations in Policy Formulation: Lessons from Policy-Based SEA Experience." Report 32783, World Bank, Washington, DC.

7. Strengthening Social Accountability

Ackerman, John. 2004. "Co-governance for Accountability: Beyond 'Exit' and 'Voice.'" *World Development* 32 (3): 447–63.

————. 2005. "Social Accountability in the Public Sector." Social Development Paper Series 82, World Bank, Washington, DC.

Adserà, A., C. Boix, and M. Payne. 2003. "Are You Being Served? Political Accountability and Quality of Government." *Journal of Law, Economics, & Organization* 19 (2): 445–90.

Ahmed, Kulsum, and Ernesto Sánchez-Triana, eds. 2008. *Strategic Environmental Assessment for Policies: An Instrument for Good Governance.* Washington DC: World Bank.

Batley, R. 2004. "The Politics of Service Delivery Reform." *Development and Change* 35 (1): 31–56.

Blair, Harry. 2008. "Building and Reinforcing Social Accountability for Improved Environmental Governance." In *Strategic Environmental Assessment for Policies: An Instrument for Good Governance*, ed. Kulsum Ahmed and Ernesto Sanchéz-Triana, 127–57. Washington, DC: World Bank.

Eberlei, Walter. 2001. "Institutionalized Participation in Processes beyond the PRSP." Institute for Development and Peace (INEF), University of Duisburg-Essen, Germany.

Foti, Joseph, Lalanath de Silva, Heather McGray, Linda Schaffer, Jonathan Talbot, and Jakob Werksman. 2008. "Voice and Choice: Opening the Door to Environmental Democracy." World Resources Institute, Washington, DC.

Fung, Archon. 2002. "Collaboration and Countervailing Power: Making Participatory Governance Work." Working paper, Kennedy School of Government, Harvard University, Cambridge, MA. http://www.archonfung.net/papers/CollaborativePower2.2.pdf.

Galbraith, J. K. 1952. *American Capitalism: The Concept of Countervailing Power.* Boston: Houghton Mifflin.

Hill, Michael. 2005. *The Public Policy Process*, 4th ed. Essex, UK: Pearson.

Kaufman, Robert. 2003. "The Comparative Politics of Administrative Reform: Some Implications for Theory and Policy." In *Reinventing Leviathan: The Politics of Administrative Reform in Developing Countries*, ed. Ben Ross Schneider and Blanca Heredia, 281–302. Miami: North-South Center Press.

Malena, Carmen, Reiner Forster, and Janmejay Singh. 2004. "Social Accountability: An Introduction to the Concept and Emerging Practice." Social Development Paper 76, World Bank, Washington, DC.

O'Neill, T., M. Foresti, and A. Hudson. 2007. *Evaluation of Citizens' Voice and Accountability: Review of the Literature and Donor Approaches.* London: Department for International Development.

Schedler, Andreas. 1999. "Conceptualizing Accountability." In *The Self-Restraining State: Power and Accountability in New Democracies,* ed. A. Schedler, L. Diamond, and M. F. Plattner. Boulder, CO: Lynne Rienner Publishers.

Transparency International. 2008. *Global Corruption Report 2008: Corruption in the Water Sector.* Cambridge, UK: Cambridge University Press.

Veit, Peter, Gracian Z. Banda, Alfred Brownell, Shamiso Mtisi, Prudence Galega, George Mpundu Kanja, Rugemeleza Nshala, Benson Owuor Ochieng, Alda Salomao, and Godber Tumushabe. 2008. *On Whose Behalf? Legislative Representation and the Environment in Africa.* Washington, DC: World Resources Institute.

World Bank. 2005. "Integrating Environmental Considerations in Policy Formulation: Lessons from Policy-Based SEA Experience." Report 32783, World Bank, Washington, DC.

8. Ensuring Social Learning

Ahmed, Kulsum. and Ernesto Sánchez-Triana, eds. 2008. *Strategic Environmental Assessment for Policies: An Instrument for Good Governance.* Washington, DC: World Bank.

Argyris, Chris, and Donald A. Schön. 1996. *Organizational Learning II: Theory, Method, and Practice.* Reading, MA: Addison-Wesley.

Bennet, Colin J., and Michael Howlett. 1992. "The Lessons of Learning: Reconciling Theories of Policy Learning and Policy Change." *Policy Sciences* 25: 275–94.

Caplan, Nathan. 1979. "The Two-Communities Theory and Knowledge Utilization." *American Behavioral Scientist* 22 (3): 459–70.

Carden, Fred. 2004. "Issues in Assessing the Policy Influence of Research." Oxford, Blackwell Publishing Ltd.

Dijkstra, Geske. 2005. "The PRSP Approach and the Illusion of Improved Aid Effectiveness: Lessons from Bolivia, Honduras and Nicaragua." *Development Policy Review* 23 (4): 443–64.

Ebrahim, Alnoor. 2008. "Learning in Environmental Policy Making and Implementation." In *Strategic Environmental Assessment for Policies: An Instrument for Good Governance,* ed. Kulsum Ahmed and Ernesto Sánchez-Triana, 159–79. Washington, DC: World Bank.

Feldman, Martha, and Anne Khademian. 2008. "The Continuous Process of Policy Formulation." In *Strategic Environmental Assessment for Policies: An Instrument for Good Governance,* ed. Kulsum Ahmed and Ernesto Sánchez-Triana, 37–59. Washington, DC: World Bank.

Fiorino, Daniel, J. 2001. "Environmental Policy as Learning: A New View of an Old Landscape." *Public Administration Review* 61 (3): 322–34.

Glasbergen, Pieter. 1996. "Learning to Manage the Environment." In *Democracy and the Environment: Problems and Prospects,* ed. William M. Lafferty and James Meadocroft, 175–93. Cheltenham, UK: Edward Elgar.

Healey, P. 1997. *Collaborative Planning: Shaping Places in Fragmented Societies.* London: Macmillian Press.

IEO (Independent Evaluation Office). 2004. "IEO Evaluation Report on PRSPs and the PRGF." International Monetary Fund, Independent Evaluation Office, Washington, DC.

Innes, J. E., and D. E. Booher. 1999. "Consensus Building and Complex Adaptive Systems: A Framework for Evaluating Collaborative Planning." *Journal of the American Planning Association* 65 (4): 412–23.

IPCC (Intergovernmental Panel on Climate Change). 2007. *Climate Change Impacts: Adaptation and Vulnerability.* Report of Working Group II to the Fourth Assessment Report of the Intergovernmental Panel on Climate Change. Cambridge: Cambridge University Press, Cambridge.

Kornov, L., and W. A. H. Thissen. 2000. "Rationality in Decision- and Policy-Making: Implications for Strategic Environmental Assessment." *Impact Assessment and Project Appraisal* 18 (3): 191–200.

Lindquist, E. 2001. *Discerning Policy Influence: Framework for a Strategic Evaluation of IDRC-Supported Research.* Ottawa: International Development Research Centre Evaluation Unit.

March, James G. 1991. "Exploration and Exploitation in Organizational Learning." *Organization Science* 2 (1): 71–87.

Matland, Richard E. 1995. "Synthesizing the Implementation Literature: The Ambiguity-Conflict Model of Policy Implementation." *Journal of Public Administration Research & Theory* 5 (2): 145–74.

Neilson, Stephanie. 2001. "IDRC-Supported Research and Its Influence on Public Policy. Knowledge Utilization and Public Policy Processes: A Literature Review." Evaluation Unit, International Development Research Centre, Ottawa.

Nilsson, M. 2005. "Learning, Frames, and Environmental Policy Integration: The Case of Swedish Energy Policy." *Environment and Planning* 23: 207–26.

———. 2006. "The Role of Assessments and Institutions for Policy Learning: A Study on Swedish Climate and Nuclear Policy Formation." *Policy Sciences* 38: 225–49.

Nilsson, M., and Å. Persson. 2003. "Framework for Analyzing Environmental Policy Integration." *Journal of Environmental Policy and Planning* 5: 333–59.

Nooteboom. S. 2007. "Impact Assessment Procedures and Complexity Theories." *EIA Review* 27: 645–65.

OECD DAC (Organisation for Economic Co-operation and Development, Development Assistance Commitee). 2006. *Applying Strategic Environmental Assessment: Good Practice Guidance for Development Cooperation.* Development Assistance Committee Guidelines and Reference Series. Paris: OECD Publishing.

OED (Operations Evaluation Department). 2004. *The Poverty Reduction Strategy Initiative: An Independent Evaluation of the World Bank's Support through 2003.* Washington, DC: World Bank.

Owens, Susan. 2005. "Making a Difference? Some Perspectives on Environmental Research and Policy." *Transactions of the Institute of British Geographer* 30: 287–92.

Pillai, Poonam, 2008. "Strengthening Policy Dialogue on Environment: Learning from Five Years of Country Environmental Analysis." Environment Department Paper 114, World Bank, Washington, DC.

Sabatier, Paul A., and Christopher M. Weible. 2007. "The Advocacy Coalition Framework: Innovations and Clarifications." In *Theories of the Policy Process*, 2nd ed., ed. Paul A. Sabatier, 189–220. Boulder, CO: Westview Press.

Seppanen, Maaria. 2005. "Honduras: Transforming the Concessional State?" In *The New Conditionality: The Politics of Poverty Reduction Strategies*, ed. Paul A. Sabatier, ed., 104–34. London and New York: Zed Books.

Stern, N. 2006. *Stern Review on the Economics of Climate Change*. London: HM Treasury.

Weiss, Carol. 1977. "Research for Policy's Sake: The Enlightenment Function of Social Science Research." *Policy Analysis* 3 (4): 531–45.

World Bank. 2005. "Integrating Environmental Considerations in Policy Formulation: Lessons from Policy-Based SEA Experience." Report 32783, World Bank, Washington, DC.

9. Framework for Evaluating I-SEA Pilots

Earl, Sara, Fred Carden, and Terry Smutylo. 2001. *Outcome Mapping: Building Learning and Reflection into Development Programs*. Ottawa: International Development Research Centre.

George, Alexander L., and Andrew Bennett. 2005. *Case Studies and Theory Development in the Social Sciences*. Cambridge, MA: MIT Press.

Hilding-Rydevik, T., and H. Bjarnadóttir. 2007. "Context Awareness and Sensitivity in SEA Implementation." *Environmental Impact Assessment Review* 27: 666–84.

OECD DAC (Organisation for Economic Co-operation and Development, Development Assistance Committee). 2006. *Applying Strategic Environmental Assessment: Good Practice Guidance for Development Cooperation*. Development Assistance Committee Guidelines and Reference Series. Paris: OECD Publishing.

———. 2008. "Evaluating Development Cooperation: Summary of Key Norms and Standards." 2nd ed. http://www.oecd.org/dataoecd/12/56/41612905.pdf.

Sadler, Barry, and Barry Dalal-Clayton. 2009. "Generic SEA Quality Review Methodology." Draft commissioned by Canadian International Development Agency and presented to the Organisation for Economic Co-operation and Development, Development Assistance Committee Task Team on SEA, May 30.

Weiss, Carol, H. 1998. *Evaluation*. 2nd ed. Upper Saddle River, NJ: Prentice Hall.

Yin, Robert K. 2003. *Case Study Research: Design and Methods*. 3rd ed. London: Sage.

Appendix

Pillai, P., and L. Lunde. 2006. "CEA and Institutional Assessment: A Review of International and World Bank Tools." Environment Strategy Paper 11, World Bank, Washington DC.

Policy SEA Process Methods

THIS APPENDIX DISCUSSES METHODS FOR APPLYING SEA in policy and sector reform. The appendix is far from comprehensive, but it provides guidance and references that are complementary to the methods and approaches discussed in chapter 3.

Methods Used in Situation Assessment

In most cases, situation assessment can be desk based, drawing on existing literature and the expert knowledge of strategic environmental assessment (SEA) team members.

A significant component of the situation assessment should be an environmental study akin to a baseline study but based mainly on secondary information and expert judgement. Its main purpose is to inform the identification of key environmental and social issues, preferably those related to economic growth and poverty alleviation.

Depending on the size of the policy SEA exercise and available resources, establishment of an environmental/social baseline should involve the development of a pressure-state-impact-response (PSIR) indicator framework for the area in question. Such a framework may already exist at the national level as part of state-of-the-environment reporting. It needs to be stressed that development of PSIR indicator frameworks can be a time-consuming and expensive endeavor.

For the purposes of the situation assessment task, the environmental and social baseline work should be simple and rapid. Indicators could either be adapted from an existing PSIR framework or be developed through public consultation. The World Bank's "Generic ToR for Environmental and Social Baseline Development in a River Basin" provides some guidance.[1]

An economic profile should be produced to indicate the nature and extent of current and proposed stresses on the natural resources of the jurisdiction or sector in question. This profile would include some indication of potential industrial, agricultural, and urban development envisaged for the area. It could also be accompanied by a social study that would enable conclusions to be made about the structure, geographical distribution, income levels, income and asset endowment distribution, and land tenure arrangements in the jurisdiction. Box 3.3 of chapter 3 presents examples of situation assessment methods used in the Sierra Leone strategic environmental and social assessment (SESA) and the West Africa Minerals Sector Strategic Assessment (WAMSSA).

The situation assessment should also include a brief description of the policy, legislative, and institutional frameworks associated with management of the policy regime in question. Selective analysis of historical and cultural issues associated with the sector to be reformed is also important for understanding the context within which SEA approaches would be applied. This analysis would help to explain path dependency factors affecting policy formulation and implementation.

Methods Used in Stakeholder Analysis

Several methods can be employed to collect data on stakeholders in a comprehensive and efficient manner. Prior to the actual collection, a brief review of background literature and country studies can provide a useful understanding of the country's political economy. One method of actually collecting data is to conduct interviews directly with the stakeholders involved in the specific policy area. The second method is to interview both local experts in the field who are knowledgeable about the issue and the important groups and individuals involved in the policy area.

Country SEA team members often have extensive local knowledge and can provide a critical firsthand understanding of which stakeholders are relevant for inclusion in the stakeholder analysis. However, unless resources and time do not permit, interviewing of local and international experts in the policy area or country, and the stakeholders themselves, is imperative.

Broad, all-inclusive interviews contribute to an effective stakeholder analysis process because they uncover many facets of the sector's political economy. The content and questions used in the interviews should elicit background information concerning the policy-making process, should focus on information that identifies key stakeholders from a variety of groups in the reform process, and should seek to clarify assumptions about stakeholders' power and interest in the decision-making process.

Data from interviews—including scaled values assigned to the attributes, and relative rankings calculated accordingly—can be catalogued and presented in charts and matrixes, highlighting the following attributes: (i) the group itself, (ii) its interest (or salience), (iii) its influence (power), and (iv) its position on the reform.

An important measure called "effective power" (the degree of power the stakeholder holds over other groups in relation to a reform area) can be determined by weighting a combination of a stakeholder's salience and influence.

The level of interest or salience is the priority and importance stakeholders attach to the sector or reform area. The level of influence depends on the quantity and type of resources and power that stakeholders can marshal to promote their position with respect to the existing policies and proposed reforms. Broadly, these attributes signal the stakeholder's ability to block or promote reform, join with others to form a coalition of support or opposition, and lead the direction/discussion of the reform. Stakeholder analysis therefore provides a sufficient understanding of the potential impact of reform on interested groups, the hierarchy of authority and power among different groups, and the actual perceptions of the reform among different groups, all of which are important if the reform and policy SEA are to be effective. Stakeholder data can be organized according to stakeholders' relative power/influence and salience; this arrangement clarifies potential support for, or opposition to, the proposed reform. Often, a matrix can be used to organize and classify the stakeholder data. One form of matrix maps salience/interest and influence on the axes. This shorthand categorization and analysis indicates which stakeholders will gain or lose from a proposed reform, and whether they can significantly influence the process.

Methods Used in Environmental Priority Setting

Key environmental and social issues, identified in the situation analysis, are presented to the stakeholders for the selection of policy SEA priorities. There are different ways in which to select priorities. For example, in Sierra Leone the SESA team employed a ranking method to define which environmental and social issues were most important. Larger-scope SESAs, such as WAMSSA, involved a combination of methodologies for the selection of environmental and social priorities. For WAMSSA, focus group meetings for government, industry, and civil society were held in the capital cities of Guinea, Liberia, and Sierra Leone, and mining community surveys were conducted in 10 communities representing the range of features that characterize communities affected by mining and infrastructure development; between 22 and 25 respondents, representing a broad range of stakeholders, were selected in each community. Afterward, WAMSSA's environmental and social priorities were chosen in national workshops.

Another way of selecting priorities would be to generate scenarios based on different underlying assumptions. For example, policy SEA can be used to investigate the environmental and social impacts of different land use policies to be applied in a river basin. As a focus for policy dialogue, a small number of likely growth scenarios could be developed by considering different assumptions in the following variables: increase in domestic demand for food, power, and water; global demand for the country's exports; urban development; migration; and industrialization.

Scenario building can be an important part of environmental priority setting, because proper analysis of alternative scenarios can convince stakeholders that the policy proponent is serious about examining the different ways in which the policy might be developed and implemented. In other words, scenario analysis can build SEA legitimacy, especially when stakeholders are asked to present their own scenarios. Tools such as multicriteria analysis exist to help stakeholders sort through scenario alternatives when there are many alternatives and many criteria that can be used to compare them.[2]

Methods Used in Institutional Assessment

In some countries, an assessment of customary institutions will be necessary. This assessment addresses issues related to behaviors that stem from traditional values, which can play an important role in how stakeholders organize their economic, social, and political systems. A first step is to review available ethnographic information on the cultural attributes of the target population or indigenous group. A second step is to carry out workshops and focus groups in a sample of representative communities. The purpose of these exercises is to collect information on local perceptions of power relationships and on the traditional ways of establishing dialogue. This information is important, since a culturally sensitive approach to dialogue will reinforce local ownership of the reform process. The focus group meetings and workshops can also gather information on characteristics of groups or communities—including political features (for example, ranking of authorities, their scope of influence, and local dispute-resolution mechanisms), social features (for example, gender roles), economic features (for example, land tenure system, natural resource management, redistribution of benefits), and ideological features (for example, religious system, sacred places).

Finally, a similar process for institutional and capacity assessment as the one described in chapter 3 can be applied to assess the influence of customary institutions on the management of priority issues, and to examine the potential impact on environmental priorities of the proposed policy change or sector reform.

Methods Used in Political Economy Analysis

In practice, there is a close connection between stakeholder analysis and political economy analysis. Stakeholder analysis provides an initial mapping of the degree of influence and importance of different groups. Political economy analysis goes a step further to explain what drives the behaviors of stakeholders. In fact, some of the recent research done in this area uses the alternative term "power and drivers of change analysis" to more clearly define the focus of this work.[3]

Political economy studies supplement standard assessment methods with thorough diagnostics covering both formal and informal aspects of economic and political processes. There are substantial differences in the methods that different development agencies use when they undertake political economy analyses. World Bank studies often tend to involve extensive fieldwork, while other studies rely primarily on literature review and the experience of local consultants.

Recent reviews of how political economy analysis has been undertaken by development agencies, such as OECD DAC Network on Governance (2005), indicate that the most effective methodologies use a combination of quantitative and qualitative methods to enhance the depth of their analyses and to further understanding of the political economy of the reform process.

The recent escalation of interest in political economy analysis has brought with it an excellent collection of methodological tools. Examples include the Department for International Development's work on drivers of change; the Swedish International Development Cooperation Agency's work on power analysis; the World Bank's report on the political economy of policy reform; the Netherlands Foreign Ministry's Strategic Governance and Corruption Assessment tool; and the OECD's survey of donor approaches to governance assessment.[4]

Methods Used in Defining Policy SEA Recommendations

In general, recommendations can be framed in a policy action matrix that includes actions over the short term (one to two years), medium term (three to five years), and long term (more than five years), as well as monitoring indicators. In this manner, expected outcomes in each period can be monitored to assess the progress of reform. It is also possible to conclude with an assessment of the risks associated with the recommended actions. Risk analysis might include the potential deliberate actions that certain interest groups could take in order to bend or halt reform. Thus, possible mechanisms to safeguard the proposed institutional and governance changes should be contemplated in the analysis.

Notes

1 Available at http://web.worldbank.org/WBSITE/EXTERNAL/TOPICS/ENVIRONME
NT/0,,contentMDK:20874777~menuPK:2462263~pagePK:148956~piPK:216618~th
esitePK:244381~isCURL:Y,00.html.
2 See, for example, Annandale and Lantzke (2000).
3 See, for example, OECD DAC Network on Governance (2005).
4 All of this guidance, and more, is available at the Governance and Social Development
Resource Center's website: http://www.gsdrc.org/go/topic-guides/political-economy-
analysis/tools-for-political-economy-analysis.

References

Annandale, D., and R. Lantzke. 2000. "Making Good Decisions: A Guide to Using
Decision-Aiding Techniques in Waste Facility Siting." Institute for Environmental
Science, Murdoch University, Perth, Australia.

OECD DAC (Organisation for Economic Co-operation and Development, Development
Assistance Committee) Network on Governance. 2005. "Lessons Learned on the Use
of Power and Drivers of Change Analyses in Development Cooperation." Review
commissioned by the OECD DAC Network on Governance (GOVNET), final report.
http://www.ids.ac.uk/go/idsproject/power-and-drivers-of-change-analyses.

Summary of International Workshop, "SEA for Development Cooperation: Taking Stock and Looking Forward"

THE ORGANISATION FOR ECONOMIC CO-OPERATION and Development (OECD) Development Assistance Committee (DAC) strategic environmental assessment (SEA) Task Team and the World Bank held a combined workshop on the margins of the 30th International Association for Impact Assessment conference in Geneva on April 7, 2010. The convenors of the workshop were Fernando Loayza of the World Bank, and the current chair of the SEA task team, Peter Croal of the Canadian International Development Agency (CIDA).

The objectives of the workshop were to review progress made in the application of SEA, focusing on the recent experience of the OECD DAC SEA Task Team and the World Bank's Pilot Program on SEA; to receive feedback from workshop participants on how SEA can be used more effectively for environmental integration in development policy and poverty reduction; and to discuss the relevance of SEA in the New Environment Strategy of the World Bank Group (International Development Association, International Bank for

Reconstruction and Development, International Finance Corporation, and Multilateral Investment Guarantee Agency).

The rest of this appendix presents the agenda for the day, an outline of the process used to direct the afternoon's workshop session, a summary of the workshop outcomes, and a full transcript of comments made by break-out groups during the workshop.

Agenda

09.00–09.15	Welcome and introduction
	Peter Croal (CIDA and OECD DAC SEA Task Team) and
	Fernando Loayza (World Bank)

Session 1: *OECD DAC SEA Task Team Progress and News on the Implementation of SEA for Development Cooperation.* Session chair: Peter Croal

09.15–09.30	Introduction and SEA task team overview
	Peter Croal (CIDA and OECD DAC SEA Task Team, Canada)
09.30–09.45	SEA quality tool
	Barry Dalal-Clayton (International Institute for Environment and Development, UK)
09.45–10.05	SEA in practice in development cooperation
	Peter Nelson (Land Use Consultants, UK)
10.05–10.25	SEA activities in China
	Kin Che Lam (Centre of Strategic Environmental Assessment for China, Chinese University of Hong Kong, China)
10.25–10.45	Questions and answers
10.45–11.15	*Coffee break*

Session 2: *SEA and the New Environment Strategy of the World Bank Group.* Session chair: Anna Axelsson (Swedish EIA Centre, Swedish University of Agricultural Sciences)

11.15–11.30	The World Bank's Pilot Program on SEA
	Fernando Loayza (World Bank, U.S.)
11.30–11.55	Main findings of the evaluation of the pilot program
	David Annandale (Consultant, Canada)

11.55–12.05	Scaling up SEA in development cooperation
	Anders Ekbom (Environmental Economics Unit, University of Gothenburg, Sweden)
12.05–12.25	Questions and answers
12.25–12.45	Environmental governance and institutions
	Urvashi Narain (World Bank, U.S.)
12.45–13.00	Questions and answers
13.00–14.00	*Lunch*

Session 3:	***Break-out groups.*** Session chair: Daniel Slunge (Environmental Economics Unit, University of Gothenburg, Sweden)
14.00–15.10	Groups focused on answering questions presented in "dialogue maps"
15.10–15.30	*Coffee break*

Session 4:	***Plenary.*** Session chair: Rob Verheem (Netherlands Commission for Environmental Assessment [NCEA])
15.30–16.30	Reporting back from break-out groups
16.30–16.45	Wrap-up and conclusion
	Rob Verheem (NCEA, the Netherlands)
16.45–17.00	Next steps and closure
	Fernando Loayza (World Bank, U.S.) and Peter Croal (CIDA and OECD DAC SEA Task Team, Canada)

Process Used for the Workshop Break-Out Groups

The afternoon workshop session used a process known as "dialogue mapping" to focus discussion on the following four topics:

1. obstacles to and enabling factors for SEA effectiveness in development cooperation and poverty reduction
2. the role of the World Bank in strengthening environmental governance and institutions for sustainable development
3. SEA as a tool for strengthening environmental governance and institutions
4. main steps for scaling up SEA in development policy

Groups were organized around these topics, and participants were asked four questions under each topic heading.

Approximately 70 people attended the morning session, and 45 stayed to participate in the afternoon workshops.

Summary of the Workshop Outcomes

The following summary of results derives from analysis of the dialogue maps, combined with observations made of the group discussions:

- There is no objection to the idea of institution-centered SEA (policy SEA), or to its possible scaling up.
- There is a tendency not to focus specifically on policy SEA but on SEA more generally defined.
- SEA is predominantly thought of as a "product"; participants spoke of "doing a SEA." There is some uncertainty about the idea of SEA as a process.
- There is some uncertainty about the purpose of and differences between "varieties" of SEA.
- Policy SEA is quite different from impact-centered SEA. Real inefficiencies eventuate when policy or plan making take place in addition to policy appraisal (reference the English system of sustainability appraisal/SEA).
- The issue of ownership is important. There is disagreement about the role of development agencies and whether they have a mandate to encourage demand.
- There remains some sense that I-SEA/policy SEA is just "taking account of the environment in policy making."

With regard to the issue of "obstacles to and enabling factors for SEA effectiveness in developing countries," the following comments were made by participants:

- Need to (widely) show evidence of benefits, for example:
  - SEA leading to economic efficiency (good example: the hydropower plan SEA in central Vietnam).
  - Improving the lot of the poor (West Africa Minerals Sector Strategic Assessment).
  - SEA as a forum for conflict resolution.
- Capacity building
  - The idea of policy SEA "champions."
  - Should tap into networks of finance, budget, and planning people (reference to the recent phases of PEI [Poverty-Environment Initiative]). The need to "convert" traditional sector and national planners.

With regard to the role of development agencies and the issue of scaling up SEA in development policy, the following comments were made by participants:

- Policy SEA should be "sold" by recognizing that it often adds value to existing processes.
- The role of SEA should be considered in intergroup donor discussions.
- It is important to be clear about what donors should not do, as well as what they should do.

Finally, with regard to "SEA as a tool for strengthening environmental governance and institutions," the following issues were raised by participants:

- Policy SEA is most appropriate in connection with new/weak governments, postconflict situations, and new sectors.
- Do we need to differentiate between "SEA" and "decision making"?
- How can SEA contribute to a policy dialogue that extends beyond the completion of the SEA report?
  - Involve stakeholders in post-SEA follow-up.
  - Set up process/responsibility for following up SEA outcomes.
  - Record institutional memory.
  - SEA becomes a key component of policy making, not a separate track.

Transcript of the Workshop Outcomes

The dialogue maps used by each of the four groups were collected and transcribed. The full transcription is presented below.

Group A: Obstacles to and Enabling Factors for SEA Effectiveness in Developing Countries

Question 1.   What kind of value added must SEA demonstrate for developing countries to want to use SEAs?

- Long-term cost savings.
- Success stories from other countries.
- Evidence of SEA leading to economic efficiency.
- Evidence that SEA can deal with cumulative impacts and overcome the limitations of environmental impact assessment.
- Evidence of SEA improving the lot of the poor. WAMSSA's influence on regionalism should result in cheaper shared physical infrastructure, and hence help alleviate poverty.
- Risk reduction.
- Well-being.
- Solidification of politicians' power base.
- Answer will differ depending on the country.
- Improved and more efficient policy making.
- Ability to become a process/forum for overcoming conflict over resource management (the example was given of public protest in China).

Question 2.   What kind of capacity (individual, organizational, institutional) needs to be developed for successful use of SEAs in developing countries?

- Individual practitioner, auditors, politicians.
- Identify champions with the ability to influence and empower.

- Match knowledge needs with the different groups.
- Have organizational bodies to coordinate SEA work at the national level.
- Doing SEA: technical ability; getting the message across; diplomatic skills; understanding needs.
- Using SEA: environmental understanding.
- Public: how is SEA related to the daily lives?

Question 3.   What activities, mechanisms, and networks already exist that can be used to advance SEA practice in developing countries?

- Should tap into networks of finance, budget, and planning people. These are the people that we need to influence. There are existing networks for these people. UNDP-UNEP (United Nations Development Programme–United Nations Environment Programme) PEI phase 2 and 3 is already working with environmental mainstreaming in budget and planning processes at the national level.
- Example given of a planning secretary in a developing country who became an environmental mainstreaming "convert" when sent to a mainstreaming workshop.
- Examine the UNDP-UNEP PEI "champions" model. Nonenvironmental people are nominated as PEI champions and sent to short-course training. A fuss is made of these people when nominated. This is a competition.
- Make use of networks for insurance corporations, banks, nongovernmental organizations.
- Use social network media to get to young people.
- Legal frameworks.
- EPA-type agencies.
- Professional associations.
- Regional organizations.
- SEA road shows.

Question 4.   What could be priority actions to promote developing country use of SEA?

a. SEA practitioners

- Build capacity with respect to communication skills, understanding policy-making processes, and technical analysis/best practice.
- Incentives.
- Pilot SEAs.
- Capacity strengthening.

b. Government agencies

- Link to national priorities.

- Solicit more public support.
- Media.
- International obligations and legal agreements.

c. Other actors
- Media: successful stories.
- Champions.
- Big corporations.
- EITI (Extractive Industries Transparency Initiative).
- Industry bodies.

Group B: The Role of the World Bank in Strengthening Environmental Governance and Institutions for Sustainable Development

Question 1. *The World Bank has traditionally not done as much to increase the demand for better environmental governance and institutions. What role can it realistically play in this area?*

- In the past, poorly defined goals may have increased demand in an untested fashion.
- Need to overcome the limitations of individual-project lending focus.
- Increase local-level partnerships with other development agencies.
- Need more outreach for follow-up after lending.
- World Bank may well have a "global mandate" to strongly encourage the use of policy SEA as an institutional strengthening tool (due to significance of global problems that are not taken on board by national governments).

Question 2. *How can the World Bank do a better job of measuring the effectiveness of its interventions aimed at strengthening environmental institutions and governance?*

- Find means to show that SEA is subject to participation and public hearings.
- Degree of compliance of governments with own legislation.
- Make sure that clear disclosure rules are widely known.
- Audit country systems.

Question 3. *Should World Bank engagement in strengthening environmental governance and institutions differ between countries?*

- Yes. Political economy analysis is extremely important.
- Priorities based on issues of global concern. Not all engagement needs to be demand driven.

Question 4. *Other comments?*

(The group did not provide additional comments.)

Group C: SEA as a Tool for Strengthening Environmental Governance and Institutions

Question 1. *In which situations should institutional and governance strengthening be an important focus of an SEA?*

- New/weak governments.
- Postconflict.
- New sectors.

Question 2. *How can SEA best contribute to multistakeholder participation in strategic decision making?*

- Differentiate between "SEA" and "decision making."
- Train SEA practitioners re "participation" continuum.
- Connection to governance and accountability: will decision makers allow stakeholders a "participatory" role in decision making?

Question 3. *How can SEA contribute to a policy dialogue that extends beyond the completion of the SEA report?*

- Involve stakeholders in post-SEA follow-up.
- Set up process/responsibility for following up SEA outcomes.
- Record institutional memory.
- SEA becomes a key component of policy making, not a separate track.

Question 4. *Indicate three outcomes that SEA should achieve in order to contribute to strengthening of environmental governance and institutions.*

- Change! New becomes normative.
- Raising awareness—widely, beyond politicians/bureaucrats.
- Stronger ownership/accountability.

Group D: The Role of Development Agencies: Main Components and Steps for Scaling Up SEA in Development Policy

Question 1. *What kind of value added must SEA demonstrate for development agencies to want to support the development of SEA capacity and use of SEAs?*

- Demonstrate that the environment has been considered.
- Local buy-in.
- Work with poverty agenda.
- Peer-group support.
- Recognize that SEA often adds value to existing processes—simply enhancing.

Question 2. *What can different development agencies (both bilateral and multilateral) do to support the use of SEA at the policy level in developing countries?*

- Example of Finland/Denmark giving sector support in Zambia.
- Honoring the outcomes of SEA, after validation.
- Ensure real ownership within the developing country and clarify individual roles.
- Be clear about what donors should *not* do, as well as what they should do.
- Consider role of SEA in intergroup donor discussions (a good model is the SEA donor framework in Vietnam, which was recognized as a good example of donor harmonization by the Accra aid effectiveness meeting).

Question 3. *How should different development agencies (both bilateral and multilateral) work together to promote SEA at the policy level? In other words, what are the partnership options for development agencies?*

- Rotation of ideas between agencies (less formal dialogue).
- Cooperation, such as World Bank with the Swedish International Development Cooperation Agency, NCEA, and the University of Gothenburg.
- SEA as a way to manage environmental risks.

Question 4. *Other comments?*

(The group did not provide additional comments.)

INDEX

Page numbers followed by *b, f,* or *t* refer to boxed text, figures or tables, respectively.